Confronting Poverty

Brief Contents

Detailed Contents

Introduction

One of the most pressing economic and social problems facing the United States today is the persistence of widespread poverty. Among the industrialized nations, the United States consistently ranks near the top in terms of the percentage and severity of its population that is poor. A wide range of social problems, from mass incarceration to lowered life expectancy, are associated with impoverishment. A fundamental conundrum lies in the question of why the wealthiest country in the world has such high rates of poverty? This paradox of poverty amidst plenty has perplexed social commentators and academics for decades.

Furthermore, the conditions of economic hardship amidst plenty have become increasingly visible and pronounced in recent years. Over the past five decades, the divide between the top and bottom of the income distribution has grown steadily wider (Stiglitz 2012). The distance between those at the 90th percentile of the income distribution compared with those at the 10th percentile currently stands at 13 to 1 (U.S. Census Bureau 2020a). This difference is far wider than that found in other OECD (Organisation for Economic Co-operation and Development) countries.

Even more extreme are the current patterns of wealth holdings in the United States. The top 1 percent of the U.S. population possess 46 percent of the entire financial wealth in the country, while the bottom 60 percent hold less than 1 percent of the wealth (Wolff 2017). As with income inequality, the patterns of wealth inequality have been widening over recent decades. In fact, the extent of income and wealth inequality now surpasses the extreme inequality found during the Gilded Age and the 1920s (Piketty and Saez 2014).

The vulnerability of those in the bottom half of the United States can be seen in a variety of other settings. Approximately 45 percent of all jobs in the United States are considered low-paying, with median wages of $10.22 an hour (Ross and Bateman 2019). Real median wages for full-time male workers were lower in 2019 than they were in 1973 (U.S. Census Bureau, 2020a). Greater numbers of Americans are living one paycheck away from poverty. A recent study from the Federal Reserve found that 37 percent of Americans do not have enough savings put aside to protect them from a 400 dollar emergency (Federal Reserve Bank 2020). Moreover, the social safety net that is designed to protect families from economic calamities has been weakened over recent decades (Tach and Edin 2017). One result has been increasing numbers of individuals living in deep or extreme poverty, with the numbers of homeless remaining stubbornly high (Parolin and Brady 2019). In short, more Americans are at risk of losing ground economically (Chetty et al. 2017; Hout 2018), leading to an increased likelihood of poverty across the life course (Sandoval, Rank, and Hirschl 2009).

These conditions are alarming for many reasons. Perhaps most disconcerting is that poverty undermines the very concept of a just and livable society. In an affluent nation such as the United States, it appears patently wrong that not only are many left out of such prosperity, but that they are living in such debilitating economic conditions. Furthermore, these conditions have resulted in a host of social and economic problems that the United States must grapple with on an ongoing basis.

For these and many other reasons, this book will argue that understanding and confronting poverty must become a top priority for the nation. It is an issue of vital importance to the well-being and vitality of our country. And yet it is one that has been surrounded by misunderstanding and misperception. The purpose of this book is to provide you with a solid foundation on which to understand and confront American poverty.

Background

Much of my teaching and research over the years has focused on the topics of poverty and inequality. I first began teaching my poverty course in the late 1980s and have taught it every year since. During this time I have had the great privilege of interacting with hundreds of students interested in learning more about this topic. Without a doubt, they have enriched my thinking with their insights and questions. This book is the result of 30 years of engagement on the subject.

With respect to research, *Living on the Edge: The Realities of Welfare in America* was the title of my first book. In that work I attempted to understand what it was actually like to try to survive on the safety net from the perspective of those who were living this experience. Needless to say, the realities of such a life were quite different than the many stereotypes surrounding welfare recipients.

My next book, *One Nation, Underprivileged: Why American Poverty Affects Us All*, set out to articulate a new understanding of American poverty. As argued throughout, part of the problem behind poverty in the United States has been a serious misunderstanding by both policy makers and the general public. Much of this misunderstanding centers around the dynamics and causes of poverty. The common perception of the poor is that they are predominately nonwhite, in poverty for years at a time, and find themselves impoverished because of a lack of motivation. It turns out these assumptions are simply incorrect. As we shall see in the upcoming chapters, the dynamics of poverty are quite fluid, and in fact, a majority of Americans will experience poverty first-hand at some point in their lives.

In my third book, *Chasing the American Dream: Understanding What Shapes Our Fortunes*, I sought to explore the meaning of the American Dream and its viability in today's society. In researching that book, I interviewed dozens of individuals who were struggling economically to stay afloat. They confided in me their struggles as well as their hopes for a better day ahead. It was clear that while many still believed in the American Dream, it was becoming increasingly difficult to achieve it in today's society.

I have written several more books along the way, and all of them have to varying degrees dealt with the issues of poverty and inequality. In the process of working on these manuscripts, I have been struck by the similarity between organizing a course and writing a book. Each week of a class can be thought of as analogous to each chapter in a book, and in fact, the organization of this book closely follows the organization of my poverty course. In that course, we focus on four basic questions which we will also address in this book. These questions and their answers are designed to provide a solid introduction into the subject matter.

Finally, an issue I have been interested in for some time is how can we as academics and students make our research more accessible and relevant to a broader audience? Part of this thinking has led me to develop with my colleague at Cornell University, Tom Hirschl, a companion website also called "Confronting Poverty." We will turn to a number of interactive and online tools on the website that allow us to interact and engage with the topic of poverty in a dynamic way. The combination of the book with these online resources is intended to provide an engaging experience into this critical issue facing the United States.

Organization

Confronting Poverty is organized around answering four major questions: (1) What is the nature, extent, and makeup of poverty?; (2) Why does poverty exist and persist?; (3) What are the effects and consequences of poverty?; and (4) How can we address and alleviate poverty? In teaching my poverty course over the years, I have found that these four questions are key to providing a solid understanding into the subject. Each of these questions and their answers are designed to build upon the prior questions in order to deepen your understanding of poverty.

We begin by examining the nature and scope of poverty in the United States. As one sets off to explore a social problem, a logical starting place is to examine the size and characteristics of that problem. In Part I of the book, we review different dimensions of poverty. We begin in Chapter 1 by exploring some of the ways to define and measure poverty. Several distinctions are discussed, including economic versus noneconomic approaches to conceptualizing poverty, absolute versus relative measures of poverty, and pretransfer versus posttransfer definitions of poverty. The manner in which the U.S. official poverty line is drawn is also reviewed, followed by a brief discussion of the Census Bureau's alternative measure of poverty.

In Chapter 2 we turn our attention to understanding the patterns and dynamics of poverty. Issues explored include the length of time that individuals are poor, events leading households into and out of poverty, and the risk of poverty across the life course. In addition, we will look at how the United States compares to other countries.

Chapter 3 focuses on particular groups that have had traditionally elevated rates of poverty. These groups include nonwhites, women, single-parent families, children and young adults, rural and inner-city residents, and those with less education and skills. We will also examine the composition of the poverty population with respect to these characteristics.

In Part II, we turn our attention to the various ideas and theories that have been offered to explain poverty in the United States. These are discussed in the next three chapters of the book. In Chapter 4, we explore those explanations that focus primarily upon individual failings as the cause of poverty. Such explanations tend to dominate the popular discussion and they can be divided into several different lines of thought. One approach focuses on deficient attitudes and behavior that are viewed as leading individuals into poverty. In particular, the lack of an industrious work ethic is seen as critical. Another prominent individual explanation focuses upon a scarcity of what economists call human capital (e.g., skills, job training, education, etc.), which is then seen as leading to a greater risk of poverty. In addition, we will examine those theories that emphasize culture as a primary reason for poverty. The most well known of these explanations is the culture of poverty theory. The argument here is that individuals and families living in deep poverty develop a way of life that helps them to cope with their environment, but also prevents them from escaping poverty.

Chapter 5 shifts gears and focuses on those explanations that view poverty resulting from failings at a structural level, including the economic, social, and political environments. A range of theories will be discussed, including functionalism, structural critiques of capitalism, and social welfare state theories. Each of these theories posits that structural constraints limit the opportunities for individuals to get ahead in life.

In Chapter 6, we attempt to make sense of the various theories we have been examining through the development of what I have called a structural vulnerability perspective. This approach combines elements of human capital theory with the importance of structural constraints. Consequently, while characteristics such as the lack of education help to explain who in particular is more likely to experience poverty, the fact that there is a shortage of livable wage jobs helps to explain why the United States has such elevated rates of poverty in the first place.

In Part III, we explore the impact that poverty has upon individuals, families, communities, and the nation as a whole. Such impacts demonstrate why poverty alleviation must become an important objective of social policy, and why we should be vitally concerned about the issue. In Chapter 7 we review the negative effects that poverty has upon individuals and families. These include detrimental effects upon health, psychological well-being, and the ability of children and adults to reach their full potential. Chapter 8 outlines several of the ways in which poverty impacts upon the well-being of communities. Issues discussed include neighborhood crime, quality of schools, environmental effects, and employment opportunities. The sizeable impact of poverty upon the nation as a whole is examined in Chapter 9. Research will be utilized to demonstrate that the annual economic cost of poverty is enormous. In addition, we will explore the social, civic, and psychological costs of poverty upon the nation.

As we move into the final part of the book (Part IV), an array of ideas and strategies for alleviating poverty in the United States are presented. We begin in Chapter 10 by discussing the ways in which the social safety net might be strengthened. We also will discuss the development of policies and programs that can build the long-term assets of lower-income Americans.

Chapter 11 argues that beyond a strong social safety net, there are certain key public goods and services that should be made available to all. These include a first-rate education, comprehensive health care, and affordable housing. Each of these allows individuals and families to achieve an economically secure life.

As covered in Chapter 3, single-parent families are at a heightened risk of falling into poverty. Policy ideas to better support such families are detailed in Chapter 12, including stronger child support measures, quality childcare, and programs to prevent teenage pregnancies.

In Chapter 13, we explore policies to create enough jobs that pay a living wage. We will review the Earned Income Tax Credit, raising the minimum wage to a living wage, along with economic policies designed to encourage job creation. In addition, we will explore the idea of a basic guaranteed income as a supplemental strategy to employment policies.

A final approach for reducing poverty in the United States is through organizing for social change, discussed in Chapter 14. Such organizing can take place on a variety of levels, but in this chapter we focus on three—at the job; in the community; and across the nation. As we think about ways to address poverty, organizing for better working conditions, stronger communities, and a greater federal effort in addressing poverty would appear excellent places to begin.

Our book comes to a conclusion in Chapter 15. Here we will recap the major ideas and themes in the book, as well as point to what might lie ahead in the future. In particular, each of you is challenged to consider your role in helping to confront poverty in the years ahead.

At the end of each chapter are various online activities and exercises designed for use with the different topics and issues covered. These activities are intended to take advantage of the many resources available on the internet. In particular, we will use the companion *Confronting Poverty* website as our jumping-off point for all of these activities. This website has been designed to provide an online understanding into the issues surrounding poverty and inequality. You can access it through your PC, laptop, or smartphone. In order to arrive at the homepage, simply type "confronting poverty" into any search engine, and the link to the website should appear at the top of the page. If it does not, you can directly access the website by typing the URL: confrontingpoverty.org.

The website began as a way to make available the poverty risk calculator that my colleague, Tom Hirschl, and I developed. Since that time, a number of components have been added, including a discussion guide, a facts and myths section, and a section to learn about additional research. The site has been used by hundreds of thousands of visitors from over 200 countries around the globe. As we work our way across the chapters in this primer, we will use this resource to add to your understanding of American poverty.

Each chapter has several activities to engage in. These are designed to expand your knowledge pertaining to the chapter's subject matter. Of course, once you begin your explorations, you may very well find other topics and questions to investigate further.

Concluding Thoughts

Few issues are as consequential to the well-being of the United States as that of poverty. Many of the social problems that we see in America today can be traced back to elevated levels of poverty and inequality. But it is also a condition that undermines us as a people and as a nation. America has always placed utmost importance upon equality of opportunity, which, in turn, allows individuals to reach their full potential. Widespread poverty calls this goal into question. It casts serious doubts upon this broadly held ideal and it diminishes us in the process.

As we embark together on this journey, I will do my utmost to be an engaging and enlightening guide through the troubling landscape of poverty and inequality. Its terrain is marked by twists and turns, roadblocks, and detours. Yet hopefully as we reach the end of the book, you will have a deeper appreciation of this challenging landscape, as well as the rewards of beginning to alter its contours.

The fact that there is widespread poverty in the United States is not written in stone. Poverty can be reduced. We will discuss examples of countries that have confronted and reduced the extent of their poverty, as well as periods of U.S. history where this has occurred as well. A starting point in confronting poverty is with a thorough understanding of its dimensions and scope. The first chapter begins that exploration.

PART

I

Nature, Extent, and Characteristics of Poverty

Our first overall question to be explored in this book revolves around what is the nature, extent, and makeup of poverty? Regardless of the issue being examined, a logical starting point is to understand the scope of the problem. Specific topics explored include how to define and measure poverty, the manner in which the official poverty line in the United States is constructed, and to what extent have the overall rates of poverty changed over the past 70 years? In addition, we will look at how long people are in poverty; what is the lifetime risk of poverty; how do the rates of poverty in the United States compare to other countries; and which groups are more likely to experience poverty and why?

As we examine these questions, consider how the research and evidence being presented in these chapters at times differ from the mainstream images of poverty portrayed in the popular media and political arena. The reality of who experiences poverty is in some ways more disturbing than the stereotypes and myths.

CHAPTER 1 Defining and Measuring

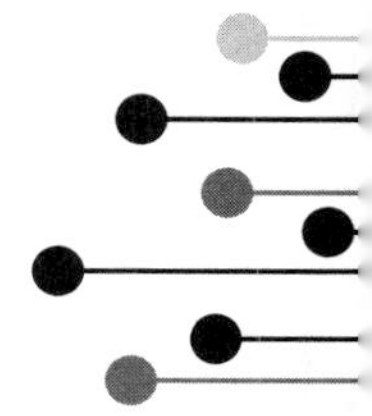

If you were asked to provide an image of poverty, what comes to mind? Hardship and struggle? A lack of money and overdue bills? Deteriorating neighborhoods? What about the neighbor down the street or the family next door? Maybe a small-town fast-food worker or a struggling farmer? Perhaps yourself sometime in the next 20 years?

As we shall see, all of these and more might be a part of a broad conception of what is meant by poverty. In our examination of the nature and scope of poverty, we begin with what is denoted by the term itself.

Defining Poverty

Over the centuries, poverty has been conceptualized and defined in a number of different ways. In ancient societies, the poor were often thought of as those who fell into particularly unfortunate categories such as beggars, the sick, or the widowed. In medieval times, those in poverty would have been considered the peasant class, which encompassed most of society.

More recently, Adam Smith in his landmark treatise, *The Wealth of Nations* (1776), defined poverty as a lack of those necessities that "the custom of the country renders it indecent for creditable people, even of the lowest order, to be without." This type of definition is what is known as an absolute approach to defining poverty. A minimum threshold for adequate living conditions is determined, and individuals falling below that threshold are considered poor.

On its surface, many of us might agree with Smith's description. However, our consensus would probably begin to break down over what exactly such necessities should encompass. Certainly most of us would include items such as food, clothing, and shelter, but what kind of food, clothing, and shelter? Furthermore, what additional items might we include—a cell phone, health insurance, internet access, a car, and so on?

If we turn to the dictionary for contemporary guidance in defining poverty, Webster defines poverty in three ways: "1. the state or condition of having little or no money, goods, or means of support; 2. deficiency of necessary or desirable ingredients, qualities, etc.; 3. scantiness; insufficiency." Here again we have the notion that poverty consists of a shortage of basic goods and resources and that the lack of money is the cause of this shortage. Similarly, in defining poverty, the World Bank (2018) says, "A person is considered poor if his or her income level falls below some minimum level necessary to meet basic needs."

Yet another way of thinking about how we might define poverty is to conceptualize what such a shortage means in the daily lives of individuals. It is within this context that many countries speak of poverty in terms of social exclusion or deprivation. To be poor is often to be on the outskirts of society. The economist and social philosopher Amartya Sen defines poverty in terms of a lack of basic capabilities. According to Sen (1992), poverty implies an overall absence of individual freedom and agency. Individuals in poverty are less able to exert control over their lives. They are more likely to be stigmatized and discriminated against, less likely to be able to take advantage of certain fundamental rights such as voting, plagued by a lower life expectancy, and affected by a host of other constraints.

This introduces the idea that poverty may be more than simply a lack of money. It includes aspects of life that are diminished as a result of an inadequate income. The United Nations (UN) incorporates such a perspective into its definition of poverty for high-economy countries. The UN includes not only a lack of income but also long-term unemployment, lower life expectancy, and overall rates of illiteracy (United Nations Development Programme 2019).

Consequently, there are many ways in which we might define who is poor. Yet all of these definitions touch upon the idea that those in poverty are lacking the necessities to maintain a minimally adequate life.

Measuring Poverty

In 1964 President Lyndon Johnson historically declared a war on poverty. Delivering his State of the Union address to Congress and the American people, the President announced,

> *This Administration today, here and now, declares unconditional war on poverty in America, and I urge this Congress and all Americans to join with me in that effort. It will not be a short or easy struggle, no single weapon or strategy will suffice, but we shall not rest until that war is won. The richest nation on earth can afford to win it. We cannot afford to lose it.* (New York Times, *January 9, 1964)*

Yet as the administration was to learn on both the domestic and foreign battlefields, a country marching off to war must have a credible estimate of the enemy's size and strength. Surprisingly, up until this point in our nation's history, we had no official measure of poverty and therefore no statistics on its scope, shape, or changing nature. The task was therefore to come up with a way of measuring how many people in America were poor.

There are several basic distinctions that can be made when seeking to measure poverty (Iceland 2005, 2013). Three of the most important are whether one should use an absolute versus a relative measure, whether one should use a pretransfer versus a posttransfer measure, and whether one should use income or assets as the measuring stick for poverty.

Absolute Versus Relative Measures

A first distinction in measuring poverty is between what is known as an absolute measure of poverty versus a relative measure. An absolute measure defines poverty as a household failing to have a particular amount of income to purchase those goods and services that are necessary for a minimally adequate life. As discussed earlier, these would include food, shelter, transportation, utilities, and so on. An absolute measure of poverty determines how much these items cost annually, and based upon that, estimates an overall dollar amount for the year. Households whose total annual income falls below this amount would be counted as poor, while those above this amount would be considered nonpoor.

The assumption is that there is an income floor that can be empirically calculated, and that living below that floor constitutes poverty. In this sense, such a measure is considered absolute—there is an absolute amount drawn dividing the poor from the nonpoor, with below that line representing material hardship.

On the other hand, a relative measure of poverty looks at where a household's income falls relative to the rest of the population. One relative measure of poverty would be to consider the poor as falling into the bottom 20 or 10 percent of the income distribution. Another relative measure widely used throughout the European Union is to consider those in poverty as having incomes below 50 percent of a country's median income. Consequently, if median income was $60,000, then those earning less than $30,000 would be counted as poor. If median income were to rise to $70,000, then those below $35,000 would be considered in poverty.

Underlying this type of measure is the concept of relative deprivation. Individuals are considered poor not because they fall below a particular set amount of income but rather by the fact that they fall at the bottom of the income distribution. One major advantage of a relative measure such as falling below 50 percent of median income is that it allows us to make comparisons across countries with respect to the extent and depth of poverty.

Pretransfer Versus Posttransfer Measures

A second important distinction in measuring poverty is between what is known as a pretransfer versus a posttransfer measure of poverty. A pretransfer measure of poverty is based on a household's overall annual income but excludes any cash, in-kind benefits, or tax credits that it might have received from the government. On the other hand, a posttransfer measure of poverty will include personal earnings along with government cash programs (such as Social Security or unemployment insurance) and/or in-kind programs (such as food stamps) and tax credits in calculating a household's overall income.

Policy analysts will often compare the difference in poverty rates between a pretransfer and posttransfer measure as a way of gauging the impact that government programs have upon reducing poverty. A posttransfer measure of poverty will always be lower than a pretransfer measure. How much lower varies widely across countries.

Income- Versus Asset-Based Measures

A third important distinction to be made in measuring poverty is the difference between using income or assets as the measuring stick to determine whether or not a family is considered in poverty. The standard economic approach has been to use a household's income to determine whether or not they fall into poverty. It is through income that households are able to purchase those goods and services necessary for a minimally adequate lifestyle. Such a measure, however, does not take into account the value of any assets that the household may hold.

On the other hand, an asset-based measure of poverty gets at the idea of whether individuals have enough assets (i.e., savings and checking accounts) to allow them to get over a period where their stream of income has been stopped. The concept is one of protection from a rainy day. This type of measure often defines asset poverty as not having enough liquid assets to keep a household above the poverty line for three months.

How the Official Poverty Measure Is Constructed

All of these approaches have been, and continue to be, discussed in policy circles (for an extended discussion on various ways of measuring poverty, see Smeeding 2016). At the time of President Johnson's declared war on poverty, any one of these approaches could have been taken to assess the federal government's efforts. The task fell upon an economist working for the Social Security Administration—Mollie Orshansky—to devise the country's yardstick for measuring poverty (see Fisher 1992, and Orshansky 1965, for a descriptive history of her approach).

The method that Orshansky took was consistent with Adam Smith's definition 200 years earlier. That is, poverty was conceptualized as a failure to have the income necessary to purchase a basic basket of goods and services that allows for a minimally decent level of existence. The approach was therefore absolute rather than relative.

The way that this was (and still is) calculated is straightforward. One begins by estimating the household costs of obtaining a minimally adequate diet during the course of the year. For example, in 2019 a family of three would need to spend $6,778 to purchase such a diet. This figure is then multiplied by three (in the above case $\$6,778 \times 3 = \$20,335$), which constitutes the official poverty line for a family of three. The reason for using three as a multiplier is that Orshansky relied upon a 1955 Department of Agriculture survey showing that families with three or more persons spent approximately one-third of their income on food, and the remaining two-thirds on other items such as clothing, housing, heating, and so on. Thus, the logic in the above example is that if $6,778 will purchase a subsistence diet for a family of three, then the remaining $13,557 should provide enough income to purchase the other basic necessities needed for a minimal level of existence.

Several other points are important regarding the measurement of poverty. Each year the poverty levels are adjusted to take into account inflation. Obviously it costs more to purchase that basic basket of goods today than it did 55 years ago. Second, the measuring stick to determine whether individuals fall above or below the poverty threshold is household income. Household income is based on the annual income from all members in the household, calculated from pretax dollars, and does not include in-kind program benefits such as Medicaid or Food Stamps, or tax credits such as the Earned Income Tax Credit. It does include government cash programs such as Social Security. Third, the actual estimates of how many Americans fall below the poverty line are derived from the annual Current Population Survey of approximately 60,000 households conducted by the U.S. Bureau of the Census each March. Fourth, the levels of poverty established each year are for the entire nation and do not differentiate between the cost of living differences found in various parts of the country. Finally, the monetary amount necessary for a small household's basic needs will obviously differ from those of a larger household, and therefore the poverty levels are adjusted for household size. For example, in 2019 the poverty level for a household of one was $13,011, while that of a household of nine or more was $52,875 (U.S. Census Bureau 2020a).

In Table 1.1, we can see the percentage of the U.S. population experiencing various levels of poverty. Three different levels are shown: the official poverty measure (below 100 percent of the official poverty line), poverty and near poverty (below 150 percent of the official poverty line), and extreme poverty (below 50 percent of the official poverty line). For 2019, 10.5 percent of the population fell below the official poverty line representing 34.0 million individuals, 18.1 percent experienced poverty or near poverty, and 4.7 percent were living in extreme poverty.

In addition to the official measure of poverty, the Census Bureau has developed an alternative measure of poverty, called the Supplemental Poverty Measure (U.S. Census Bureau 2020b). This is intended to refine the official poverty measure by taking into account a wider variety of expenditures, adjusting for cost of living differences, and including noncash benefits along with received tax credits in determining income. The estimates of poverty using the Supplemental Measure tend to be slightly higher than when using

Table 1.1 Percent and Number of the Population in Poverty for 2019

Level of Poverty	Percent (%)	Number (in millions)
Official Poverty Measure		
0.50 Poverty	4.7	15.3
1.00 Poverty	10.5	34.0
1.50 Poverty	18.1	58.3
Supplemental Poverty Measure		
0.50 Poverty	3.9	12.7
1.00 Poverty	11.7	38.2
1.50 Poverty	25.7	83.6

Source: U.S. Census Bureau (2019)

the official measure of poverty. In addition, poverty rates for children tend to be lower than the official measure, while poverty rates for those over age 65 years tend to be higher.

In the bottom panel of Table 1.1, the extent of poverty in the United States using the Supplemental Poverty Measure is shown. According to this measure, 11.7 percent of the population fell into poverty, representing 38.2 million Americans. Furthermore, a quarter of Americans (25.7 percent) were in poverty or near poverty, while 3.9 percent experienced extreme poverty. We can see from this table that some differences exist between the official and supplemental measures, particularly with respect to the size of the population experiencing near poverty.

What Does Living Below the Poverty Line Mean?

As discussed earlier, the manner in which poverty is officially defined in the United States is by falling below a specific level of income. Households earning less than a minimum level income are considered to be in poverty. Yet what exactly does it mean to be living below the U.S. poverty line?

In 2019, the poverty line for a household of three was set at $20,335. Consequently, a three-person household that earned less than this amount would be counted as in poverty. This comes out to an average monthly income of approximately $1,695. As noted above, the Census Bureau estimates that poor families will spend one-third of their income on food and the remaining two-thirds on other necessities such as housing, clothing, and transportation.

To illustrate what these numbers mean in a day-to-day sense, let us take the poverty level for a family of three. Using the one-third/two-thirds split, our hypothetical family would have $6,778 available for food during the year. This comes out to $130 a week, $18.62 a day, or $6.21 a day for each member of that family. Assuming that family members eat three meals per day, this works out to approximately two dollars per person, per meal, per day.

Taking the remaining two-thirds of the poverty line's threshold—$13,557—provides our family with $261 per week for all other expenses. Using the MIT Living Wage Calculator developed by Amy Glasmeier (2020), it is estimated that a family of two adults and one child in the St. Louis region (which is fairly representative of the country as a whole) would need to earn $39,094 for the year in order to meet all of their other basic needs beyond food. This comes out to $752 per week. We can quickly see that a family in poverty falls well short of what is considered minimally necessary to purchase an adequate basket of goods and services. Their $261 a week for expenses is only one-third of what they really need to get by to cover their basic housing costs, utilities, medical expenses, and so on. Bringing the poverty line down to this level allows for a more meaningful sense of what these numbers represent in terms of people's lives and the extreme difficulty in trying to survive at this level.

However, it is important to keep in mind that this example captures poverty at its most opulent level, that is, families fall to varying degrees below the poverty line. In 2019, 45 percent of all poor persons were living in households where their incomes fell below one-half of their respective poverty thresholds, otherwise known as extreme poverty (U.S. Census Bureau 2020a). Therefore, rather than an annual income of $20,335 for a family of three, many are trying to survive on an income of $10,178 or less for a three-person household. If living at the poverty line is difficult, imagine trying to live below one-half of the poverty line.

It is also interesting to contrast what Americans feel is the minimum amount of income needed to get by on versus the poverty line. In 2013, the Gallup Poll asked a national sample, "What is the smallest amount of money a family of four needs to make each year to get by in your community." The average amount given was $58,000 (Gallup Poll 2013). In 2013, the poverty threshold for a family of four was $23,550. Consequently, it is obvious that most Americans would perceive surviving below the poverty line as extremely precarious.

Yet another way of translating the meaning of poverty into one's own life can be illustrated with the following statistic. In 2019, the median income for a household of three in the United States was $91,894 (U.S. Census Bureau 2020a). On the other hand, as noted, the poverty threshold for such a household was $20,335. Therefore, the income for a family of three at the edge of poverty is just 22 percent of the overall median income for such a family.

For some of you reading this book, your family may be near the median in terms of household income and may occasionally find it difficult to keep up with various household expenses and needs. Now imagine that instead of the income you currently have coming in for this month, next month you will be receiving only 22 percent of your income. The other 78 percent is suddenly gone. That 78 percent is the distance between the median standard of living and the standard of living for those at the edge of poverty. And as noted earlier, this represents poverty at its most opulent level. Forty-five percent of poor individuals fall below one-half of the poverty line. For a family of three this would be $10,168, which represents 11 percent of the national median income.

Finally, in an important respect, today's poverty is harsher than it was 70 years ago. In 1947 the poverty threshold for a family of four would have stood at 69 percent of the median four-person family income. In 1959, it had dropped to just under 50 percent of the median. In 1980 it was 35 percent, and by 2019, the poverty threshold had dropped further to 25 percent (U.S. Census Bureau 2020a). Being categorized as poor today has meant living further afield from the economic mid-point than in the past. If we were to apply the economic distance that families in poverty were from the median income found in 1959, the poverty threshold for a family of four would rise from its current $26,172 to $53,074. As Howard Glennerster noted,

> *Very few American voters can realize that the measure of poverty that dominates political discussion has been getting more and more mean as the years pass.... If the present rate of income growth continues and the poverty line remains unchanged, the poverty line will soon be equivalent not to half of median earnings, as it was when Mollie Orshansky invented the number, but to a quarter of median earnings. That would be twice as harsh a measure as other countries in the world adopt (2002, 90).*

In this sense, poverty has become more severe today than it was 70 years ago.

Poverty Rates Over Time

As noted earlier, when President Johnson declared a war on poverty in 1964, there was a need to create an overall measure of poverty. As a result, a poverty line was established that determined how many people in the United States were in poverty in any given year. The measure was then backdated to 1959, which is why official statistics always begin with that year.

In Figure 1.1 we can see how the overall official poverty rates have changed over the 60-year period from 1959 to 2019, as well as the rates for children and the elderly. Several patterns are apparent. From 1959 to 1973, overall poverty in the United States was cut in half. In 1959, the poverty rate stood at 22.4 percent and by 1973 it had fallen to 11.1 percent.

Figure 1.1 Poverty Rate, 1959–2019

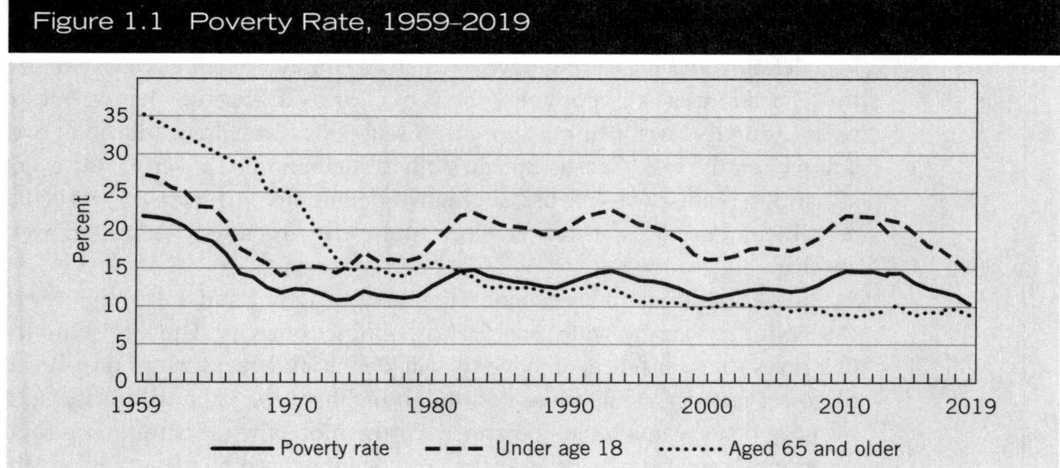

Source: Semega, Jessica, Melissa Kollar, John Creamer, and Abinash Mohanty, U.S. Census Bureau, Current Population Reports, P60-266(RV), Income and Poverty in the United States: 2018, U.S. Government Printing Office, Washington, DC, 2020.

Consequently, during a fairly short period of time, the overall rate of poverty was substantially reduced.

We can also see that since the early 1970s, poverty has varied between 10 and 15 percent. It has tended to go up during periods of recessions (e.g., the early 1980s and 2008–10) and has declined during periods of economic growth (e.g., the later 1990s and 2010s).

The overall rate of poverty is influenced by several broad factors. First, as mentioned, how well the economy is performing will influence the rate of poverty. Second, changes in the size of particular population groups can influence the overall poverty rate. The growth or decline of groups at a higher risk of poverty (i.e., single-parent families) can influence the percentage of the population in poverty. Finally, government programs directed at financially assisting those with low incomes can have an impact on reducing overall poverty. As such programs are expanded or contracted, poverty rates will often fall or rise.

With respect to the elderly, in 1959 those 65 years and over was the age group most at risk of poverty. Their rate of poverty was 35.2 percent. By 2019 it had fallen to 9.4 percent. This drop represents America's greatest success story in reducing poverty. On the other hand, for children the story is different. Their rate of poverty fell from 26.9 percent in 1959 to 14.2 percent in 1973. However, since the mid-1970s poverty among children has not improved, standing at 14.4 percent in 2019.

Concluding Thoughts

In this chapter, we have reviewed various aspects of defining and measuring poverty. These are important considerations to keep in mind as we explore the contours and dimensions of poverty in the pages ahead.

The manner in which we define and measure poverty can be considered somewhat arbitrary. While there are many important considerations that go into defining and measuring poverty, there is simply no definitive way to do this. Therefore, it is important to be very clear as to exactly what we mean when using this term. In many of our discussions throughout this book, we will rely on the U.S. Census Bureau's official definition of poverty. However, at various points, we will use alternative definitions of poverty as well. In certain circumstances, it may be more appropriate to use one definition over another.

It is also important to recognize that how we define and measure poverty can be influenced by wider social and political concerns. Those wishing to downplay the existence of poverty will define and measure poverty in a narrower manner, while those desiring to highlight the issue will define and measure poverty in a broader manner. Furthermore, the narrative that is told regarding American poverty over time can be influenced by the way in which poverty is defined and measured. The bottom line is that rather than just an academic question, the defining and measuring of poverty can have significant real-world implications.

ONLINE ACTIVITIES

confrontingpoverty.org

Let us begin by going to the "Confronting Poverty" website (confrontingpoverty.org). On the homepage, select the "Discussion Guide" box, and then select the "Module 1" box. On the sidebar, select the "MIT Living Wage Calculator" link.

This will take you to the Living Wage calculator that has been created by Amy Glasmeir at MIT. The idea behind this calculator and website was to develop a way of measuring what a living wage should be in various parts of the country by using cost of living data from hundreds of localities.

A logical starting point is to begin where you live right now. First, select the state that you are residing in. Once you do that, you can then select your county within the state you are living in. What will appear on the page is several sets of information. The first chart shows you what a living wage should be in your locality depending on the type of family one is in. This represents the wage at which someone who is working full-time is able to purchase the basic necessities of living for their family, including housing, food, and so on.

You can see that across the different household types, the living wage is much higher than the current minimum wage. In most states and localities, the minimum wage is significantly below what a living wage should be. In addition, you can also observe what the poverty wage is. This represents the wage at which someone working full-time would be at the poverty threshold through their earnings.

On the next chart are the average expenses that have gone into calculating a living wage. Here we find the annual estimates for food, childcare, medical, housing, and transportation in a specific county. These give you a sense of the yearly expenses for someone earning a living wage.

Finally, after this chart you can observe what the average salaries are for a range of occupations in your region. You will notice that some of these are quite low. For example, someone who is working in a sales job is likely to be earning well below what a living wage should be.

After examining your own location, you can compare the costs of living and a living wage in other locations in the United States. As you explore these regions, you will discover that some areas of the country have extremely high costs of living, and therefore require a much higher living wage in order to get by. For example, the San Francisco Bay area on the West coast or the Boston and New York City areas on the East coast have extremely high costs of living, largely as a result of their expensive housing costs. These comparisons illustrate that for households earning minimum wages in these regions, their material conditions may be particularly dire.

We will return to the issue of a living wage in Chapter 13, but what this analysis shows is that much of poverty is the result of people not earning enough at their jobs to get them out of poverty or near poverty. We will also take up this issue in Chapters 5 and 6.

There are many other important pieces of information and research on this website. Take some time to explore these offerings with respect to the relationship between poverty and the lack of a living wage.

CHAPTER 2 Patterns and Dynamics

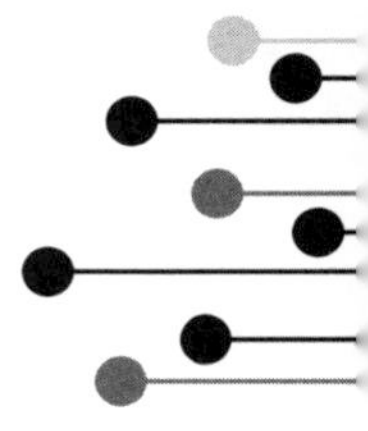

In the prior chapter we examined the questions of how to define and measure poverty. We also looked at how many people are poor in any given year. This background is a logical starting point for understanding the scope of the problem.

In this chapter we expand upon these topics by exploring the dynamics and patterns of poverty. Here the elements of time and space are introduced. Consequently, how long are people poor? How often do they experience poverty? What is their lifetime risk of experiencing poverty? How does the United States compare to other countries? We explore each of these questions in the pages ahead.

The Dynamics of Poverty

Before the advent of large longitudinal data sets tracking the same people and households over extended periods of time, it was often assumed that those who were in poverty this year were roughly the same people who were in poverty last year and the next year. These assumptions were primarily based on anecdotal stories. However, beginning in the mid-1970s, social scientists have acquired substantial information from large panel data sets (following the same people over time) about the actual patterns and length of time that individuals find themselves in poverty (Pfeffer, Fomby, and Insolera 2020). It turns out that a much more accurate picture is that poverty spells tend to be short but frequent. Poverty is typically fluid rather than the static image often portrayed.

Table 2.1 displays the percentage of new poverty spells in the United States that end after a given number of years. As we can see, within one or two years, the majority of people have escaped from poverty. Within one year, 53 percent of new spells have ended, 70 percent have ended after two years, and over three-quarters within three years. Less than 15 percent of spells will last more than five years. If we consider long-term poverty as five or more consecutive years, then the vast majority of American poverty spells do not meet such a standard. As Mary Jo Bane and David Ellwood explained years ago in one of the first analyses of American poverty spells, "Most people who slip into poverty are quite successful in getting out" (1986, 12).

Another way of seeing the relatively short-term nature of poverty spells is through a U.S. Census analysis of monthly poverty. Using a large longitudinal data set known as the SIPP (Survey of Income and Program Participation),

Table 2.1 Spell Length Distribution for New Poverty Spells

Years in Poverty	Percent of New Spells that Ended (%)
1	52.5
2	69.7
3	77.9
4	82.9
5	86.1
6	88.3
7	90.1
8	91.3
9	92.3

Source: Adapted from Ann Huff Stevens, "Climbing Out of Poverty, Falling Back In Measuring the Persistence of Poverty over Multiple Spells," *Journal of Human Resources* 34, no. 3 (Summer 1999), p. 568.

poverty can be analyzed on a monthly rather than an annual basis. During the 36 months of 2009, 2010, and 2011, 31.6 percent of the U.S. population experienced poverty at some point (defined as being in poverty for two or more consecutive months). For those experiencing poverty, 72.1 percent did so for 12 months or less, while only 15.2 percent of individuals experienced poverty for more than 24 consecutive months (U.S. Census Bureau 2014). Again, the vast majority of those experiencing poverty do so over a fairly short period of time.

Research has also shown that the reasons for entering and exiting poverty are most often caused by changes in employment status and/or financial resources (Cellini, McKernan, and Ratcliffe 2008). As individuals lose jobs or have their hours cut back, the likelihood of poverty increases. Other causes of entrances/exits include changes in family structure (such as divorce/marriage, childbirth, or a child leaving home to start their own household), and health-related issues. These are common events that most of us will experience over our life course. However, some Americans live closer to the poverty line than others, making these events more consequential in their lives. But they can happen to any of us, and for those close to the line who fall into poverty as a result, most will fight hard to escape poverty and succeed relatively quickly.

Poverty spells triggered by moving out of one's parents' house tend to be the shortest, while spells triggered by the birth of a child tend to be the longest. Employment, education, and marriage are helpful in avoiding poverty along with faster exits if one does become poor, and avoiding multiple spells. African Americans, women, female-headed households, and those with low educational attainment are at higher risk of new spells, multiple spells, and longer-lasting spells (Rank 2020a).

Data on time spent on government assistance in terms of the social safety net are also useful to this discussion. A little over a quarter (27 percent) of Americans use at least one major means-tested program (Medicaid, the Supplemental Nutrition Program or SNAP, Housing Assistance, the Supplemental Security Income Program or SSI, the Temporary Assistance for Needy Families Program or TANF, and/or General Assistance) at some point during the year, with an average of about a fifth (21 percent) participating in at least one program each month (U.S. Census Bureau 2015). Participation within a given year is higher for female-headed households (58 percent versus 20 percent for married couples), African Americans and Hispanics (49 and 46 percent versus 18 percent for whites), children (47 percent versus 23 percent for working-age adults), those without a high school degree (45 percent versus 29 percent for high school graduates), and the unemployed (42 percent versus 11 percent for full-time workers). Within a four-year period, a majority of participants (57 percent) will use these programs for three years or less (U.S. Census Bureau 2015). Medicaid and SNAP are the most heavily used programs (15 percent and 13 percent monthly participation, respectively).

The program that Americans most often strongly associate with "welfare"—TANF—is used much less than other programs (1 percent of the population monthly, 1.7 percent over a four-year period) (U.S. Census Bureau 2015). Spells on TANF are also very short: half (50.5 percent) end within 4 months, and over three-quarters (79.6 percent) within a year (U.S. Department of Health and Human Services 2018).

While short-term poverty and welfare use is the norm, long-term poverty is nevertheless a concern. Some analyses show that, at any given moment, a majority of the poor are enduring long-term poverty spells of 10 years or more. How could this be, if most new poverty spells end within one or two years? Bane and Ellwood explain with a helpful metaphor:

> *Consider the situation in a typical hospital. Most of the persons admitted in any year will require only a very short spell of hospitalization. But a few of the newly admitted patients are chronically ill and will have extended stays in the hospital. If we ask what proportion of all admissions are people who are chronically ill, the answer is relatively few. On the other hand, if we ask what fraction of the number of the hospital's beds at any one time are occupied by the chronically ill, the answer is much larger. The reason is simple. Although the chronically ill account for only a small fraction of all admissions, because they stay so long they end up being a sizable part of the hospital population and they consume a sizable proportion of the hospital's resources. (1986, 11)*

So while most Americans who find themselves in poverty will be there for only a matter of a few years, persistent poverty is in fact a concern. This minority of the poor does indeed present unique challenges to policy makers compared to the majority of short-termers.

The risk of experiencing multiple spells is also a concern. Despite the norm of short spells for most people, slightly more than half of those who escape poverty will return for an additional spell within five years (Stevens 2012). The longer one experiences poverty, the harder it is to escape and the more likely one is to return as well. While a majority will exit poverty within the first year, the likelihood of escaping declines rapidly after that. For those who have been in poverty for five years, their likelihood of exit is less than 20 percent. And for those who have been in poverty for at least five years prior to exit, more than two-thirds will return within five years (Cellini, McKernan, and Ratcliffe 2008).

The Life Course Risk of Poverty

Another way of thinking about the scope of poverty is to consider the lifetime risk of experiencing poverty. Rather than asking the question of how long are people in poverty, the question becomes what percentage of the American population will at some point in their lives experience poverty?

Background

The longitudinal research of sociologists Mark Rank and Thomas Hirschl has helped shed light on the issue of the life course risk of poverty. Over two decades ago, Rank and Hirschl were interested in asking a very basic question, "How likely is it that an American will experience poverty firsthand?" Furthermore, "What are the chances that an American will use a social safety net program at some point during their adulthood?" In order to answer these questions, they turned to an invaluable longitudinal data set—the Panel Study of Income Dynamics, otherwise known as the PSID.

The PSID is a nationally representative, longitudinal sample of households interviewed from 1968 onward (Pfeffer, Fomby, and Insolera 2020). It has been administered by the Survey Research Center at the University of Michigan, and it constitutes the longest-running panel data set both in the United States and the world. The PSID initially interviewed approximately 5,000 U.S. households in 1968, obtaining detailed information on roughly 18,000 individuals within those households. These individuals have since been tracked annually (biennially after 1997), including children and adults who eventually break off from their original households to form new households (for example, children leaving home or adults following a divorce). Thus, the PSID is designed so that in any given year the sample is representative of the entire U.S. population.

As its name implies, the PSID is primarily interested in household information about economics and demographics. For each wave of the study, there is detailed information about the annual income for each household. Consequently, one can easily determine whether households fell into poverty across the various years of the study. The survey also asks questions

the benefits of an antipoverty policy or of an economic safety net in terms of their own self-interest. The research findings discussed in this section directly challenge such beliefs. In doing so, they provide a vital piece for making a self-interest argument—most Americans in fact will be touched directly by poverty.

These findings have an additional implication. Much of the general public's resistance toward assisting poor people and particularly those on welfare is that they are perceived to be undeserving of such assistance (examined in Chapter 4). That is, their poverty is the result of a lack of motivation, questionable morals, and so on. In short, poor people are fundamentally culpable, and therefore, do not warrant sacrifices on our behalf.

Although the causes of poverty have not been examined in this section, the findings presented here suggest that given its widespread nature, poverty appears systematic to our economic structure. In short, we have met the enemy, and they are us.

Such a realization can cause a paradigm shift in thinking. For example, the economic collapse during the Great Depression spurred a fundamental change in the country's perceptions and policy initiatives as citizens realized the full extent and systematic nature of poverty during the 1930s. Given the enormity of the collapse, it became clear to many Americans that most of their neighbors were not directly responsible for the dire economic situation they found themselves in. This awareness helped provide much of the impetus and justification behind the New Deal.

Or take the case of unemployment as described by sociologist C. Wright Mills,

> *When, in a city of 100,000, only one man is unemployed, that is his personal trouble, and for its relief we properly look to the character of the man, his skills, and his immediate opportunities. But when in a nation of 50 million employees, 15 million men are unemployed, that is an issue, and we may not hope to find its solution within the range of opportunities open to any one individual. The very structure of opportunities has collapsed. Both the correct statement of the problem and the range of possible solutions require us to consider the economic and political institutions of the society, and not merely the personal situation and character of a scatter of individuals.* (1959, 9)

In many ways, poverty today is as widespread and systematic as in these examples. Yet we have been unable to see this because we are not looking in the right direction. By focusing on the life-span risks, the prevalent nature of American poverty is revealed. At some point during our adult lives, the bulk of Americans will face the bitter taste of poverty. Consequently, unless the general public is willing to argue that the majority of us are undeserving, the tactic of using character flaws and individual failings as a justification for doing as little as possible to address poverty loses much of its credibility.

In short, by conceptualizing and measuring impoverishment over the adult life course, one can observe a set of proportions that truly cast a new light on the subject of poverty in the United States. For the majority of

American adults, the question is not if they will experience poverty, but when. Such a reality should cause us to reevaluate seriously the very nature, scope, and meaning of poverty in the United States.

Poverty Rates Across Countries

Yet another way to think about the scope of U.S. poverty is to ask how do we compare to other countries? Is the extent of poverty similar or dissimilar to other Western industrialized countries?

It is certainly true that if we compare the United States to countries in sub-Saharan Africa, physical poverty in the United States is much less extreme. The United States does not have the widespread famine and severe stunting of children that is sometimes found in extremely poor countries. However, most analysts would argue that the more relevant comparison would be the group of other high-economy countries such as those found in the European Union, Canada, Japan, Australia, and so on. In comparing poverty in the United States to these Organisation for Economic Co-operation and Development (OECD) countries, we find that American poverty is both more prevalent and more extreme.

In Table 2.4, we can compare poverty rates across 26 OECD countries. In this table, poverty is being measured as the percent of the population falling below one half of a particular country's median household income. As discussed in Chapter 1, this is what is known as a relative measure of poverty, and is used extensively in making cross-national comparisons. The first column shows the overall poverty rate for each country; the second column displays the poverty rate for children; and the third column indicates the distance between the average income of those in poverty compared to the country's overall poverty threshold.

What we find is that the U.S. rates of poverty are substantially higher and more extreme than those found in the other 25 nations. The overall U.S. rate using this measure stands at 17.8 percent, compared to the 25 country average of 10.7 percent. The Scandinavian and Benelux countries tend to have the lowest rates of poverty. For example, the overall rate of poverty in Denmark is 5.5 percent.

Looking at the poverty rates for children, we see similar patterns. The United States leads all nations in having the highest rates of child poverty at 20.9 percent, while the overall average stands at 11.7 percent. Again, we see the Scandinavian countries having the lowest rates of child poverty, with Denmark seeing only 2.9 percent of its children falling into poverty.

Finally, the third column indicates the poverty gap, which is defined as the percentage by which the average income of the poor falls below the poverty line. This gives us an overall gauge of the depth and severity of poverty in each country. Once again we find that the United States is at the very high end in terms of this measure. The distance between the poor's average income and the poverty line is nearly 40 percent. Only Italy has a greater poverty gap than the United States.

Table 2.4 Extent of Poverty Across 26 OECD Countries			
Country	**Overall**	**Children**	**Poverty Gap**
Iceland	5.4	5.8	27.2
Denmark	5.5	2.9	31.0
Finland	6.3	3.6	21.0
France	8.3	11.5	23.9
Netherlands	8.3	10.9	31.6
Norway	8.4	8.0	34.3
Switzerland	9.1	9.5	26.2
Sweden	9.3	9.3	22.5
Belgium	9.7	12.3	21.6
Austria	9.8	11.5	35.4
Ireland	9.8	10.8	23.3
Hungary	10.1	11.8	29.2
Poland	10.3	9.3	28.4
Germany	10.4	12.3	26.5
New Zealand	10.9	14.1	26.2
Luxembourg	11.1	13.0	28.9
United Kingdom	11.1	11.8	35.5
Australia	12.1	12.5	28.7
Canada	12.4	14.2	30.4
Portugal	12.5	15.5	29.4
Italy	13.7	17.3	40.8
Greece	14.4	17.6	35.3
Japan	15.7	13.9	33.7
Mexico	16.6	19.8	33.5
Korea	17.4	14.5	35.5
Overall 25 Country Average	10.7	11.7	29.6
United States	17.8	20.9	39.8

Source: OECD Data (2019).

To summarize, when analyzing poverty as the number of persons who fall below 50 percent of a country's median income, we find that the United States has far and away the highest overall poverty rate in this group of 26 developed nations. Furthermore, the distance of the poor from the overall median income is extreme in the United States. At the same time, the United States is arguably the wealthiest nation in the world.

This paradox is revealed in additional analyses that have examined both income and wealth inequality across OECD countries (Balestra and Tonkin 2018; Tridico 2018). Not surprisingly, the United States has the highest standards of living at the middle and upper ends of the income distribution scale, yet for children at the lower end, their standards of living fall behind most other industrialized nations. The conclusion to be drawn from these divergent patterns regarding American children is that,

> *Compared to other high-income counterpart nations, the US constantly experienced higher child poverty rates, regardless of the relative or absolute terms. Social insurance and universal programs in the US tend to be meager compared to those in high-income countries, and the overall portion that the US contributes to reducing its deep child poverty is far lower. (Cai and Smeeding 2019, 19)*

The reasons for such poverty are twofold. First, as discussed in Chapter 10, and as indicated in the above quote, the social safety net in the United States is much weaker than in virtually every other country in Table 2.4. Second, the United States has been plagued by relatively low wages at the bottom of the income distribution scale when compared to other developed countries (discussed in Chapter 6). These factors combine to contribute to both the relative and absolute depths of US poverty in comparison to other industrialized nations.

Concluding Thoughts

Introducing the elements of time and space into the discussion of the extent of American poverty expands our understanding of this question. In any given year, the U.S. poverty rate varies between 10 and 15 percent. However, when looking across longer periods of time, the percentage of the population exposed to poverty increases dramatically. Furthermore, although the length of time spent in poverty tends to be short, recidivism is quite common. Finally, when we compare the United States to other OECD countries, the United States is at the high end in terms of the extent and severity of its poverty.

The upshot of these findings is that regardless of how we measure poverty, its reach is quite wide. The fact that a majority of Americans will experience poverty indicates the extent of its range.

Furthermore, the fact that poverty varies widely across countries indicates that much can be done to reduce poverty. For example, although single parenthood results in high poverty rates in the United States (as we will see in the next chapter), in other countries this is not necessarily the case. Likewise, U.S. poverty can be dramatically reduced for particular groups over time. A case in point has been the significant reduction in senior poverty over the past 60 years that we saw in Chapter 1. Consequently, the scope of poverty can be quite fluid over time and space.

ONLINE ACTIVITIES

confrontingpoverty.org

The Organisation for Economic Co-operation and Development (OECD) is a group of 37 high-income economy countries. For our purposes, they represent the relevant group to compare the United States to in terms of poverty and inequality. The data in Table 2.4 in Chapter 2 come directly from its website, which we will now explore.

In order to do so, go to the "Facts and Myths" page of the *Confronting Poverty* website. Once there, go to Fact 4. On the sidebar is a link to OECD data, and click on that. This will take you directly to the OECD data on poverty.

As you can see in this first chart, the various countries are listed at the bottom of the chart, ranging, on the left side, from those with the lowest rates of poverty, to those, on the right side, with the highest rates of poverty. Throughout the OECD data, poverty is being measured as the percent of the population falling below one half of a country's median income. As we discussed in Chapter 1, this is what is known as a relative measure of poverty. One of the advantages of such a measure is that it allows us to compare poverty across a range of countries using a similar metric.

We can observe that the countries with the lowest rates of poverty tend to be the Scandinavian countries, while the United States is located near the highest end. Under the heading "Perspectives" below the table, you can choose to examine poverty for the total population, for children, for the working-age adult population, and for the elderly. First, uncheck the "Compare variables" box, and now choose each of the age categories separately to see how the rates of poverty vary across the countries. In general, you will see that poverty for the elderly tends to be lower than for the other groups. However, you will also see that regardless of the age group being looked at, the order of the countries largely remains the same.

Next, click on the tab "Poverty gap" under "Indicators" on the left side of the page. This will then give you a new chart and data to look at. The poverty gap is the distance between the average income of those in poverty and the poverty line or threshold. What this tells us is how severe poverty is in each country. The greater the gap, the worse off the poor are. This is expressed as a ratio, which can also be interpreted as a percentage. So for example, if the poverty gap for a country is .30, this means that the average income of the poor is 30 percent below what the poverty line is for that country.

If we begin looking at the total population, we can see on the left side of the chart those countries where the poverty gap is smallest, and on the right side are the countries where the poverty gap is widest. Once again, the United States is on the high end with respect to the depth of its poverty. Consequently, not only does the United States have a greater percentage of its population in poverty than the comparison countries, but the severity of its poverty is also quite high.

Under the "Perspectives" box, you can change which age group you would like to examine. Select "18–65-year-olds," and then "66-year-olds or more" to see how the numbers change. You can also compare all three at once by checking the box "Compare variables" and then selecting all three groups within the "Perspectives" box.

Finally, let us now examine the extent of income inequality across the OECD countries. In order to do so, click under the "Indicators" box on the left side of the page the category "Income inequality." This will take you to the income inequality page.

Here the countries are again lined up from left to right, with those having less income inequality on the left side and those with more income inequality on the right side. Under the "Definition of income inequality" box you can click on the "more" button to read about how the different inequality measures are defined. All of these measures attempt to describe with a number how narrow or wide the income distribution within a country is.

Regardless of the measure used, we can see that once again the United States tends to be on the far right hand side of this chart. Consequently, not only does the United States exhibit high rates of poverty compared to other OECD countries, but it also has high rates of income inequality as well.

There are many other social and economic indicators that can be explored on this website. Spend a few minutes examining some of these indicators. Taken as a whole, they provide a look into how OECD countries compare with respect to their overall quality of life.

CHAPTER 3

The Face of Poverty

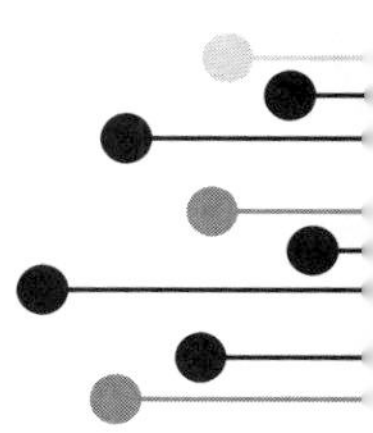

In thinking about who specifically in the U.S. population experiences poverty, there are at least two ways of approaching this question. The first is to focus on which groups have a higher or lower rate of poverty compared to the general population. This allows us to easily examine to what extent various population characteristics are associated with the risk of poverty.

The second approach looks at the overall poverty population with respect to group composition. This informs us as to what the face and makeup of poverty looks like. Each of these approaches tells us something slightly different about who the poor are.

Consider the example of race. Nonwhites (specifically African Americans, Hispanics, and Native Americans) have much higher rates of poverty than do whites. However, the majority of the poor are white. How can this be? The answer is that whites comprise a much larger segment of the overall population, and therefore, even though their rate of poverty is lower than nonwhites, they still make up a majority of the poor. Throughout this chapter, we are interested in examining both of these questions in order to understand the risk and composition of the poverty population. We begin with the role that demographics plays in influencing who the poor are.

The Role of Demographics

In Table 3.1, we can see how the rate of poverty and the composition of the poor population vary by demographic attributes. It should first be noted that with respect to race, Hispanic is considered an ethnic rather than a racial category. Consequently, one could self-identify as both white and Hispanic, or as black and Hispanic.

For whites (not of Hispanic origin), the poverty rate in 2019 was 7.3 percent. In contrast, the rate for other groups is considerably higher. The black poverty rate is 18.8 percent; for Hispanics, 15.7 percent; for Native Americans, 23.7 percent; and for Asians and Pacific Islanders, 7.3 percent.

These differences reflect the disparities found across many economic measures. They include significant racial and ethnic differences in income, unemployment rates, net worth, educational attainment, and occupational status (Shapiro 2017). The result is a much higher overall rate of poverty for nonwhites when compared to whites.

On the other hand, we can also see that approximately two-thirds of the poor self-identify as white. As noted above, this is primarily the result of the relatively larger size of the overall white population, so that while the

Table 3.1 Poverty Rates and Demographic Composition of the Poor 2019

Demographic Characteristics	Poverty Rate (%)	Percent of Poor Population (%)
Total	10.5	100.0
Race and Ethnicity		
White	9.1	66.2
Not of Hispanic Origin	7.3	41.6
Black	18.8	23.8
Asian and Pacific Islander	7.3	4.3
Native American*	23.7	1.7
Hispanic	15.7	28.1
Age		
Under 5 years	15.7	8.9
5–17 years	14.0	21.9
18–24 years	13.3	11.3
25–34 years	10.0	13.4
35–44 years	8.4	10.3
45–54 years	7.4	8.6
55–59 years	8.6	5.3
60–64 years	9.7	6.0
65–74 years	7.9	7.5
75 years and over	10.3	6.8
Gender		
Female	11.5	55.9
Male	9.4	44.1
Household Structure		
Married Couple	4.6	26.8
Female Headed	24.3	33.4
Male Headed	11.3	6.3
Single Female	20.9	19.1
Single Male	16.6	14.4

*Data is for 2018.
Source: U.S. Census Bureau (2019).

face of poverty is largely white, the risk of poverty is much greater for nonwhites.

Turning to age, the groups most at risk of poverty are children and young adults. Furthermore, very young children are at a particularly high risk. The poverty rate for children under the age of five is 15.7 percent. Those who are in their prime earning years (mid-30s to mid-50s) tend to have the smallest risk of poverty. This makes perfect sense in that this period of life represents the time in life where individuals tend to be earning the most from their jobs. Approximately 42 percent of those in poverty are under the age of 25 years, and an additional 14.3 percent are age 65 years and older.

Women are more likely to experience poverty than men. As with racial differences, this reflects gender differences across a wide range of key economic measures. Household structure, combined with gender, is also strongly related to the risk of poverty. Married couple households have an overall poverty rate of 4.6 percent, female-headed households (headed by a woman, usually with children) have a poverty rate of 24.3 percent, and households comprising of a single female have a poverty rate of 20.9 percent.

Consequently, we can see that certain demographic characteristics are closely associated with an elevated risk of poverty. These characteristics have been consistently correlated with poverty over many decades.

Human Capital

A second group of characteristics strongly related to the risk of poverty are what economists label human capital. As discussed in the next chapter, human capital refers to those attributes that individuals have acquired that allow them to compete more or less effectively in the labor market. These would include the level, quality, and type of acquired education, various skills and talents, job experience, and others. We can also think of human capital as including those attributes that may help or hinder an individual's ability to compete in the labor market, such as having a physical or mental disability.

In Table 3.2, the impact of three specific components of human capital is shown. First, greater levels of education are clearly related to a lowered risk of poverty. Those who have not graduated from high school have a poverty rate of 23.7 percent. The poverty rate for high school graduates falls to 11.5 percent, while those with some college education have a poverty rate of 7.8 percent. Finally, college graduates have an overall poverty rate of 3.9 percent. Considerable research has shown that greater levels of education are strongly related to greater levels of earned income. This is clearly reflected in the patterns found in Table 3.2. In terms of group composition, three-quarters of those in poverty have a high school degree or higher, with 39.6 percent having some amount of college education.

Table 3.2 Poverty Rates and Human Capital Composition of the Poor 2019

Human Capital	Poverty Rate (%)	Percent of Poor Population (%)
Education (25 and over)		
Less than 12	23.7	24.4
12	11.5	36.0
13 to 15	7.8	22.8
16 or more	3.9	16.8
Disability Status (18–64)		
Disability	22.5	17.5
No Disability	8.4	82.5
Work Experience (18–64)		
Did Not Work	26.4	60.8
Worked Part-Time	12.0	27.0
Worked Full-Time	2.0	12.3

Source: U.S. Census Bureau (2019).

Disability status is also strongly related to the risk of poverty. Those between the ages of 18 and 64 years with a disability have a poverty rate of 22.5, while those without a disability have a poverty rate of 8.4 percent. Clearly having a physical or mental disability makes it more difficult to compete effectively in the labor market. It may shrink the number of jobs one is competitive for and/or reduce the number of hours one is able to work.

Finally, whether one is employed or not is strongly related to the risk of poverty. Those not working during the year had a poverty rate of 26.4 percent, while the poverty rate for those working part-time was 12.0 percent and 2.0 percent for full-time workers.

These three human capital characteristics are therefore strongly related to the risk of poverty. They serve to increase an individual's vulnerability when events happen that can precipitate a fall into poverty.

Patterns of Residence

An image of the poor often portrayed in the media and elsewhere is that of nonwhites living in high-poverty, inner-city neighborhoods. It is a picture that reinforces the idea that the poor are somehow different than other Americans—that they reside in their own neighborhoods, far away from the rest of America. As Paul Jargowsky writes,

> *When poverty is discussed, the mental image that often comes to mind is the inner-city, and particularly high-poverty ghettos and barrios in the largest cities. Many people implicitly assume, incorrectly, that most of the nation's poor can be found in these often troubled neighborhoods. (2015, 15)*

It is certainly true that the United States remains highly segregated on the basis of race, and increasingly, class. Inner cities across the country have been plagued by ongoing economic and social problems. As scholars such as William Julius Wilson have researched and written about over the years, many of these areas are comprised of the "truly disadvantaged."

It is therefore surprising to many people to discover that the vast majority of the poor do not live in high-poverty, inner-city neighborhoods. In fact, only approximately 10 to 15 percent of those in poverty do so. In this section, we explore several of these unexpected findings.

Percent of the Poor Living in High-Poverty Neighborhoods

Based upon data from the U.S. Census Bureau, researchers are able to determine what percent of the poor live in high-poverty neighborhoods. The Census Bureau allows one to analyze these data at the level of what is known as a "census tract" region. A census tract can be thought of as roughly corresponding to a neighborhood, and it averages around 4,000 people (or about 1,500 housing units). In a densely populated urban area, this might comprise a ten by ten square block area, while in a rural location, a census tract would obviously spread out over a much larger geographical region. High-poverty neighborhoods are frequently defined as census tracts in which 40 percent or more of the residents are living below the poverty line.

Using this definition, Paul Jargowsky (2019) has analyzed the percentage of the poor that are living in impoverished neighborhoods. We can see in Table 3.3 these percentages for 1990, 2000, 2010, and 2015. In 1990, 15.1 percent of the poor were residing in high-poverty neighborhoods. That figure dropped to 10.3 percent by 2000, rose to 13.6 percent for 2010, and then fell to 11.9 percent for 2015.

The second column shows the percentage of all the census tracts in the United States that are considered high poverty. In 1990, 5.7 percent of all census tracts were counted as high-poverty areas. In 2000, this percentage was 3.9 percent; by 2010, it had risen to 5.6 percent; and then it fell to 5.0 percent for 2015. Consequently, although there has been some fluctuation in the percentage of the poor living in high-poverty neighborhoods, most individuals in poverty have not and do not live in such neighborhoods.

Table 3.3 Percent of Poor Living in High-Poverty Census Tracts and the Percent of Overall High-Poverty Census Tracts

Year	Percent of Poor Living in High-Poverty Census Tracts (%)	Overall Percent of High-Poverty Census Tracts (%)
1990	15.5	5.7
2000	10.3	3.9
2010	13.6	5.6
2015	11.9	5.0

Source: Paul A. Jargowsky, 2019. High poverty census tracts are defined as census tracts in which 40 percent of more of residents are below the official poverty line.

In addition, Jargowsky finds that high-poverty neighborhoods have become less concentrated during this period of time. He notes,

Ironically, the concentration of poverty has become deconcentrated, in a sense. In 1990 and the years prior to that, most high-poverty census tracts in a metropolitan area could be found in one or two main clusters. These huge high-poverty neighborhoods—such as Bedford-Stuyvesant, Harlem, the South Side of Chicago, North Philadelphia, and Watts—have become embedded in the public consciousness as iconic representations of urban poverty. But in the more recent data, even though the number of high-poverty census tracts has returned to levels comparable to 1990, the individual high-poverty tracts are more decentralized and less clustered. (2015, 11–13)

The overall finding of a minority of the poor living in high-poverty neighborhoods is consistent with the results presented in Chapter 2—that only a small percentage of those experiencing poverty do so for a long, extended period of time. Certainly it is important to keep the deeply entrenched poor in mind when discussing poverty, but it is equally important to keep in mind that they constitute a relatively small proportion of the entire poverty population.

Suburban Poverty

The words suburban and poverty are rarely uttered together. Yet it turns out that in terms of sheer numbers, there are now more poor people living in suburban areas of the country than are living in central cities (Anacker 2015; Lacy 2016).

Elizabeth Kneebone and Alan Berube have addressed this phenomenon in their book *Confronting Suburban Poverty in America* (2013). They analyzed where the poor were living in 100 of the largest metropolitan areas. Approximately two-thirds of the country's population currently reside in these 100 urban areas. Suburbs were defined as those municipalities within a metropolitan area beyond the first-named city. For example, the city of St. Louis would be counted as the city in the region, while the surrounding municipalities such as Ferguson would be counted as suburban.

In Figure 3.1, we can see that the number of poor residents in suburban areas is greater than the size of poor residents in city areas. While it is true that poverty rates remain higher in central cities than suburbs, because of the population growth in suburbia over the past 50 years, the actual number of poor people is now greater in suburban neighborhoods. In discussing these changes, the authors observe,

> *Poverty is a relatively new phenomenon in many suburbs.... As such, it upends deeply fixed notions of where poverty occurs and whom it affects. As poverty becomes increasingly regional in its scope and reach, it challenges conventional approaches that the nation has taken when dealing with poverty in place.... Poverty rates do remain higher in cities and rural communities than elsewhere. But for three decades the poor population has grown in suburbs. The especially rapid pace of growth in the 2000s saw suburbs ultimately outstrip other types of communities so that they now account for the largest poor population in the country. (Kneebone and Berube 2013, 3)*

Some of this poverty can be found in older, inner-ring suburban areas. These were among the first suburbs developed, often at the beginning of the twentieth century. By the end of the twentieth century, their infrastructure and housing stock were aging and frequently in need of repair. Likewise, many of these communities saw their school districts deteriorate over time. Consequently, they represent some of the areas where the more affluent have

Figure 3.1 Numbers of Poor in Suburbs and Cities, 1970–2017

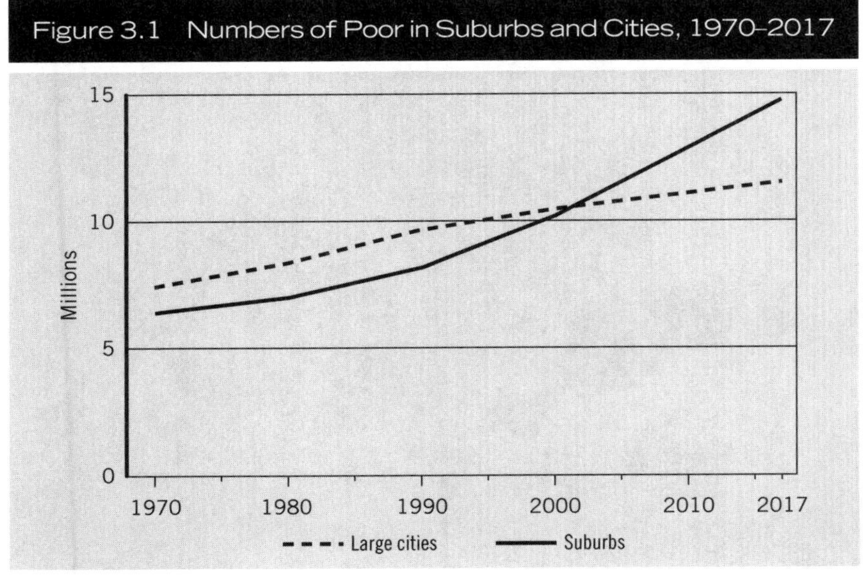

Source: Elizabeth Kneebone, "The changing geography of US poverty". The Brookings Institution, February 15, 2017. Retrieved from https://www.brookings.edu/testimonies/the-changing-geography-of-us-poverty/

left in order to relocate further afield. The result has been a rising number of poor households in these communities.

Rural Poverty

Like suburban poverty, poverty in rural areas is an unlikely image for many people when asked to describe where the poor live (Gurley 2016). However, it turns out that the most deeply seated poverty in this country is generally found in rural America. Figure 3.2 shows a map of the most persistently poor counties in the United States over recent decades. These are counties that have had poverty rates of over 20 percent from the 1990 Census onward.

We can see that the vast majority of these counties are rural or nonmetropolitan. Of the 353 counties with persistent poverty, 301 are nonmetropolitan. We can also observe from the map that there are certain distinct regions of the country where these counties are found. Each of these areas has a unique historical legacy of poverty.

The area of Appalachia, found predominately in West Virginia and Kentucky, is a region of long-standing white poverty. It is characterized by the dominance and gradual disappearance of the coal mining industry. As a result, low-paying service sector types of jobs are often all that remain (Lobao et al. 2016).

A second area of long-standing rural poverty can be found across the Deep South and the Mississippi Delta region. This is an area with a history of

Figure 3.2 Persistently Poor Counties (1990–2010)

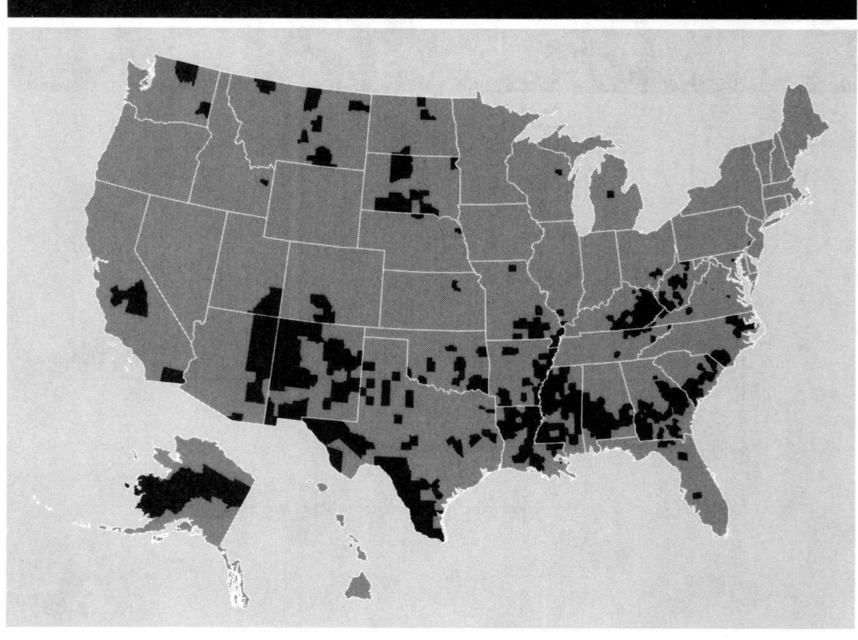

Source: Housing Assistance Council, http://www.ruralhome.org/sct-initiatives/mn-persistent-poverty

slavery and cotton plantations. Many of the poor in this region are the descendants of slaves and sharecroppers. Again, good job opportunities are often far and few between (Hattery and Smith 2007; O'Connell, Curtis, and DeWaard 2018).

The Texas–Mexico border along the Rio Grande constitutes a third area of deeply entrenched rural poverty. Here one finds a largely Latino population with a long history of being exploited. The presence of colonias along the border represents largely impoverished communities that are lacking basic public services (Anderson 2003).

The southwest and northern plains (including parts of Alaska) are also marked by high poverty. Much of this poverty is specific to Native Americans, often on reservations (Davis, Roscigno, and Wilson 2015; Mauer 2016). These counties frequently have some of the highest rates of poverty in the country. The history here is one of exploitation, broken treaties, and the decimation of Native people.

Finally, the central corridor of California represents an area of high poverty especially among migrant labor. It is a region marked by historically low wages paid to farm laborers and their families. Most of these workers are of Hispanic origin (Martin, Fix, and Taylor 2006).

The fact that poverty is greater in rural than urban America contradicts the bucolic image that we often have of small towns dotting the countryside. In fact, many of these areas have been crippled by the economic changes that have taken place in the past 50 years (Ziliak 2018). Small towns have seen their main streets bordered up, and small farming in particular has witnessed devastating changes.

Inner-City Poverty

Poverty is also found in urban, inner cities across the United States. These are areas largely segregated on the basis of race, consisting of African American and Latino populations, often residing in barrios or ghettos. Social policies of the past have largely created these areas through transportation, planning, and zoning laws, as well as discriminatory real estate practices such as red lining and the denial of home loans on the basis of race. As Jargowsky notes,

> *It is worth noting that those poor living in urban high-poverty areas face significant challenges. Not only must they cope with their own lack of resources, but they reside in neighborhoods that often have low-quality housing stock, vacant buildings, crime and violence, and underperforming schools. Recent research has found significant negative effects on children who grow up in such environments. The existence of these neighborhoods has resulted to a large degree from unwise public policies regarding mortgage lending, exclusionary zoning, and large-scale subsidies for suburban sprawl. While we should improve the social safety net for all poor people, wherever they live, we must also reverse the process that creates economically and*

racially segregated neighborhoods that make all the problems of poverty worse. (Rank, Eppard, and Bullock 2021, 23)

These areas are characterized by a shortage of viable job opportunities. As the economy has shed millions of manufacturing and blue-collar jobs over the past decades, many of the hardest hit areas have been in central cities across the Rust Belt. The result has been rising levels of poverty and unemployment, with residents often unable to escape these conditions as a result of residential segregation (Wilson 2016). Furthermore, as we will discuss in Chapter 8, those residing in inner-city, poverty-stricken neighborhoods are exposed to a wide range of detrimental social and environmental conditions. These conditions are exacerbated by the isolation and segregated nature of inner cities across the American landscape.

Concluding Thoughts

We can ask the question, "What do the various attributes that we have been exploring in this chapter have in common?" One answer is that they each increase or decrease the vulnerability of individuals vis-à-vis the labor market. We will discuss this concept in greater detail in the next section, but suffice it to say that the risk of poverty for specific individuals can be largely understood in terms of their economic vulnerability. As we saw in Chapter 2, individuals move into poverty largely due to detrimental events such as the loss of work, a reduction in earnings, families breaking up, or medical emergencies. Those with less advantageous characteristics (i.e., a lack of education or skills) will be more likely to experience such events and more fully exposed to the negative brunt of these events. This results in a greater likelihood of falling below the poverty line for some amount of time until getting back on one's feet. Consequently, nonwhites, children and young adults, women heading households, residents in economically depressed regions, and individuals with less education or a disability all face greater risks of poverty. These factors have held steady across decades of cross-sectional, yearly poverty data.

The other question we have explored in this chapter is what the face of poverty looks like in terms of group makeup. Perhaps the best summary of these data would be that the composition of the poor is diverse. Those in poverty can be found across all geographic regions of the United States. Furthermore, although certain characteristics are associated with an elevated risk of poverty, the face of poverty includes a wide range of demographic and human capital attributes. For example, 40 percent of the poor have attained some level of college education, 27 percent are in married couple families, and 66 percent identify as white. As discussed in Chapter 2, although the grip of poverty is relatively weak, its reach is quite wide. This is reflected in the fact that the life course research discussed in Chapter 2 indicates that three-quarters of the American population will at some point experience poverty or near poverty during their adulthood years.

ONLINE ACTIVITIES

confrontingpoverty.org

In Chapter 3, we have been examining the composition of those experiencing poverty. We have seen that certain demographic characteristics increase or decrease the risk of experiencing poverty. Five of the most important are age, education, marital status, race, and gender. Those who are younger, have less education, are not married, are nonwhite, and are women are at a greater risk of poverty than the overall population.

Our discussion of these characteristics in Chapter 3 is based on U.S. Census data taken at a point in time. While these data are helpful in understanding these dynamics, we should also consider how these characteristics might influence our own personal risk of poverty in the future.

Therefore, let us now go to the *Confronting Poverty* website, and click on the "Risk Calculator" box on the home page. You can read more about the calculator on the website, but it is based on hundreds of thousands of cases from the longitudinal data set known as the Panel Study of Income Dynamics, or PSID. Cases have been followed since 1968, and in any given year the sample is representative of the nonimmigrant U.S. population.

There are three steps involved in using the calculator. The first, as you can see, is to select the time period that you wish to look at in terms of the risk of poverty. You can select either the next 5, 10, or 15 years.

After selecting a time period, we then go to step 2 of the calculator. Here you are asked to select the level of poverty that you are interested in predicting. The three choices are near poverty (below 150 percent of the official poverty line), poverty (the official poverty line), or extreme poverty (below 50 percent of the official poverty line). Click which of these levels you wish to examine, and let us go to step 3.

In step 3, you can check off responses for race, education, gender, marital status, and age. A logical place to start might be with yourself. Try putting in your own characteristics for each of these categories (if you are younger than 20, select the 20–24 age box, it will be close enough). Once you have entered your responses, click the submit button, and you will see the future risk of poverty for someone such as yourself with these characteristics.

For many individuals, their risk is far from trivial. As we discussed in Chapter 2, a majority of Americans will at some point in their lives experience poverty. Also keep in mind that the calculator only projects out to a maximum of 15 years. If the calculator were able to extend the time period out to 20 or 30 years, these percentages would be even higher.

What you can now do is examine several changes on the fly. First, you can easily see how your risk varies depending on how far out you want to project. By changing the 5-, 10-, or 15-year boxes at the top left of the calculator, you can see how your risk changes. As we look further into the future, the risk of poverty increases. This is because we are examining more years in which the possible event (in this case, poverty) can occur. As the years increase, the risk also increases (for a further discussion of this topic, look at the sidebar in Discussion Guide Module 4, and click on the Harvard lecture).

Next, you can see how the risk of poverty increases or decreases depending on the severity of poverty. The three boxes on the top right of the risk calculator allow you to change the level of poverty that you want to predict. Try changing these levels to see how your risk also changes.

Finally, and perhaps most interesting, you can compare your profile with someone who has different characteristics. This allows you to look at the specific impact that these characteristics have upon increasing or decreasing the risk of poverty. Begin by changing just one of the five characteristics, and hit "submit another." This will show how you might compare with someone who has the same characteristics as yourself except for the one that you have changed. Next you might enter various profiles to examine how the different combinations of characteristics increase or decrease the odds of experiencing poverty (you can enter up to five profiles before you will need to reset).

Within the calculator, these five characteristics are quite powerful for understanding who in particular experiences poverty. They range from a high of 90.1 percent (nonwhite, high school, female, not married, age 20–24 years, predicting the 15-year risk of experiencing near poverty) to a low of 1.6 percent (white, beyond high school, male, married, 45–49 years, predicting the five-year risk of experiencing extreme poverty).

However, as we will discuss in Chapter 6, while these characteristics help to explain who loses out at the game, they do not explain why there are losers in the first place. In order to answer that question, we must look at the broader structural forces that affect the number of opportunities available in a society. In particular, the robustness of the economy and the effectiveness of the social welfare state both exert a sizeable impact on the levels of poverty in a country.

PART II

Reasons for Poverty

Why is there poverty? It is a question that people have been grappling with for at least 2,000 years. Hesiod of Boetia, in his poem *Work and Days*, vividly portrays what poverty was like in early Greece, discusses its causes, and questions its justice. Biblical references to the poor and their condition are scattered throughout the Old and New Testaments. The debate continued through medieval and early modern times and was particularly intense in the nineteenth century (Hartwell 1986). Many of the explanations in vogue today have existed over long periods of time (Desmond and Western 2018).

The question of why poverty exists is fundamental for at least two reasons. First, the strategies for addressing poverty should be based upon our understanding of why poverty exists. To use an analogy, an effective doctor must base their prescription and cure upon an accurate diagnosis.

Second, the extent to which there is a collective responsibility for addressing poverty is predicated on why poverty exists. If poverty is viewed as an individual failing, then solving poverty is generally thought to be the responsibility of the individual. On the other hand, if poverty is understood to be the result of a structural failing and a lack of opportunity, then this implies a collective responsibility for alleviating poverty.

In the next three chapters, we review a variety of explanations for understanding why poverty exists. Social scientists have divided these explanations into various classifications (Brady 2019; Calnitsky 2018; Royce 2019). I have chosen to group them into individual, cultural, and structural level theories. I then discuss a framework for explaining poverty that combines aspects of several theories into an overall framework.

CHAPTER 4

Individual- and Cultural-Level Explanations

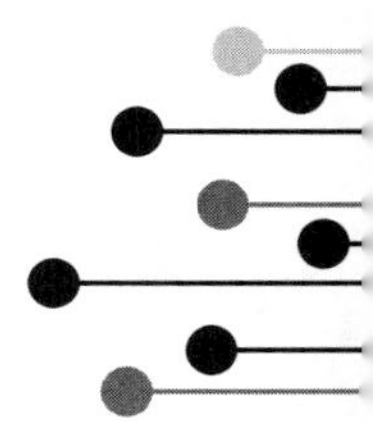

We begin our exploration into the causes of poverty by reviewing those explanations that focus on either individual deficiencies or on cultural processes and norms. These types of explanations tend to have greater support in the overall population than those that focus on structural failings (examined in the next chapter).

Individual-Level Explanations

If we were to ask a random sample of Americans why people are poor, the most likely response would be one that emphasized some aspect of individual failing. Indeed, surveys that have asked this question have found that such factors tend to predominate (Hunt and Bullock 2016). Consequently, poverty is often explained through individual shortcomings and faults. These include not working hard enough, making poor life decisions, failing to get enough education or job experience, lack of ability, and so on. While these surveys also indicate that structural factors (such as the lack of good paying jobs) are cited, it is the individual deficit reasons that are most often mentioned as important. This should not be surprising given that America has been steeped in the ethos of rugged individualism (Eppard, Rank, and Bullock 2020). As a result, individuals are viewed as being in control of their destiny.

Interestingly, even those in poverty often hold these beliefs. For example, in my *Living on the Edge* book, I asked respondents why they were having to use a social welfare program. For the vast majority, they referred to the types of events mentioned in Chapter 2—losing a job; families splitting up; medical emergencies; and so on. However, when asked why most people were using social welfare programs, their responses were typically along the lines of welfare recipients not working hard enough or making bad decision in their lives. Such is the power of individual-level explanations (Rank 1994).

Attitudes/Motivation/Behavior

The most common set of individual reasons surrounding why poverty exists pertain to deficient attitudes, motivation, and/or behavior. The argument is that the poor simply do not have the "right" attitudes necessary to get ahead in life. These include traits such as fortitude, self-responsibility, knowing right from wrong, and so on. The result of these deficiencies is that the poor are not working hard enough to lift themselves out of poverty.

The phrase "Pull yourself up by your own bootstraps" is one embedded in the American lexicon and is the predominate mindset when it comes to explaining poverty (Davidai 2018). There is a widespread belief that with hard work and effort, anyone can avoid poverty. George Gilder, in his 1981 book *Wealth and Poverty*, exemplifies this,

> *The only dependable route from poverty is always work, family, and faith. The first principle is that in order to move up, the poor must not only work, they must work harder than the classes above them. Every previous generation of the lower class has made such efforts. But the current poor, white even more than black, are refusing to work hard. (1981, 68)*

In addition, these negative attitudes and outlets are viewed as leading individuals into bad decision-making, which further increases the likelihood of poverty. As Isabel Sawhill notes,

> *The challenge is to find ways of providing generous support to the poor without disregarding the unpleasant facts about their behavior. Ideally, we need to nudge them toward a different set of behaviors by linking generous governmental assistance to staying in school, delaying childbearing, getting married, and working full-time. What areas of behavior are we talking about? As I have suggested, three are critical. The first is education; the second is family formation; and the third is work. These have always been the sources of upward mobility in advanced democracies. Those who graduate from high school, wait until marriage to have children, limit the size of their families, and work full-time will not be poor. (2001, 83)*

From this perspective, the United States is endowed with abundant opportunities for all who are willing to work for them. The way to avoid poverty is to exert oneself through hard work, to make responsible decisions as one goes through life, and to take advantage of the opportunities that are available. Doing so will ensure economic prosperity and will allow individuals the ability to climb the ladder of success (Davidai 2018).

Cognitive Ability and Talent

A second type of individual-level poverty explanation focuses on innate ability and talent. A particular version of this argument is that those experiencing poverty are lacking in intelligence and cognitive ability. This was the approach taken in the controversial book by Richard Herrnstein and Charles Murray, *The Bell Curve* (1994). The authors argue that although both social class and cognitive ability are important for economic success, cognitive ability or intelligence is much more important. According to the authors, those experiencing poverty are more likely to be lacking in intelligence.

For example, Herrnstein and Murray describe the process for single parents in the following way:

> *The smarter the woman is, the more likely she will be able to find a job, the more likely she will be able to line up other sources of support (from parents or the father of the child), and the more farsighted she is likely to be about the dangers of going on welfare. Even within the population of women who go on welfare, cognitive ability will vary, and the smarter ones will be better able to get off.* (1994, 193–194)

Another variation of this argument is that those in poverty are lacking in innate abilities, skills, and talents. These are viewed as the attributes that allow one to get ahead in life. As a result, such individuals are unable to compete effectively in the labor market, and are therefore much more prone to experiencing poverty.

Human Capital

A third individual-level explanation attributes poverty to a lack of what economists refer to as human capital. Human capital represents that basket of acquired skills and resources that allow individuals to compete in the labor market. These would include the quantity and quality of education that one has received, job experience and training, talent and skills developed, good health, and so on.

The labor market is conceptualized as a competitive system, in which wages are determined by supply and demand, as well as the resources or human capital that people possess. Those who do well in the labor market do so primarily as a result of the human capital they have acquired. Such people are in greater demand and hence enjoy brighter job prospects. Those experiencing poverty tend to be lacking in human capital and therefore cannot compete as effectively in the labor market. Research has shown that those with greater human capital will generally do better economically than those with less human capital (Rank 2020a). And as we saw in the previous chapter, human capital characteristics, such as education, are related to the risk of poverty.

According to this perspective, the way to reduce poverty is to concentrate on upgrading individual skills. This might include ensuring graduating from high school, teaching people marketable trades, enabling them to acquire job experience, and so on. This premise underlies most job training programs directed to the poor (Holzer 2013; Sommer et al. 2018).

Cultural-Level Explanations

Rather than focusing on the inadequacies of the individual, a second group of theories focus on the inadequacies of the culture in which individuals are raised as a dominant factor in maintaining poverty. Three major explanations fall under this perspective: (1) culture of poverty; (2) social isolation; and (3) group membership theory.

Culture of Poverty

The culture of poverty thesis arose from the ethnographic work of Oscar Lewis. His study *Five Families* (1959) examined lower-class Mexican family life, while a later work, *La Vida* (1966a), focused on Puerto Rican families residing in slum communities in both New York City and Puerto Rico. Based on these ethnographies, Lewis argued that a culture of poverty existed.

The argument is that individuals and families living in communities that have been mired in long-term poverty develop a way of life that allows them to better cope with their difficult circumstances, but in turn make it more difficult to escape from poverty. Lewis writes that the term *culture of poverty*,

> *... is the label for a specific conceptual model that describes in positive terms a subculture of Western society with its own structure and rationale, a way of life handed on from generation to generation along family lines. The culture of poverty is not just a matter of deprivation or disorganization, a term signifying the absence of something. It is a culture in the traditional anthropological sense in that it provides human beings with a design for living, with a ready-made set of solutions for human problems, and so serves a significant adaptive function. (1966b, 19)*

Lewis felt that this way of life applied to only perhaps 20 percent of those in poverty. He argued that it is found in those areas of long-standing impoverishment such as rural Appalachia or inner-city, racially segregated ghettos. Lewis goes on to write that

> *It is both an adaptation and a reaction of the poor to their marginal position in a class-stratified, highly individuated, capitalist society. It represents an effort to cope with feelings of hopelessness and despair that arise from the realization by the members of the marginal communities in these societies of the improbability of their achieving success in terms of the prevailing values and goals. (1966b, 22)*

Those within this culture are viewed as displaying certain traits and behaviors that reflect the environmental conditions they face. These include having a present-time orientation, feelings of alienation and fatalism, and a greater acceptance of alternative avenues and behaviors for achieving success (e.g., criminal activity, out-of-wedlock births, etc.). Lewis argued that once the culture of poverty has come into existence, it tends to perpetuate itself across generations.

The culture of poverty is understood as a rational response of attempting to survive in an environment plagued by severe poverty. However, while such a culture makes coping with the present more tolerable, it also hinders the ability of individuals to climb out of poverty. For example, although a present-time orientation makes perfect sense for dealing with the daily turmoil of poverty, it works against long-term planning and goal setting, which can facilitate escaping poverty.

More recent uses of the culture of poverty perspective have largely followed in this tradition (Dahl, Kostol, and Mogstad 2014). For example, Mario Small, David Harding, and Michele Lamont note that "Culture is back on the poverty research agenda. Over the past decade sociologists, demographers, and even economists have begun asking questions about the role of culture in many aspects of poverty and even explicitly explaining the behavior of the low-income population in reference to cultural factors" (2010, 6). In addition, the literature on "poverty traps" largely falls within this tradition as well (Bowles, Durlauf, and Hoff 2006).

The Social Isolation Explanation

William Julius Wilson offers a somewhat different perspective on the contribution of culture to poverty, noting that the "key theoretical concept is not culture of poverty but social isolation" (1987, 61). Wilson's theory is based on an analysis of the increasing problems found within inner cities and the reasons such problems have worsened over the past 50 years. Wilson deals with a specific group in poverty, those he terms "the truly disadvantaged." He argues that many of the problems found in inner cities today are the result of what he labels concentration effects: "The social transformation of the inner city has resulted in a disproportionate concentration of the most disadvantaged segments of the urban black population, creating a social milieu significantly different from the environment that existed in these communities several decades ago" (58).

In addition, the inner city has become increasingly isolated from mainstream social behavior. As the black middle and working classes have left the inner cities, fewer positive role models remained in the community. The inner city has therefore become more socially isolated, while at the same time experiencing a greater concentration of deviant behavior.

> *The communities of the underclass are plagued by massive joblessness, flagrant and open lawlessness, and low-achieving schools, and therefore tend to be avoided by outsiders. Consequently, the residents of these areas, whether women and children of welfare families or aggressive street criminals, have become increasingly socially isolated from mainstream patterns of behavior. (1987, 58)*

Wilson repeatedly points out that the ultimate cause of inner-city conditions is not the culture itself but rather the social structural constraints and the lack of opportunities. Thus, "the key conclusion from a public policy perspective is that programs created to alleviate poverty, joblessness, and related forms of social dislocation should place primary focus on changing the social and economic situation, not the cultural traits, of the ghetto underclass" (1987, 137). Wilson further distinguishes his concept of social isolation from that of a culture of poverty by arguing that cultural traits are not self-perpetuating but rather adaptations to structural conditions. When structural conditions change, culture will change along with it. Nevertheless,

Wilson emphasizes that a distinct culture exists in the inner city and that this culture helps to maintain poverty. Thus, while it may not be the ultimate factor, it does contribute heavily to Wilson's understanding of poverty.

Group Membership Theory

A third cultural-level perspective is what has been referred to as membership theory. The economist Steven Durlauf (2001, 2006) has been a major proponent of this perspective. He emphasizes the importance of group membership and peer influence in the maintenance and reproduction of poverty.

Substantial research in sociology, anthropology, social psychology, and economics has demonstrated the importance of groups and peers on affecting behavior. The earlier discussed research of William Julius Wilson, along with others, has shown the influence that peers and a lack of positive role models can have on negatively affecting the aspirations and behaviors of inner-city impoverished youth. For example, if one's peers display little motivation to graduate from high school, their lowered aspirations can then downwardly affect their fellow students' academic outlooks and efforts. As Durlauf notes, "If the educational effort and aspirations of one child are influenced by the efforts of his friends and peers, then neighborhoods can create powerful forces promoting or retarding social mobility" (2001, 398). In this way, certain norms and expectations may be created that exist not only on a group level but on a community level as well. Similar types of arguments could be made regarding the effects of peers and group membership on teenage pregnancy, criminal activity, drug use, and so on, which in turn may influence neighborhood expectations.

Membership theory thus seeks to understand particular counterproductive behavior through the influence of peers and groups. It is argued that cultural norms operate through these groups, resulting in lower aspirations and a greater likelihood of engaging in deviant behavior. These, in turn, substantially increase the risk of poverty in the future.

Concluding Thoughts

In this chapter, we have reviewed several explanations that fall under the rubric of individual- and cultural-level factors. As noted earlier, these types of explanations have always been more popular within the general public than structural-level theories. One reason for this is undoubtedly that America has historically had a strong undercurrent emphasizing the importance of rugged individualism. Such an outlook assumes that each of us has the ability and agency to shape our own destiny. Consequently, those who fail to succeed have no one but themselves to blame.

However, a second possible reason for why these explanations are popular is because individual and cultural shortcomings may be easier to physically observe than structural processes. For example, when one looks at an economically depressed inner-city neighborhood, one sees the physical deterioration of that neighborhood—one does not see the structural factors that may have led that neighborhood down the road to deterioration.

Yet another reason behind the popularity of these explanations may be that they let the wider community off the hook with respect to any shared responsibility for addressing poverty. If poverty is viewed as an individual failing, then it is up to that individual to pull themselves out of poverty.

Yet in spite of these reasons, the empirical research to support the idea that those in poverty have a different set of attitudes and beliefs is weak (Duina 2018; Rank 1994, 2004). On the other hand, evidence does indicate that human capital is related to the risk of poverty—those with less education and skills are at a much greater risk of encountering poverty. We take up this issue in Chapter 6.

ONLINE ACTIVITIES

confrontingpoverty.org

In this chapter, we have been exploring individual explanations for why poverty exists. As we reviewed, these types of explanations are generally the most popular when the overall public is asked to explain why poverty exists. Yet interestingly, when Americans are asked about the national spending on assistance to the poor, many feel that we are not spending enough.

This is a question (along with many others) that has been asked in an ongoing national social survey called the General Social Survey (GSS). The GSS is a nationally representative survey that asks American adults various questions about their attitudes pertaining to a wide range of issues. It began in 1972 and is conducted every two years.

We can go to "General Social Survey Data Explorer Tool" found on the National Research Opinion Center website. First go to the *Confronting Poverty* website and click on the "Discussion Guide." Then click on Module 8, and the sidebar link to the General Social Survey will take us to the data. Here you can see the data over the last 35 years regarding the question of whether the country is spending too much, too little, or about right on its efforts to assist the poor. This chart can be explored in a number of ways. Begin by looking at the total population. You can examine individually the three responses (too little; about right; or too much). What this chart basically shows is that a majority of Americans have felt for many years that we spend too little in terms of assistance to the poor.

Next, you can see how these numbers compare depending on a variety of background characteristics. Under the breakdown box, you can click on a range of characteristics to see how these influence people's perceptions of poverty spending. In general, conservative-leaning individuals are more likely to feel we are spending too much, while liberal-leaning individuals are more likely to say we are spending too little.

Now let us go to a second question that the GSS asks about a related topic. Click on the down arrow at the end of "National spending on assistance to the poor" and a drop-down menu will appear listing a variety of subjects. On the left side, you will see the topic "National spending on welfare." Click on this.

Here we have data on a related question, but eliciting a much different response. When assistance to the poor is phrased as spending on welfare, a much higher percentage of the population feels that we are spending too much. Repeat the various steps that you took with the previous question, and look at how the responses vary depending on the background characteristics.

Why then the discrepancy between the American public's responses to these two questions? One reason is that the term *welfare* is highly stigmatized in American society. Many researchers have found this to be the case in a variety of settings. The term often conveys an image of someone not working hard and taking advantage of the system. There are also racialized overtones to welfare programs as well. Welfare is often seen as being used mostly by nonwhites. These mental images are consistent with several aspects of the individual explanations of poverty that we discussed in this chapter.

CHAPTER 5 Structural-Level Explanations

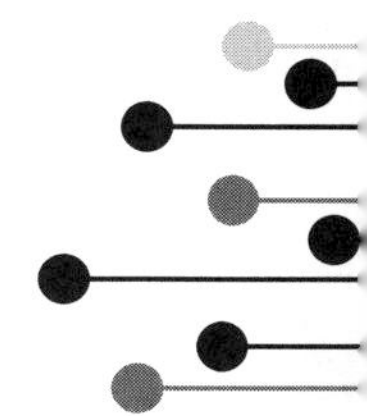

We now turn to those theories that focus on the structural level to explain the existence of poverty. Rather than looking to individual failings as the reason for poverty (discussed in the last chapter), these theories emphasize the importance of failings at an economic, societal, and/or political level to understand why poverty exists.

These perspectives argue that poverty is largely the result of a shortage of opportunities. This lack of opportunities is generated by economic and political forces found within society. The answer as to why there is poverty is hypothesized to be found in the mechanisms behind these forces.

Marxist Critique of Capitalism

The most influential structural critique of capitalism can be found in the writings of Karl Marx. Marx was researching and writing during the middle and latter part of the nineteenth century. Considerable political and economic turmoil was occurring in Europe during this period. Much of Marx's work focused on attempting to answer two broad questions. First, what has been the dynamic that has driven societal change over time? Second, how might we better understand the manner in which exploitation occurs within capitalism?

According to Marx, history can be seen as an ongoing conflict between two broad classes in society—those who Marx called the owners of the means of production, and the rest of society. The means of production refers to those goods or commodities capable of generating or reproducing greater wealth. In today's society, they would include factories, intellectual property, real estate, and so on. There is an inherent antagonism and conflict between these two classes. In ancient societies, this was represented by the master/slave; in feudal times, the lord/serf; under capitalism, the bourgeoisie/proletariat. This conflict eventually leads to a broad economic and societal transformation.

Much of Marx's writing was concerned with capitalist societies and the exploitative class relations found within them. In feudal times, workers had produced their own goods and bartered or sold them. Capitalism brought about a dramatic change—people began to work in settings other than the home (i.e., a factory). Furthermore, they worked not for themselves but for the capitalists who owned the factories, and they were paid a wage in return for their labor.

Competition is inherent within capitalism. In order for capitalists to remain competitive and profitable in the economic marketplace, they must try to keep the costs of their products low. In order to do so, there is pressure to pay their employees as low a wage as possible. This pressure also encourages technological developments to replace labor, such as automation and computerization, or relocating jobs to other parts of the globe where labor costs might be significantly lower.

Marx argued that workers are not paid at rates that reflect the true value of what they produce. The difference between what they are paid and what the product is actually worth—Marx called this the surplus value—is what the capitalists take for their own profit. This, according to Marx, represents the exploitation of workers by capitalists. It is in the nature of capitalism for the owners of the means of production to increase profits at the workers' expense.

> *What then, is the general law which determines the rise and fall of wages and profit in their reciprocal relation? They stand in inverse ratio to each other. Capital's share, profit, rises in the same proportion as labour's share, wages, falls, and vice versa. Profit rises to the extent that wages fall; it falls to the extent that wages rise. (Marx and Engels 1968, 86–87)*

As capitalism develops, it brings about a greater division of labor, which allows the capitalist to produce more goods with fewer workers, resulting in even greater profits. Many of the remaining jobs become increasingly simplified, requiring fewer skills. This, in turn, makes individual workers more expendable, driving wages down even further.

With a decreased need for workers and easily replaceable labor, more individuals are reduced to what Marx called the industrial reserve army. The soldiers in this army live much of their lives in or near poverty and are able to work and fully support themselves only during periods of boom or economic expansion. As Marx wrote, "Thus the forest of uplifted arms demanding work becomes ever thicker, while the arms themselves become ever thinner" (Marx and Engels 1968, 94).

According to Marx, then, poverty is simply inherent in the economic structure of capitalism—it is an inevitable by-product of the exploitation of workers by capitalists. As capitalism further develops, it will leave in its wake more and more individuals and families that are on, or have fallen over, the economic precipice (Wright 1994).

Dual Labor Market Theory

The dual labor market theory arose as a reaction against the perceived failings of human capital theory (discussed in the last chapter). Whereas human capital theory assumes that there is one labor market in operation, the dual labor market perspective posits the existence of two quite distinct markets that operate according to different rules (Pula 2017). In the primary market, jobs are characterized by stability, high wages and benefits, and good working conditions. This market is limited to a certain sector of the private economy, called the core or monopoly sector. Firms within the monopoly sector tend to be large and capital intensive and to possess sizable and often international markets (e.g., the automobile industry, pharmaceuticals, etc.). Within such firms, there exists what is called an internal labor market. Individuals from the outside can only enter this internal labor market at certain points, often the bottom rung of a career ladder. Jobs higher up the ladder are filled within the firm through promotion.

On the other hand, jobs in the secondary labor market are characterized as menial, having poor working conditions, low wages, little stability, and few benefits. The secondary market exists primarily within what is called the peripheral or competitive sector of the private economy. Firms within the competitive sector tend to be small and labor intensive, with lower productivity per worker and more local markets. In addition, an individual's labor and skills can be easily replaced by another individual's. Examples include restaurants, retail sales, custodial work, and so on.

The determinants of earnings vary between markets. In the primary market, earnings are determined by the worker's position in the career structure, as well as seniority. In contrast, wages in the secondary labor market are largely determined by market forces. Since workers in this market are generally considered homogeneous and have little union power, their wages are the product of supply and demand. Thus, differences in earnings are due primarily to the number of hours worked.

The dual labor market approach seeks to explain the persistent poverty of different social groups and persistent racial and gender wage differences. It argues that, for a variety of reasons (e.g., statistical discrimination, fewer skills, employers' perceptions of a lack of worker commitment), women and minorities are more likely to begin their work careers in the secondary labor market. As Randy Hodson and Robert Kaufman note, "Once workers enter the secondary market, they acquire unstable work histories" (1982, 730). Employers in the primary labor market then use these histories as evidence that they are inadequate workers, and thus they are blocked from moving into the primary market. This in turn helps to perpetuate income inequality and poverty.

People are poor not because they do not participate in the economy but because of the way in which they participate in the economy. Because of the instability and low wages in the secondary labor market, workers in such jobs experience unemployment and turn to the social safety net in order to survive lean times. Individuals in these jobs routinely face economic insecurity and hardship, with poverty being a frequent companion.

Functionalism

Functionalism has a long history in the social sciences. Its origins began at the end of the nineteenth and early twentieth centuries as European anthropologists traveled to non-Western cultures such as those in the Pacific Islands. There they observed cultural adaptations and traits that, at first glance, were hard to understand from a Western European lens. However, after immersing themselves in these cultures, they realized that such traits and adaptations served a number of purposes for specific groups and for the society as a whole. Out of this ethnographic work arose the perspective known as structural functionalism.

The sociologist Robert Merton defined functions as "those observed consequences which make for the adaptation or adjustment of a given system; and dysfunctions, those observed consequences which lessen the adaptation or adjustment of the system" (1949, 50). Functions can be both intended (manifested functions) and unintended (latent functions). For an institution or phenomenon to survive in a society, it must somehow be functional for that society. If it is not, it eventually disappears or is modified.

Using this perspective, Herbert Gans (1972, 1991, 2012) sought to explain the persistence of poverty in the United States. He begins his argument by stating that the reason poverty has remained at high levels is because it must be serving a number of important functions for society in general, and specifically, that it serves important economic, social, and political functions for the well-to-do. Although this may at first seem counterintuitive, Gans goes on to detail a number of potential functions that are served by the presence of poverty. For example, the existence of poverty ensures that undesirable, low-wage work gets done. Because those in poverty have few job alternatives, they are forced to take these unpleasant but necessary jobs. Poverty also creates a number of occupations and professions that serve and rely on the poor (i.e., academics writing books about poverty). Or that the poor can be identified and punished as deviants (such as welfare freeloaders) by political actors in order to uphold the legitimacy of dominant norms and to further their own political careers. He concludes by writing,

> *My analysis suggests that the alternatives for poverty are themselves dysfunctional for the affluent population, and it ultimately comes to a conclusion which is not very different from that of radical sociologists. To wit: that social phenomena which are functional for affluent groups and dysfunctional for poor ones persist; that when the elimination of such phenomena through functional alternatives generates dysfunctions for the affluent, they will continue to persist; and that phenomena like poverty can be eliminated only when they either become sufficiently dysfunctional for the affluent or when the poor can obtain enough power to change the system of social stratification. (Gans 1972, 288)*

Some have also argued that the social safety net itself is functional for society, not because it provides help to the needy, but because it placates and regulates the poor (Piven and Cloward 1971). As Carol Stack argues,

> *It is clear that mere reform of existing programs can never be expected to eliminate an impoverished class in America. The effect of such programs is*

> *that they maintain the existence of such a class. Welfare programs merely act as flexible mechanisms to alleviate the more obvious symptoms of poverty while inching forward just enough to purchase acquiescence and silence on the part of the members of this class and their liberal supporters.... These programs are not merely passive victims of underfunding and conservative obstructionism. In fact they are active purveyors of the status quo, staunch defenders of the economic imperative that demands maintenance of a sizable but docile impoverished class. (1974, 127–28)*

Such analysts point out that safety net programs tend to expand during times of social upheaval precisely for this reason. For example, the beginnings of the modern welfare state in the United States can be traced back to the Social Security Act of 1935. This Act was signed into law at a time when the country was in its deepest depression, and food riots were occurring on the streets. Likewise, the War on Poverty initiatives that began in the mid-1960s also took place at a time of tremendous turmoil and unrest. From this perspective, the welfare state is designed to placate the poor so that they are not so desperate as to revolt against the government and status quo.

Big Brother Argument

A fourth structural perspective regarding poverty and welfare use is what Bradley Schiller (2008) has labeled the "Big Brother argument." The emphasis here is on the role of misguided social policies in exacerbating poverty. The argument is that human nature is shaped by incentives and disincentives and that individuals generally desire the easiest way out of difficult situations. In the case of poverty, welfare and public assistance can create work and marriage disincentives. Individuals may exert themselves less when in dire straits because they know they can fall back on the safety net of public assistance. As they become more accustomed to receiving welfare, they can eventually settle into this lifestyle.

Like many of the perspectives discussed in this part of the book, these arguments have a long history behind them. Alexis de Tocqueville noted in his 1835 lecture to the Royal Academic Society of Cherbourg, "Any measure which establishes legal charity on a permanent basis and gives it an administrative form thereby creates an idle and lazy class, living at the expense of the industrial and working class. This, at least, is its inevitable consequence, if not the immediate result" (1983, 113).

This argument has been used to explain what conservatives have called the counter-productivity of the War on Poverty programs. Charles Murray (1984) is the most widely cited analyst working within this framework. Murray argues that from 1964 onward, measures of poverty, employment, education, crime, and family structure have been deteriorating for low-income black families and that this coincides with the War on Poverty programs. Murray's thesis is that by violating several basic assumptions—people respond to incentives and disincentives; people are not inherently hard working; and people must be held accountable for their actions—these programs played on individuals' worst instincts, eventually trapping many into lives of poverty and welfare dependency, instead of helping them escape. It became easier (and economically more rational in the short term) from the mid-1960s onward to rely on welfare rather than to work at the minimum wage. As a result, Murray argues that the welfare system itself is largely to blame for the fact that millions of Americans are currently in poverty.

This has been the long-running conservative argument against welfare spending, particularly since Ronald Reagan's rise to presidency in 1980. As Reagan often remarked, "We fought a War on Poverty and poverty won." Or to reiterate another of President Reagan's favorite sayings, "Government is not the solution to our problem, government is the problem."

From this point of view, the answer to the problem of poverty is to cut back substantially on social welfare programs and to ensure that work disincentives are minimized in the remaining programs. Governmental intrusion into private initiative must be curtailed so that people have no choice but to work themselves out of poverty.

Distribution of Welfare State Resources

In sharp contrast to the Big Brother argument, distribution of welfare state resource theories argues the opposite. They focus on variation in poverty rates across countries. The argument is that lower poverty rates are the result of more generous and effective social welfare state programs. As David Brady writes,

> *What explains this tremendous variation in poverty across the affluent Western democracies? This question represents a serious challenge to any theory of poverty. Theories of poverty should be able to explain why some affluent Western democracies maintain substantial poverty and others are more egalitarian and accomplish low levels of poverty. Yet, the conventional approach in poverty studies is to analyze only the United States and to compare the characteristics of poor people (perhaps in poor neighborhoods) to nonpoor people. It is not an exaggeration to say that the vast majority of poverty studies explain why one group of people within a country are more likely to be poor, or why some individuals are poor while others are not. Thus, conventional poverty research stops short of confronting the enormous cross-national differences.* (2009, 5–6)

Brady goes on to argue,

> *In contrast, I contend that these cross-national and historical differences in poverty are principally driven by politics. This book makes the simple claim that the distribution of resources in states and markets is inherently political. I explicitly seek to challenge the mainstream view that poverty is an inescapable, if perhaps unfortunate, outcome of an individual's failings or a society's labor markets and demography. Instead, I argue that societies*

make collective choices about how to divide their resources. These choices are acted upon in the organization and states that govern the societies, and then become institutionalized through the welfare state. Where poverty is low, equality has been institutionalized. Where poverty is widespread, as most visibly demonstrated by the United States, there has been a failure to institutionalize equality. (2009, 6)

As we discussed in Chapter 2, poverty rates vary widely by country. The United States is at the high end in terms of the extent and depth of its poverty. From this perspective, the reason lies in its extremely weak and limited social safety net programs. As specific events occur to households that can trigger spells of poverty (e.g., loss of a job, families splitting up, health problems), the programs designed to protect households from poverty come up short. When comparing pretransfer with posttransfer rates of poverty, the United States has the smallest rate of reduction compared to the other OECD countries. As a result, the United States is plagued by high rates of poverty and inequality.

In more recent work, Brady argues that the United States in particular attaches a much higher penalty to specific behaviors (Brady, Finnigan, and Hubgen 2017). These include single parenthood, unemployment, and low educational attainment. While other countries provide support for those who fall into these categories, U.S. policy has sought to punish those who engage in this behavior by withholding economic support. The result is a much higher overall rate of poverty (Brady 2019).

Concluding Thoughts

In this chapter, we have reviewed several different structural-level theories of poverty. These theories view poverty as the result of a lack of opportunities caused by processes occurring at a systemic level. These include an economy that does not create enough jobs to support families, a weak social safety net, or a social system that depends on poverty to fulfill certain needs.

With the exception of the Big Brother argument, such theories tend to resonate more with liberal-leaning thinkers. The Big Brother argument, on the other hand, is most often held by conservatives.

The implication of these approaches is that poverty is endemic to the overall social and economic structure. In order to address poverty, one must address these various systemic shortcomings.

ONLINE ACTIVITIES

confrontingpoverty.org

The economist Raj Chetty has been at the forefront of the effort to bring "big data" to bear on social and economic issues. In particular, his work has revolved around understanding patterns of economic inequality and opportunity. He has been able to use millions of records from the Internal Revenue Service and merge this information with data from the U.S. Census in order to look at patterns of economic mobility over time. One of his key research findings has been that more recent generations of Americans are having greater difficultly surpassing their parents' overall economic well-being. One of the premises of the American Dream has been that each generation should do economically better than the previous generation. This may no longer be the case.

Chetty and his colleagues have also shown that patterns of upward economic mobility are not evenly divided across the regions and municipalities of the United States. Rather, there are some areas of the country where children are able to achieve much more than in other areas. From this body of research, Chetty has constructed an "Opportunity Atlas" that we will now explore for our online activity.

The atlas is based on administrative data representing 20 million children born between 1978 and 1983, which is then linked to their parents' information acquired from the U.S. Census Bureau. The analysis in the atlas then looks at how well children do as adults depending on where they grew up.

Let us begin by going to the *Confronting Poverty* website and clicking on the "Facts and Myths" box. Then, click on the "Fact 3" box and click on the "Opportunity Atlas" link on the sidebar. This will take you directly to the website.

A helpful place to begin is with either the tutorial or the frequently asked questions (FAQs) link at the bottom of the page. As the description on the homepage states, what the atlas allows us to do is to look at how well children with different backgrounds perform as adults in various parts of the United States. There are a range of outcomes that one can look at, including levels of income and likelihood of incarceration.

As with several of our other online exercises, a logical place to begin might be where you yourself grew up. You can enter your city or zip code at the top left of the page. Next, you can choose what outcome variable you would like to examine. Let us start with household income (which has already been selected). The third step is to choose on the top right hand side box the parental income, race, and gender for the child that you wish to examine. These variables allow you to look at what impact they have upon children's earnings as adults.

After you have entered the categories that you are interested in exploring, you can see on the left what the value for the outcome variables is (in this case, income). Now change parental income, race, or gender to see what effects these variables have on the various outcomes.

There are many other ways that you can analyze the data. You can use the drop-down menu to enter a more advanced mode that allows you to have additional options in analyzing the data. One of the dynamics that becomes quite apparent as you explore this website is that opportunities are largely shaped by structural forces, such as parental income, the neighborhood that one grows up in, race, and gender. As we have discussed in this chapter, these structural forces have a significant impact upon the risk of poverty.

CHAPTER 6 Putting It Together—Structural Vulnerability

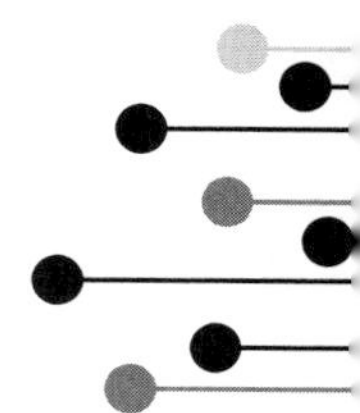

Given the explanations we have been examining, how might we better understand the specific patterns of poverty and how they play themselves out on a daily basis? In order to answer this question, this chapter develops what I have referred to as a structural vulnerability explanation of poverty. This perspective has developed out of my prior work examining the lives of welfare recipients (Rank 1994), those in poverty (Rank 2004), and the pursuit of the American Dream (Rank, Hirschl, and Foster 2014). It is intended to provide a framework for understanding who loses out at the economic game, while emphasizing that the game itself is structured in a way that ultimately produces economic losers. In this sense, it brings together the prior research focusing on individual human capital and demographic characteristics discussed in Chapters 3 and 4, with the structural roots of poverty discussed in the prior chapter.

There are three basic premises underlying the structural vulnerability perspective. The first is that particular characteristics, such as the lack of human capital, tend to place individuals in a vulnerable position when detrimental events and crises occur. The incidence of these events (e.g., the loss of a job, family breakup, ill health) often results in poverty. In addition, the lack of human capital also increases the likelihood of such events occurring (particularly those related to the labor market). In this sense, human capital characteristics help to explain who in the population is likely to encounter poverty more frequently and for longer periods of time.

Second, the acquisition of such human capital is strongly influenced by the impact that social class has upon this process. Those who find themselves growing up in a working-class or lower-income home will face greater odds against them in terms of acquiring marketable education and skills during their lifetime. The process of cumulative inequality serves to accentuate these earlier disadvantages across the life course. Additional background characteristics also play a role in the acquisition of human capital, including race, gender, and particular innate abilities.

And finally, while individual characteristics help to explain who loses out at the economic game, the structural forces described earlier ensure that there will be losers in the first place. In this sense the dynamic of poverty can be described as a game of musical chairs in which those with the least advantageous characteristics are likely to find themselves without a chair and left standing with a heightened risk of economic vulnerability. Each of these components is discussed in this chapter.

Economic Vulnerability and Human Capital

Essential to an initial understanding of poverty are the concepts of economic vulnerability and the importance of the lack of human capital in accentuating such vulnerability (discussed in Chapter 4). Individuals more likely to experience poverty tend to have attributes that put them at a disadvantage vis-à-vis their earnings ability within the labor market.

These attributes can be thought of largely in terms of human capital, or that basket of skills, attributes, education, and qualifications that individuals bring with them into the economy (Becker 1981, 1993; Karoly 2001; Sommer et al. 2018). Those who do well in the labor market often do so as a result of the human capital they have acquired (in particular, they possess marketable skills and training). As a result, they are in greater demand by employers, and consequently will enjoy brighter job and earnings prospects (Bills, Di Stasio, and Gerxhani 2017).

On the other hand, those facing an elevated risk of poverty tend to have acquired less valuable human capital. For example, education may be truncated or of an inferior quality, while job experience and skills may be less marketable. This results in individuals being less attractive in the job market. Additional attributes can also limit the ability to effectively compete in the labor market. Households residing in inner cities or remote rural areas often face diminished job prospects. Single mothers with young children experience reduced flexibility in their ability to take a job as a result of having to arrange childcare. Likewise, those with a physical or mental disability may be more limited in terms of the type of jobs and number of hours they can work. In addition, factors such as race and gender can result in employers using such characteristics to screen and/or limit the promotion of potential employees. In short, those who experience poverty are more likely to have attributes that place them at a disadvantage in terms of competing in the labor market.

However, these factors alone do not directly cause poverty. If they were solely responsible, how might we explain the fluid movements of people in and out of poverty as indicated by the research into the longitudinal dynamics of poverty? As we saw in Chapter 2, the typical pattern is that individuals may be poor for one or two years and then get themselves above the poverty line, perhaps experiencing an additional spell of poverty in the future. Furthermore, the life course patterns of poverty also indicate the commonality of short but recurring periods of impoverishment. For many people, their personal characteristics have remained constant while their poverty status has not. An explanation that focuses solely on human capital cannot in and of itself account for such transitions.

What is argued here is that the lack of human capital results in certain life crises occurring more often and with greater intensity. This would appear particularly true in the case of labor market difficulties. Those with less human capital are more likely to experience job instability, longer periods of unemployment, lower wages, and part-time work. Each of these, in turn, is associated with an elevated risk of poverty.

In addition, the lack of human capital places the individual in a more economically vulnerable position when faced with the loss of employment, changes in family status, illness and incapacitation, and so on. Individuals and families who are marginalized in terms of their ability to participate in the free market system will have a more difficult time weathering such storms. It will take them longer to find a job, or to earn enough to tide them through the breakup of a family. When such events take place, they often throw individuals into poverty for a period of time until they are able to get back on their feet.

Thus, a lack of human capital increases the likelihood that particular detrimental economic events will occur, such as not having a job that can sustain a family, as well as making it more difficult to weather such events when they do occur. As a result, those who are lacking in human capital might be thought of as walking a very fine line. If nothing out of the ordinary happens, many of these families are able to just get by. However, should a crisis occur, such as the loss of a job, an unanticipated medical problem, or a costly but needed repair of an automobile, it generally places the household into an economic tailspin.

Many of the families that I interviewed for my book, *Living on the Edge*, were households straddling the borderline between self-sufficiency and dependence. One wrong step, and they were likely to land back in poverty and on welfare. They simply did not have the resources and assets necessary to tide them over for more than several weeks. For example, I asked Cindy and Jeff Franklin, a married couple with two children, to describe these types of situations,

> CINDY: *Well, I think it's running out of money. (Sighs) If something comes up—a car repair or (pause) our refrigerator's on the fritz.... We have enough money for a nice, adequate, simple lifestyle as long as nothing happens. If something happens, then we really get thrown in a tizzy. And I'd say that's the worst—that's the worst.*
>
> JEFF: *Yeah, 'cause just recently, in the last month, the car that we had was about to rust apart. Sort of literally. And so we had to switch cars. And my parents had this car that we've got now, sitting around. They gave it to us for free, but we had to put about two hundred dollars into it just to get it in safe enough condition so that we don't have to constantly be wondering if something's gonna break on it.*
>
> CINDY: *I think that sense of having to choose—the car is a real good example of it—having to choose between letting things go—in a situation that's unsafe, or destituting ourselves in order to fix it. Having to make that kind of choice is really hard. (Rank 1994, 57)*

The phrase "one paycheck away from poverty" is particularly apt in describing the situations for many of these households.

Other work has revealed parallel findings. Studies examining blue-collar or working-class families have found a similar dynamic (Eppard, Rank, and Bullock 2020; Goldstein 2017; Morduch and Schneider 2017). As a result of less marketable skills and education, these households experience a heightened vulnerability to economic deprivation and poverty. For example, the title of Lillian Rubin's book *Families on the Faultline* exemplifies this notion with regard to working-class families. As Rubin writes,

> *These are the men and women, by far the largest part of the American work force, who work at the lower levels of the manufacturing and service sectors of the economy; workers whose education is limited, whose mobility options are severely restricted, and who usually work for an hourly rather than a weekly wage.... They go to work every day to provide for their families, often at jobs they hate. But they live on the edge. Any unexpected event—a child's illness, an accident on the job, a brief layoff—threatens to throw them into the abyss.* (1994, 30–31)

The first factor therefore in understanding the occurrence of poverty is the concept of economic vulnerability and the role that the lack of human capital plays in accentuating such vulnerability. People who have fewer skills and education, or who possess other attributes putting them at a disadvantage in terms of competing in the labor market (such as single parenthood or having a disability), are more likely to experience detrimental economic events, while at the same time being more adversely affected when they occur. These episodes often result in pushing individuals and families below the poverty line.

The Impact of Social Class and Cumulative Inequality Upon Human Capital Acquisition

Given that skills and education bear upon poverty (by causing varying degrees of vulnerability), why are individuals lacking these in the first place? A major reason often neglected in such discussions is the importance of social class and cumulative inequality. This is the second component of the structural vulnerability framework.

Analyses of the American system of stratification have shown that while some amount of social mobility does occur, social class as a whole tends to reproduce itself (Bowles, Gintis, and Groves 2005; Ermisch, Jantti, and Smeeding 2012). Those with working- or lower-class parents are likely to remain working or lower class themselves (Mazumder 2018). Similarly, those whose parents are affluent are likely to remain affluent (Pfeffer and Killewald 2018). Why? The reason is that parental class differences result in significant differences in the resources and opportunities available to their children. These differences in turn affect children's future life chances and outcomes, including the accumulation of skills and education. This process of cumulative advantage or disadvantage results in widening inequalities over time (Rank 2020b).

While it is certainly possible for someone to rise from rags to riches, that tends to be much more the exception rather than the rule. Again turning to Lillian Rubin's analysis,

> *Our denial notwithstanding, then, class inequalities not only exist in our society, they're handed down from parents to children in the same way that wealth is passed along in the upper class. True, American society has always had a less rigid and clearly defined class structure than many other nations. Poor people climb up; wealthy ones fall. These often well-publicized figures help to fuel the myth about equality of opportunity. But they're not the norm. Nor is the perpetuation of our class structure accidental. The economy, the polity, and the educational system all play their part in ensuring the continuity and stability of our social classes.* (1994, 36)

The impact of differences in income and social class from one generation to the next is therefore a critical factor in understanding the human capital and skill differences that exist in today's society.

A game analogy helps to illustrate this process. Imagine three players beginning a game of Monopoly. Normally, each player would be given $1,500 at the start of the game. The playing field is in effect level, with each of the players' outcomes determined by the roll of the dice as well as their own skills and judgments.

Now let us imagine a modified game of Monopoly, in which the players start out with quite different advantages and disadvantages, much as they do in life. Player 1 begins with $5,000 and several Monopoly properties on which some houses have already been built. Player 2 starts out with the standard $1,500 and no properties. Finally, Player 3 begins the game with only $250.

Who will be the winners and losers in this modified game of Monopoly? Both luck and skill are still involved, and the rules of the game have remained the same, but given the differing sets of resources and assets that each player begins with, they become much less important in predicting the game's outcome. Certainly, it is possible for Player 1, with $5,000, to lose, and for Player 3, with $250, to win, but that is unlikely given the unequal allocation of money at the start of the game. Moreover, while Player 3 may win in any individual game, over the course of hundreds of games, the odds are that Player 1 will win considerably more often, even if Player 3 is much luckier and more skilled.

In addition, the way each of the three individuals are able to play the game will vary considerably. Player 1 is able to take greater chances and risks. If he or she makes several tactical mistakes, they probably will not matter much in the larger scheme of things. If Player 3 makes one such mistake, it may very well result in disaster. In addition, Player 1 will easily be able to purchase assets in the form of properties and houses that Player 3 is largely locked out of. These assets, in turn, will generate further income later in the game for Player 1, and in all likelihood result in the bankrupting of Player 3.

This analogy illustrates the concept that Americans are not beginning their lives at the same starting point. Parental differences in income and resources exert a major influence over their children's ability to acquire valuable skills and education. These differences in human capital will, in turn, strongly influence how well such children are able to compete in the labor market and therefore determine the extent of their economic vulnerability during the course of their lives.

This process is what is known as cumulative inequality. The argument is that as a result of the position one starts in life, particular advantages or disadvantages may be present (Merton 1968, 1988). These initial advantages or disadvantages can then result in further advantages or disadvantages, producing a cumulative process in which inequalities are widened across the life course (Rank 2020b).

The assertion that the economic race is run as an altered game of Monopoly has been confirmed in an array of empirical work. For example, if a father has a level of income that falls in the bottom 20 percent of the income distribution, 42.2 percent of the sons from such a father will wind up in the bottom quintile of the income distribution when they grow up, while only 7.9 percent will reach the top quintile in terms of the income distribution. On the other hand, if a father has an income in the top 20 percent of the income distribution, 36 percent of his sons will be earning an income in the top quintile of the income distribution, while only 9.5 percent will fall into the bottom quintile (Jantti et al. 2006).

Another way of conceptualizing this association is that research over the past 25 years has revealed a sizeable correlation between father's and son's incomes, averaging around .5 (Connolly, Corak, and Haeck 2019). A correlation of .5 is approximately the correlation between fathers' and sons' heights. Thus, "if people's incomes were represented by their heights, the similarity in income between generations would resemble the similarity observed in the heights of fathers and sons" (Krueger 2002). More recent studies have found even higher correlations. For example, using Social Security records and PSID data for fathers' and sons' earnings, Bhashkar Mazumder (2018) reports an intergenerational correlation between .6 and .7. This results in an even greater narrowing within our visual image of fathers' and sons' heights.

Research focusing on the transmission of occupational status has also found a strong connection between parents and children (Hout 2018). For example, Daniel McMurrer and Isabel Sawhill report that children of professionals are "significantly more likely to become professionals as adults, and children of blue collar workers significantly more likely to work in blue collar occupations.... Men with white collar origins are almost twice as likely as those with blue collar origins to end up in upper white collar jobs" (1998, 2).

Or if one looks at the transmission of wealth, a similar pattern emerges (Bentron and Keister 2017; Killewald, Pfeffer, and Schachner 2017). William Gale and John Scholz (1994) estimate that intended family transfers and bequests account for 51 percent of current U.S. wealth, while an additional

12 percent is acquired through the payment of college expenses by parents. Consequently, nearly two-thirds of the net worth that individuals have acquired is through family transfers. Parents with considerable wealth are able to pass on these assets and advantages to their children. As a result, it is estimated that "children of the very rich have roughly 40 times better odds of being very rich than do the children of the poor" (Gokhale and Kotlikoff 2002, 268).

Additional work has focused on the impact that growing up specifically in poverty has upon one's later economic well-being (Duncan and Murnane 2016; Crowder and South 2003). In our Monopoly example, this might represent the player beginning the game with 250 dollars. Joan Rodgers (1995) has found that of those who experienced poverty as an adult, 50 percent had experienced poverty as a child, while an additional 38 percent had grown up in homes that were defined as near poor (below 2.00 of the poverty line).

Once again we see that the social class a child is reared in has a profound impact upon their later economic well-being and outcomes. This is not to say that economic movement is nonexistent. Individuals do move up and down the economic ladder across adulthood (Rank and Hirschl 2015). However, when such movement does happen, it often transpires over relatively short distances from their economic origins. In fact, contrary to popular myth, the United States tends to have less intergenerational mobility than a number of other industrialized countries (Corak 2010; Fox, Torche, and Waldfogel 2016; Rank, Eppard, and Bullock, 2021) and such mobility has been declining over time (Chetty et al. 2017; David and Mazumder 2020; Song et al. 2020). The empirical evidence clearly points to the fact that children from a lower-class background will be much more at risk of economic vulnerability in their adult lives than children from wealthier families.

The reasons for this are that children from a working- or lower-class background simply do not have the range and depth of opportunities as children from a middle- or upper-class background. This then affects the quantity and quality of human capital they are able to acquire. The discussion in Chapter 7 regarding the impact of poverty upon children's development will illustrate this point. Likewise the vast differences in educational quality by residence and income quickly illuminate the magnitude of these opportunity differences (discussed in Chapter 8) (Hertel and Pfeffer 2020).

For example, the work of Thomas Shapiro (Shapiro 2004, 2017; Shapiro, Meschede, and Ossoro 2013) illustrates the manner in which wealthier families are able to utilize their assets (a significant portion of which have been received through inheritance and/or gifts from parents) in order to acquire a high-quality primary and secondary education for their children. This is accomplished through either purchasing a home in an affluent school district or sending their children to private schools. In-depth interviews conducted with scores of parents in Boston, St. Louis, and Los Angeles made this point abundantly clear. As Shapiro and Johnson note, "By accessing quality school systems parents ensure specific kinds of schooling for their children and in this way help to pass their own social position along to the next generation" (2000, 2).

And of course this process continues with higher education. Children from wealthier families are often able to attend elite private universities, children from middle-class backgrounds may enroll at state public universities, while children from lower-class backgrounds will probably not continue on to college, and if they do, will likely attend a community or two-year college. As McMurrer and Sawhill note,

> *... family background has a significant and increasing effect on who goes to college, where, and for how long. With the rewards for going to college greater than ever, and family background now a stronger influence over who reaps those rewards, the United States is at risk of becoming more class stratified in coming decades. (1998, 69)*

Beyond social class there are several other factors that clearly play a role in the acquisition of human capital. A sizeable amount of research over the years has established that race exerts a powerful effect upon the life chances of children above and beyond social class (Bloome 2014; Chetty et al. 2020; Conley 1999; Feagin 2010; Rank 2009). For example, patterns of racial residential segregation further ensure that black children with similar social class backgrounds to white children find themselves in more heavily segregated schools with inferior resources (Massey 2007, 2016; Owens 2018; Orfield and Lee 2005). These patterns apply to Latino children as well.

Gender has also been shown to impact upon the acquisition of human capital (Wiswall and Zafar 2018). For example, throughout their schooling, girls are more likely to be steered into less lucrative career paths.

Finally, differences in innate abilities such as cognitive reasoning can play a role in the acquisition of human capital. All of these factors will influence the ability of children to acquire human capital and compete effectively in the labor market.

Consequently, where one begins one's life exerts a powerful effect throughout the life course. This process was succinctly described by Howard Wachtel.

> *If you are black, female, have parents with low socioeconomic status, and [are] dependent upon labor income, there is a high probability that you will have relatively low levels of human capital which will slot you into low-paying jobs, in low wage industries, in low wage markets. With this initial placement, the individual is placed in a high risk category, destined to end up poor sometime during her working and nonworking years. She may earn her poverty by working fulltime. Or she may suffer either sporadic or long periods of unemployment. Or she may become disabled, thereby reducing her earning power even further. Or when she retires, social security payments will place her in poverty even if she escaped this fate throughout her working years. With little savings, wealth, or private pension income, the retiree will be poor. (1971, 6)*

Thus, in order to understand why people are lacking in skills and education in the first place, one important place to look is the impact that a child growing up in a lower-income family versus a child growing up in a well-to-do family has on that child's acquisition of human capital, which then impacts upon their economic outcomes. This process of cumulative inequality is often neglected in political and policy discussions, but unfortunately the class you are born into has wide-ranging implications upon your life course. As Billie Holiday sang 80 years ago, "Them that's got shall get, them that's not shall lose. So the Bible says, and it still is news."

Two Levels of Understanding Poverty

A third element of the structural vulnerability perspective is that there are two levels to understanding impoverishment. On one hand, we can understand who is more likely to experience poverty through the earlier discussed impact that human capital exerts upon creating individual economic vulnerability. On the other hand, why poverty occurs in the first place can largely be ascertained through the structural failings discussed in Chapter 5. To illustrate these two levels, another analogy is used—that of musical chairs. The key is whether one chooses to analyze the losers of the game or the game itself.

Let us imagine eight chairs and ten players. The players begin to circle around the chairs until the music stops. Who fails to find a chair? If we focus on the winners and losers of the game, some combination of luck and skill will be involved. In all likelihood, the losers will be those in an unfavorable position when the music stops, somewhat slower, less agile, and so on. In one sense, these are appropriately cited as the reasons for losing the game.

However, if we focus on the game itself, then it is quite clear that given only eight chairs, two players are bound to lose. Even if every player were suddenly to double his or her speed and agility, there would still be two losers. From this broader context, it really does not matter what the loser's characteristics are, given that two are destined to lose.

I would argue that this musical chairs analogy can be applied to what has occurred in America economically, socially, and politically. Given that there is unemployment that translates into a shortage of jobs; given that we are producing more and more low-paying jobs lacking benefits; given that countless inner-city and rural communities have been devastated by economic restructuring; given the weak safety net in place to provide economic protection to the vulnerable; given that there is a scarcity of decent-quality, affordable childcare; given that there are few provisions to care for those who can no longer participate in the economy because of an illness—someone is going to lose at this game.

The losers will generally be those who are lacking in skills, education, and training, and therefore cannot compete as effectively and are more vulnerable than their counterparts who have acquired greater skills and education. In one sense, we can focus on these deficits, such as a lack of education, as the reasons for why individuals are at a greater risk of becoming poor.

Yet if we focus on the game itself, then the causes of poverty move from the individual's lack of skills or education to the fact that the economy produces unemployment, creates low-paying jobs, bypasses low-income communities, offers little social supports and protection, lacks affordable childcare, or does not provide for those who can no longer participate economically due to an illness. These then become the more fundamental reasons for why people are poor in this country. The earlier discussion in Chapter 5 provided support as to the magnitude of these structural failings, illustrating the mismatch between the number of opportunities versus the number of Americans in need of such opportunities.

Certainly the degree and intensity of these structural failings may vary over time. In our musical chairs analogy, there may be nine chairs for every ten players, or only six or seven. Likewise, the circumstances surrounding the economic game can and do change, which in turn affects the overall number of losers. Such changes result from a variety of factors, including economic upturns and downturns, public policy initiatives and changes, and demographic shifts in the population. The number of losers produced by the economic, social, and political systems in this country is therefore not written in stone.

For example, during the 1930s, the Great Depression resulted in a dramatic reduction in the number of economic opportunities, creating widespread unemployment and poverty. During this period of time, the number of available chairs versus participants in the game was significantly reduced. More recently the coronavirus pandemic has resulted in a severe economic downturn, resulting in millions facing unemployment.

On the other hand, the 1960s saw a booming economy coupled with federal initiatives to address poverty. The result was a dramatic increase in the number of chairs available, resulting in a significant drop in the overall rates of poverty during the decade. While the ratio of opportunities to participants fluctuates over time, nevertheless at any given point there tends to be a significant number of losers produced by the overall game.

What this means is that when we focus solely on personal characteristics, such as education, we can shuffle individual people up or down in terms of their being more likely to find a job, but we are still going to have somebody lose out if there are not enough decent-paying jobs to go around. In short, we are playing a game of musical chairs in this country with ten players but only eight chairs.

Many examples of this mismatch exist in today's society. Perhaps the most important is the earlier mentioned imbalance between the number of jobs that can support a family in the current economy versus the number of families in need of such jobs. In his study of long-term unemployment, Thomas Cottle talked with one man who had worked for 25 years with the same company, only to be downsized. After two and half years of searching, he eventually found a job at a much lower pay scale but felt fortunate to have such a job nonetheless. He referred to his job search using the musical chairs analogy discussed above,

> *The musical chairs of work still have me in the game. The music plays, we run around, the music stops and I dive for a chair. Took me two and half years to find this last one, I don't want the music to stop again. I'm only fifty-two, but pretty soon they'll take all the chairs away. Then what? That's the part I don't want to think about.* (Cottle 2001, 216)

Or take the spatial mismatch between the number of people in economically depressed geographical areas versus the number of opportunities in such areas. This is particularly apparent for those residing in urban inner cities or remote rural regions (as discussed in Chapter 3). Such areas are not hard to find—the rural Mississippi Delta; inner city Cleveland, Chicago, or St. Louis; American Indian reservations across the southwest; the Appalachian mountain region. In these regions, economic opportunities have largely moved away (or were never there in the first place) leaving behind many scrambling for the few chairs that are left.

William Julius Wilson documents this process in his study of inner-city Chicago residents, aptly titled *When Work Disappears* (1996). Wilson states, "The increasing suburbanization of employment has accompanied industrial restructuring and has further exacerbated the problems of inner-city joblessness and restricted access to jobs" (1996, 37).

Illustrative of this is Katherine Newman's (1999) ethnography of jobs and economic conditions in central Harlem during the mid-1990s in which she found that there were as many as 14 applicants for each fast-food job offered.

Similarly, Cynthia Duncan (2014) describes the process of diminishing jobs and opportunities in rural Appalachia, leaving behind thousands who must compete with one another for the dwindling number of viable economic opportunities. As she notes,

> *Work is hard to find. Only half the working-age men are employed, only a quarter of working-age women. "These days you can't even buy a job," complains one young man recently laid off from a mine. "Even men have a hard time getting work around here," a young single mother from Michigan explains. She was told to go on welfare when she went looking for work through the Department of Employment.* (2014, 6)

In the above cases, it is relatively easy to visualize the mismatch between the number of players and the number of chairs. Yet such a mismatch is operating on an overall national level as well. This mismatch illustrates the third point of the structural vulnerability explanation of poverty—given the structural failures, a certain percentage of the American population will experience economic vulnerability regardless of what their characteristics are. As in the musical chairs analogy, the game is structured such that some of the players are bound to lose. As Cindy Franklin (who discussed earlier her problems with unanticipated expenses) put it,

> *There are only so many good-paying jobs that exist in this society, and there are tons and tons of minimum wage jobs. And as long as we expect people to work them, there are gonna be people who can't make it without help. There's only so many people can rise to the top, and then no more can. (Rank 1994, 127)*

Increasing everyone's human capital will do little to alter the fact that there are only a limited number of decent-paying jobs available. In such a case, employers will simply raise the bar in terms of their employee qualifications, leaving behind a more qualified percentage of the population at risk of economic deprivation. Consequently, although a lack of human capital and its accompanying vulnerability leads to an understanding of who the losers of the economic game are likely to be, the structural components of our economic, social, and political systems explain why there are losers in the first place.

Visualization

As noted in Chapter 4, researchers and social commentators investigating poverty have largely focused upon individual deficiencies and demographic attributes in order to explain the occurrence of poverty in America. In doing so, they have reinforced the mainstream American ethos of interpreting social problems as primarily the result of individual failings and pathology (O'Connor 2001, 2016). In contrast, this chapter has argued that the dynamic of poverty can be better grasped through a perspective of structural vulnerability.

This framework is illustrated in Figure 6.1. It suggests that there are two ways of understanding individual vulnerability to poverty. Paths A and B deal with the question of who is at risk of poverty in America, while paths C and D focus on the question of why poverty exists in America.

The bulk of the empirical research pertaining to American poverty has focused on path A. Economists, sociologists, and demographers have concerned themselves with understanding the individual attributes that are associated with a greater risk of impoverishment. As we have discussed earlier, these attributes can largely be understood in terms of limiting an individual's ability to compete in the labor market. Consequently, those with less education, fewer job skills, and health problems; single mothers; minorities living in inner cities; and so on will face a heightened vulnerability to poverty.

Path B suggests that several background characteristics largely determine which Americans are more likely to be lacking in such human capital. The most important of these is social class—those growing up in lower- or working-class families are more likely to have their acquisition of human capital assets truncated. In addition, race, gender, and differences in innate abilities can also play a role in influencing the acquisition of human capital.

Figure 6.1 Structural Vulnerability Model of Poverty

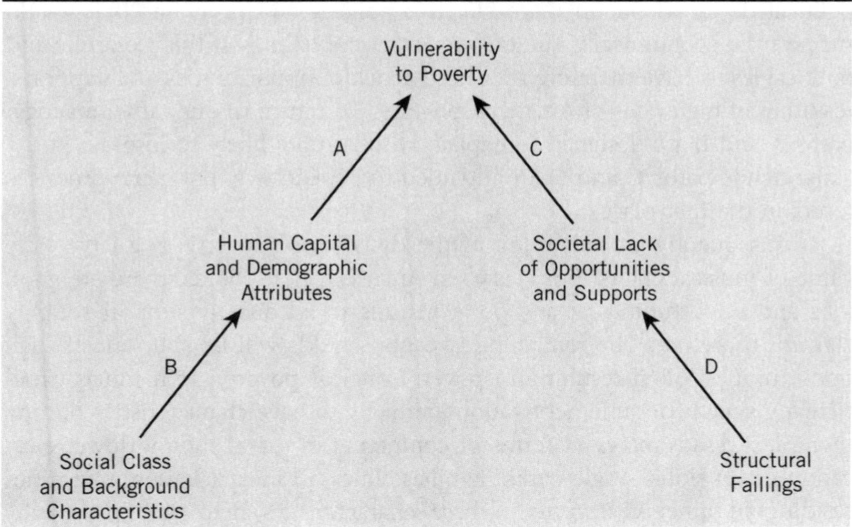

Paths A and B therefore explain who in America is at a greater risk of experiencing poverty during their lives. The critical mistake has been the following—poverty analysts have confused the question of who is at risk of poverty, with the question of why does poverty exist? They have stopped at Path A in their explanation of poverty. According to mainstream research, the question of why poverty exists is typically answered by noting that the poor are lacking in education, skills, and so on, and that these are the reasons for impoverishment. We can see in Figure 6.1 that this is an incomplete and misleading account.

The right-hand side of the structural vulnerability model includes paths C and D. These explain why so many Americans are at an elevated risk of poverty. Path C suggests that the lack of opportunities and social supports are critical reasons for this risk. As discussed earlier, there is a mismatch between the number of jobs that will adequately support a family versus the number of families in need of such jobs. Likewise, American society has failed to provide the necessary supports for those in need—the United States has been marked by a minimal safety net, inadequate childcare assistance, lack of health-care coverage, a dearth of affordable low-cost housing, and so on. This lack of economic opportunities and social supports has significantly raised the number of Americans vulnerable to the risk of poverty.

The shortage of opportunities and adequate supports has been produced by structural failings at the economic and political levels (path D). The tendency of our free market economy has been to produce a growing number of jobs that will no longer support a family. In addition, the basic nature of capitalism ensures that unemployment exists at modest levels. Both of these directly result in a shortage of economic opportunities in American society.

On the other hand, the absence of social supports stems from failings at the political and policy levels. The United States has traditionally lacked the political desire to put in place effective policies and programs that would support the economically vulnerable. Structural failings at the economic and political levels have therefore produced a lack of opportunities and supports, resulting in high rates of American poverty. To return to our earlier analogy, paths A and B are designed to explain who is more likely to lose out at the game, while paths C and D are intended to explain why the game produces losers in the first place.

Consequently we can think of the dynamic of poverty as a large-scale game of musical chairs. For every ten American households, there are good jobs and opportunities at any point in time to adequately support roughly eight of those ten. The remaining two households will be shut out of such opportunities, often resulting in poverty or near poverty. Individuals experiencing such economic deprivation are likely to have characteristics putting them at a disadvantage in terms of competing in the economy (lower education, fewer skills, single-parent families, illness or incapacitation, minorities residing in inner cities, etc.). These characteristics help to explain why particular individuals and households are at a greater risk of poverty.

Yet given the earlier discussed structural failures, a certain percentage of the American population will experience economic vulnerability regardless of what their characteristics are. The structure of the American economy, in consort with its weak social safety net and public policies directed to the economically vulnerable, ensure that millions of Americans will experience impoverishment at any point in time, and that a much larger number will experience poverty over the course of a lifetime. The fact that three-quarters of Americans will experience poverty or near poverty (at the 1.50 level) during their adulthoods is emblematic of these structural-level failings.

Concluding Thoughts

In summary, the approach taken in this chapter is intended to provide a new framework for understanding the dynamics of American poverty. Previous work has generally placed this dynamic within the framework of individual deficiencies. I have argued here that such a perspective is misdirected. Whereas individual attributes (such as human capital) help to explain who faces a greater risk of experiencing poverty at any point in time, the fact that substantial poverty exists on a national level can only be understood through an analysis of the structural dynamics of American society.

Understanding the reasons behind poverty is essential not only for appreciating the nature of poverty but also in terms of building our individual and societal responses to the condition of American poverty. If poverty is viewed as affecting a small proportion of the population who are plagued by moral failings and individual inadequacies, our individual and societal response will likely follow the familiar course we have taken in the past. That direction has been to assume relatively little collective responsibility toward the problem of poverty, while continually focusing on welfare reform initiatives that attempt to strengthen the work and family incentives for the poor. This approach has accomplished very little in terms of rectifying the problem of poverty.

On the other hand, if poverty is viewed as a failing at the structural level, this would suggest a much different approach for building an effective response to the issue (taken up in Part IV). It would also imply a reexamination into our individual and personal connections to the issue of poverty. We now embark on such an exploration.

ONLINE ACTIVITIES

confrontingpoverty.org

As a student, and now as a professor, I have always found it helpful to actually listen to someone whose work I had read. Such an experience can add insight into their way of thinking. So in order to practice what I preach, I have included for our online activity an interview that I gave several years ago. The interview format is a particularly engaging way to get to know how one frames an issue—in this case, why poverty exists.

Let us go to the *Confronting Poverty* website, and click on the "Discussion Guide." Click on "Module 6" and then click on the sidebar for the "Mark Rank interview." The interview is approximately 20 minutes long and will give you a bit more insight into my structural vulnerability perspective, which was discussed in this chapter.

After you have watched the interview, there is an interesting topic that I would like for us to think about. And that is the use of analogies to convey a concept. In the interview that you have watched, as well as in Chapter 6, I rely on several analogies to allow listeners and readers a way of better picturing the economic dynamics that I am describing.

Take the musical chairs analogy. My experience in giving talks and discussions on U.S. poverty has convinced me of the importance of this analogy. It has allowed many people to be able to picture in their mind the dynamic that I am trying to describe. It is a straightforward way of understanding that on one hand, we can predict who in particular experiences poverty through various demographic characteristics, yet on the other hand, we can understand why people are in poverty in the first place because there are not enough opportunities for all. The power of this analogy is that it allows individuals to be able to place into a wider context the common understanding of poverty being caused by individual deficiency and disadvantage. By allowing individuals to frame this dynamic differently, it provides for an "aha" experience—in fact, I have physically seen the light go on for some people when I have used this analogy.

There are many other analogies that we might consider as well. For example, you read about the altered game of Monopoly analogy in this chapter. Once again this provides a helpful way to shift our understanding of an issue. For example, the fact that primary and secondary schools vary so widely in quality depending on the economics of the neighborhood is generally quite apparent to most people. This then allows us to use the concept of cumulative inequality within the Monopoly analogy to explain unequal life outcomes.

Try to see in your discussions with others if you can come up with additional analogies in which to convey the dynamics of poverty to a wider audience. As I will argue in later chapters, one way in which we create change is through our conversations. By being able to effectively convey the realities of poverty, we allow others to understand the issue from a perspective that is perhaps different than they had originally conceived. The use of analogies can help in making such effective arguments.

Part III

Effects and Consequences of Poverty

We now turn to our third overall question to be explored—what are the effects and consequences of poverty? In the next three chapters we examine this question with respect to individuals and families, communities, and the nation as a whole. Research indicates that poverty has a wide range of negative effects upon each of these groups. The bottom line is that the cost of poverty is extremely high.

These chapters also introduce the question of why we should be concerned with alleviating poverty. Poverty is a problem with enormous ramifications. Many of the social ills that we see in society can be traced back to impoverishment. Understanding these ramifications is critical for building the political will to implement the policies suggested in Part IV.

CHAPTER 7 Individuals and Families

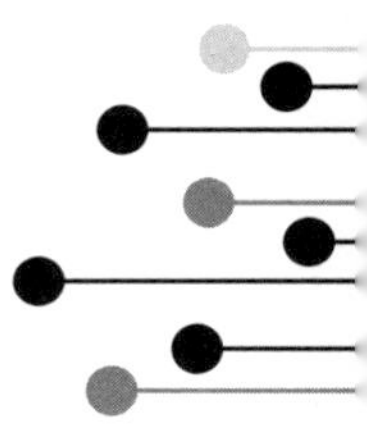

Every few years a report appears from the Heritage Foundation, a Washington conservative think tank. The author is invariably a policy analyst by the name of Robert Rector. Rector has made a reputation for himself by claiming that, among other things, economic destitution and poverty in the United States is minimal to nonexistent. The Heritage report routinely argues that America's poor are fairly well off and that they have acquired consumer goods and resources that were unheard of 100 or even 50 years ago. Quoting from the report,

> *The typical poor household, as defined by the federal government, had air conditioning and a car. For entertainment, the household had two color TVs, cable or satellite TV, a DVD player, and a VCR. In the kitchen, it had a refrigerator, an oven and stove, and a microwave. Other household conveniences included a clothes washer, clothes dryer, ceiling fans, a cordless phone, and a coffee maker. The family was able to obtain medical care when needed. Their home was not overcrowded and was in good repair. By its own report, the family was not hungry and had sufficient funds during the past year to meet all essential needs. The overwhelming majority of Americans do not regard a family living in these conditions as poor.* (Sheffield and Rector 2011, 14)

The report goes on to argue that, when compared with other countries around the globe, the poor in the United States enjoy a much higher standard of living.

The belief that the poor in the United States are not so bad off can be found in a wide range of places. It basically reflects the idea that those in poverty have nothing to complain about—that given the conditions in less developed countries, things could be much worse. In sharp contrast, this chapter presents evidence indicating that poverty extracts a very high price upon individuals and their families.

The Human Meaning of Poverty

What constitutes the human condition of American poverty? Unfortunately, as reflected in the Heritage report, the discourse coming out of Washington over the past 40 years has been marked by a remarkable lack of perception regarding the daily lives of struggling Americans. Nowhere is this more apparent than when it comes to the poor, particularly the poor who turn to welfare assistance. Rather than being guided by insight and wisdom, the debate surrounding the poor is routinely couched in ignorance, callousness, stereotypes, and political one-upmanship.

A low point in this debate came during the discussions that preceded the 1996 welfare reform bill signed by President Bill Clinton. Two House members on the Congressional floor argued that a potential cut of 69 billion dollars in public assistance programs was justified on the grounds that the use of welfare by recipients is analogous to the unnatural feeding of dangerous animals. Representative John Mica of Florida held up a sign that read, "DON'T FEED THE ALLIGATORS." He went on to say, "We post these warnings because unnatural feeding and artificial care create dependency. When dependency sets in, these otherwise able alligators can no longer survive on their own." Later in the day and not to be outdone, Representative Barbara Cubin of Wyoming continued this line of argument with the following analogy:

> *The Federal government introduced wolves into the State of Wyoming, and they put them in pens, and they brought elk and venison to them every day. This is what I call the wolf welfare program. The Federal Government provided everything that the wolves need for their existence. But guess what? They opened the gates and let the wolves out, and now the wolves won't go. Just like any animal in the species, any mammal, when you take away their freedom and their dignity and their ability, they can't provide for themselves …* (New York Times, *March 25, 1995, A9)*

Perhaps if Representatives Mica or Cubin had educated themselves to the difficulties and struggles surrounding the poor, they would not have been so quick to draw comparisons to wild animals, and they may have realized that living in poverty and on a safety net program is hardly analogous to wolves being "brought elk and venison every day."

Such an appreciation certainly does not mean that one should gloss over the problems facing the poor or glorify the downtrodden. What it does mean is a fuller and more realistic sense of the complexity and issues involved in people's lives. This complexity is too often absent in our discussions regarding poverty. Rather, they become routinely reduced to the caricatures of the lazy Cadillac driving welfare freeloader, or worse, to alligators or wolves (Levin 2019).

However, there is an additional element noticeably absent in our policy and general debates regarding the poor. It is an appreciation of the pain and suffering caused by poverty. For a host of reasons, we tend to shy away from such discussions. Yet they are essential in appreciating the deeper meaning and human costs of impoverishment. Behind each of the numbers presented in this chapter are literally millions of lives and stories. Embedded within those lives is an untold pain caused by poverty. The familiar saying that statistics represent faces with the tears wiped off is certainly apropos.

Although many experiences are associated with poverty, there are three that I believe capture the essence of the American experience of poverty in individuals' and families' lives—having to make significant compromises regarding the daily necessities in life; enduring sizeable levels of stress as a result of such insufficiencies; and experiencing a stunting of one's development and potential as a result of impoverishment. These are the painful and all-too-human costs of what it means to be poor in an American context of plenty. Each is explored below.

Doing Without

As we discussed in Chapter 1, by its very definition, poverty represents a lack or absence of essential resources. Webster defines poverty in three ways: "1. the state or condition of having little or no money, goods, or means of support; 2. deficiency of necessary or desirable ingredients, qualities, etc.; 3. scantiness; insufficiency." The experience of poverty is epitomized by having to do without.

This having to do without includes insufficiencies and compromises involving basic resources such as food, clothing, shelter, health care, and transportation. It also entails not having other items and services that many of us take for granted, from the convenience of writing a check to the small pleasure of going out for lunch. In short, poverty embodies a "deficiency of necessary or desirable ingredients" that most Americans possess. Let us examine several of these.

Living in poverty often means having to do without a sufficiently balanced diet and adequate intake of calories (Barrett and Lentz 2016). Several large-scale studies have indicated that those in poverty routinely have bouts of hunger, undernutrition, and/or a detrimental altering of the diet at some point during the month (Gundersen and Ziliak 2018). The U.S. Department of Agriculture determined that 35.3 percent of all individuals below the poverty line were in households that experienced food insecurity in 2018 (Coleman-Jensen et al. 2019). Furthermore, 46.5 million people received emergency food aid from Feeding America (the nation's largest organization of emergency food providers) in 2014, and 72 percent of these individuals fell below the poverty line (Feeding America 2014). The risk of hunger and food insecurity affects both children and adults (Popkin, Scott, and Galvez 2016) as well as the elderly (Ziliak and Gundersen 2019).

For example, an elderly woman I interviewed in the *Living on the Edge* book described how she could not afford a balanced diet, which then compounded her health problems:

> *Toward the end of the month, we just live on toast and stuff. Toast and eggs or something like that. I'm supposed to eat green vegetables. I'm supposed to be on a special diet because I'm a diabetic. But there's a lotta things that I'm supposed to eat that I can't afford. Because the fruit and vegetables are terribly high in the store. It's ridiculous! I was out to Cedar's grocery, they're chargin' fifty-nine cents for one grapefruit. I'm supposed to eat grapefruit, but who's gonna pay fifty-nine cents for one grapefruit when you don't have much*

money? But my doctor says that that's one thing that's important, is to eat the right foods when you're a diabetic. But I eat what I can afford. And if I can't afford it, I can't eat it. So that's why my blood sugar's high because lots of times I should have certain things to eat and I just can't pay. I can't afford it. (Rank 1994, 59)

This leads to a second area where families in poverty often have to do without—good health. One of the most consistent findings in epidemiology is that the quality of an individual's health is negatively affected by lower socioeconomic status, particularly impoverishment (Hudson, Gehlert, and Pandy 2020; Gregory and Coleman-Jensen 2017). Poverty is associated with a host of health risks, including elevated rates of heart disease, diabetes, hypertension, cancer, infant mortality, mental illness, undernutrition, lead poisoning, asthma, dental problems, and a variety of other ailments and diseases (Rank 2020a). The result is a death rate for the poverty stricken approximately three times higher than that for the affluent between the ages of 25 and 64 years (Pappas et al. 1993). A very large study found that the life expectancy difference between the top 1 percent and bottom 1 percent of the income distribution was approximately 15 years (Chetty, Stepner, and Abraham 2016). As Nancy Leidenfrost writes in her review of the literature, "Health disparities between the poor and those with higher incomes are almost universal for all dimensions of health" (1993, 1).

Furthermore, poverty exerts a negative effect upon children's health status, which in turn impacts upon their well-being as adults (Angel 2016; Chaudry and Wimer 2016; Hughes and Tucker 2018). According to Bradley Schiller,

A child born to a poverty-stricken mother is likely to be undernourished both before and after birth. Furthermore, the child is less likely to receive proper postnatal care, to be immunized against disease, or even to have his or her eyes and teeth examined. As a result, the child is likely to grow up prone to illness and poverty, and in the most insidious of cases, be impaired by organic brain damage. (2008, 136)

The connection between poverty and ill health exists for several reasons, including the lack of an adequate diet, less access to medical care, residing in unhealthy and stressful physical and mental environments, and less educational awareness regarding health issues. The result is an increase in pain and suffering at the doorsteps of the poor.

Although Medicaid, the CHIP program, and the Affordable Care Act have helped to increase the poor's access to health care, nevertheless when use of health services is compared to need for services, low-income households have the lowest rate. Furthermore, a number of the poor and near poor still have no insurance whatsoever—approximately 15.9 percent of those below the poverty line were uninsured for the entire year of 2019 (U.S. Census Bureau 2020c). And when insurance is carried, it is often restrictive in terms of what is covered.

Just as good health is often compromised as a result of poverty, so too is living in a safe and decent neighborhood. Although it is true that most of the poor do not live in neighborhoods that are characterized as impoverished inner-city areas, poverty nevertheless limits the choices available in terms of the overall quality of life in a neighborhood. For example, a poverty-stricken mother of two teenagers described her neighborhood as follows:

> *The territory is horrible. Across the street is the place that's been hitting the news lately. And it's really bad, 'cause when you go away, on weekends, we go down to my older son sometimes. And you really don't know what you're gonna have left when you come back. Because the apartment next door has been broken into twice. And it's bad. You can never be comfortable at night 'cause ya can never leave your windows open. You have to lock everything up, because you never know. But I guess if you want reasonable, cheap rent, you have to. (Rank 2000, 136)*

In addition, racial discrimination in the housing market further restricts the options available to nonwhites, particularly African Americans and Hispanics (Massey 2016).

Being confined to a low-income neighborhood when coupled with transportation problems often results in the poor paying more and spending more time acquiring basic necessities (Caplovitz 1968). This includes paying higher prices for food at the local grocery store (Chung and Myers 2005), not being able to buy in bulk or take advantage of items on sales, a scarcity of neighborhood retail outlets (Silber 2017), living in areas characterized as food deserts (Walker, Keane, and Burke 2010), and limited access to financial institutions, resulting in being exposed to predatory lending practices such as check-cashing stores and pawnshops (Dwyer 2018; Squires 2004). Take the case of a single mother I talked to who was living in a highly segregated, low-income black neighborhood.

> *I normally try to catch a ride with somebody or save a couple dollars and buy somebody some gas to take me somewhere. You know, you can go on the bus, but if you're grocery shoppin' it's hard to get back home. Usually I haveta grocery shop right around here where I can walk to. And then I'll have the kids meet me, and they'll help me bring the groceries back. I couldn't afford to pay somebody to go to the grocery store. I'd like to go to other places—you'd probably catch more bargains, but if you don't have no way to get there, then you have to shop where you can shop. (Rank 2004, 41)*

She went on to note,

> *I'm rentin' a washin' machine for 42 dollars a month. For two years I gotta pay that. It's a lotta money for a washin' machine. But I don't have a car to go to the laundromat, and I don't have the cash to pay cash for a washin'*

machine, so I don't have any choice. I'm stuck with one of those rent-to-own places. (Rank 2004, 41–42)

Doing without adequate transportation also affects the ability to compete for and hold a job. Likewise for those who do have a job, not having reliable transportation causes difficulties as was clear in a conversation I had with a 37-year-old, never-married mother who was working part-time as a cashier while also attending school. She was asked if not having a car caused her any difficulty.

That's a great difficulty. I use my bicycle to go to work during the winter. As long as there's a clear spot, I went on ice. With a bicycle. People told me I was crazy. But I mean, I had to do it. And I did it. And I will be doing it again this year. If there's one little patch that's been cleared, I don't care if it's in January, I will be on that bike. (Rank 2004, 42)

What is perhaps most bitter regarding all of the above hardships is that they take place within a context of abundance. In other words, most Americans have plenty to eat or clothes to wear, experience good health and safe neighborhoods, are not forced to ride a bicycle across icy streets to work, and so on. This message of abundance is seen daily from shopping malls to television advertising. The result is that poverty in America has an especially bitter taste. It imprints upon the poor a strong sense of relative deprivation and failure.

In short, living in poverty is epitomized by struggling to acquire, and at times forgoing, the daily necessities and resources that most Americans take for granted. It is the paradox and humiliation of having to do without in a land of plenty.

The Stressful Weight of Poverty

A consequence of the above struggles is that impoverishment places a heavy weight upon the shoulders of most who walk in its ranks. In essence, poverty acts to amplify the daily stress found in everyday life and its relationships. The struggle of having to juggle and balance expenses on an ongoing basis places a stressful burden upon the poverty stricken and their families (Desmond 2016; Edin and Shaefer 2015). This is illustrated in the worries a working mother conveyed to me:

My biggest worry is running out of money. You know, my kids cannot understand and I wish they could, and some day they will. But right now, every time I go shopping or even if we're sitting there and lookin' at TV—"Mom, I want this. Mom can I get this? Mom, you owe me so much for allowance. Mom can you give us so much money?" And I'm beginning to realize what my husband went through sometimes, when I said, "Gee, I wish I could have..." and knowing that he may wanted to have gotten it for me, but knowing he couldn't afford it. It's just frustrating. (Rank 2004, 43)

Rather than being able to afford her children's yearnings, this mother of three must try to juggle her ever-present array of bills within the constraints of a slightly higher than minimum wage full-time income.

> *I want to go to bed at night thinking, all the bills are paid up, I'm on the up and up with everybody and I don't have to worry about things. That's not the worry I want to have. But like last night, I got hold of the phone bill. I saw when it was due, like on the 17th. And I knew that if I didn't do something about it right away, then I wouldn't have a phone. So I went ahead and paid it and called them up today to let them know that it was in the mail so I wouldn't get one of those polite little notices. But our gas bill, that was due … I think it is coming due. I'm gonna have to hold that over until my next check and just pay the late charge, as much as I hate doing that. But they will still get paid. I wish that I were able to just go ahead and pay like I should.* (Rank 2004, 43)

Perhaps the most well-known juggling act is what has been called the "heat-or-eat" dilemma. As heating bills climb in the winter, impoverished families may be forced into the hard decision of choosing between purchasing food versus paying for heat. Bhattacharya and colleagues (2002) have empirically documented that poor families do indeed lower their food expenditures during cold-weather periods (see also Tuttle and Beatty 2017).

Such ongoing frustrations are commonplace. They result in intensifying the stress and tension within the individual, and by extension, to their relationships. Take the marital relationship. Research has consistently found that poverty and lower income are associated with a greater risk of separation and divorce, as well as spousal and child violence (Jonson-Reid et al. 2020).

What frequently happens is that unemployment precipitates a fall into poverty (as discussed in Chapter 2), which results in a tremendous strain upon a marriage (Brand 2015). Research has shown that the impact of unemployment upon marital relationships is quite deleterious (Cottle 2001; McKee-Ryan and Maitoza 2018). Yet when blended with poverty, it creates a particularly destructive combination.

For example, an out-of-work husband in Lillian Rubin's *Families on the Faultline* described his feelings as follows:

> *It's hard enough being out of work, but then my wife gets on my case, yakking all the time about how we're going to be on the street if I don't get off my butt, like it's my fault or something that there's no work out there. When she starts up like that, I swear I want to hit her, anything just to shut her mouth.* (1994, 115–16)

As Rubin writes, "The stress and conflict in families where father loses his job can give rise to the kind of interaction described here, a dynamic that all too frequently ends in physical assaults against women and children" (1994, 116).

In many ways, the stress of poverty is even greater for single-parent families. For these parents, there is no partner to turn to in order to provide a helping hand during the routine crises and struggles outlined earlier. Furthermore, most female heads of households work at two full-time jobs (within the labor force and at home). The result is stress, frustration, and exhaustion, which in turn influences the caring and raising of children (Desmond 2016; Gibson-Davis 2016).

In addition, the conditions of poverty and use of a safety net program are highly stigmatized in American society (Fabbre et al. 2020). As we discussed in Chapter 4, survey research has repeatedly indicated that the general understanding of poverty is primarily as an individual and moral failing. This stigma and shame is experienced first-hand by those in poverty. It is felt in a variety of settings, from using the SNAP program at the grocery store, to being denied health coverage at the doctor's office. This sense of shame permeates the experience of poverty and leads to individuals and families feeling additional stress as a result.

In short, the daily trials and tribulations of living in poverty put a heavy strain upon the backs of the poor. These anxieties then spill over into relationships with family and friends. It is battling head first against the formidable pressures exerted by poverty, and coming up scarred. It is no coincidence that those in poverty are particularly susceptible to the debilitating effects of toxic stress (Evans and Kim 2012; McEwen 2017).

Stunted Growth

The result of having to do without, combined with the stress of living in poverty, often produces a stunting of growth. A simple analogy is to a tree. If one denies a tree the proper nutrients, while at the same time creating stressful environmental conditions, the result is that it will fail to develop to its full potential. Often there will be a noticeable stunting of growth and deformity of its trunk and branches.

So it is with individuals in poverty for sustained periods of time. A lack of proper food, shelter, education, and other essential resources, coupled with the stress of impoverishment, results in stunted individual development. Sometimes this stunting is visibly apparent, oftentimes it lies underneath the surface. Moreover, the longer the duration of poverty and the greater the depth of poverty, the larger the negative impact.

This process is perhaps most salient in the stunting effects upon young children's physical and mental growth (Council on Community Pediatrics 2016; Hair, Hanson, and Wolfe 2015; Johnson, Riis, and Noble 2016). Poor infants and young children in the United States are much more likely to have lower levels of physical and mental growth (as measured in a variety of ways) when compared to their nonpoor counterparts (Angel 2016; Duncan and Brooks-Gunn 1997; National Academies of Sciences, Engineering, and Medicine 2019).

Furthermore, both the duration and depth of poverty intensify these negative outcomes. For example, in their research on poverty's effects upon young children's cognitive and verbal ability and early school achievement, Judith Smith and colleagues report, "Duration of poverty has very negative effects on children's IQ, verbal ability, and achievement scores. Children who lived in persistently poor families scored 6–9 points lower on the various assessments than children who were never poor. In addition, the negative effects of persistent poverty seem to get stronger as the child gets older" (1997, 164). They also found that "The effects of family poverty varied dramatically depending on whether a family was very poor (family income below 50 percent of the poverty level), poor, or near poor. Children in the very poor group had scores 7–12 points lower than did children in the near-poor group" (1997, 164).

Likewise, in a study that looked at the impact of the duration of poverty upon children's mental health, Jane McLeod and Michael Shanahan found that "The length of time spent in poverty is an important predictor of children's mental health, even after current poverty status is taken into account. As the length of time spent in poverty increases, so too do children's feelings of unhappiness, anxiety, and dependence" (1993, 360).

As children grow older and if they continue to reside in poverty, the disadvantages of growing up poor multiply. These disadvantages include attending inferior schools, coping with the problems associated with disadvantaged neighborhoods, residing in less educationally stimulating home environments, having health needs left unattended to, and a host of other disadvantages (Rank 2020).

One simple but telling example illustrating this involved a single mother of four children, ages 14, 12, 10, and 8 years. She told me how she was not able to provide the kinds of educational and social experiences for her children that she would have liked to. The case of not being able to afford a summer program was one such instance.

> *They were in a program at the elementary school. Which was five dollars per child. My one daughter was in a science program, chemistry program. And that was a three week program. That was just five dollars. But there were a lot of other programs that I didn't want to spend money for, but they weren't that much. Five or ten dollars, or maybe 25. They had a summer camp, which was for four days. That was 25 dollars through the park district. But I wasn't able to do that. For two children, that would've been 50 dollars. I did it for one child last year. But I had two. And I couldn't send one and not the other. But I mean what's 25 dollars? It's a lot if you don't have it.*
>
> *They kept 'em from eight to three. They had a camp-out. And they had swimming. And they roasted marshmallows. And they had arts and crafts. It woulda been a nice program. But I just don't have it.... And there's a lot of other additional programs that maybe I could've looked into had I the money. (Rank 2004, 46)*

This represented just one instance of how poverty diminished in a relatively small way the potential growth of two young children. Yet multiplied over hundreds of such events for these children, the effect becomes profound. This is expressed in the feelings of a mother who had been out of work for two years and could not adequately provide for the needs of her children.

> *After two years it gets to the point where you can just about start pulling out your hair. Because there is so much that you want to do, and you see your kids growing up around you, and you can't do a damn thing to help 'em out. And oooooh. It really drives you nuts.* (Rank 2004, 47)

As children continue to grow up, the disadvantages of poverty or near poverty multiply. Consequently, by the time they reach their early 20s, they may be at a significant disadvantage in terms of their ability to compete effectively within the labor market, which in turn increases their risk of experiencing poverty as adults.

As adults age, the stunting effects of poverty become less pronounced but are nevertheless still quite real. These effects include poor physical and mental health, lower productivity as workers, and reduced participation in civic activities as well as other aspects of life (Rank 2020).

Living in poverty also takes its toll in other ways as well. For example, individuals may develop strategies for coping with the stress of poverty. Some of these can be helpful, such as cultivating support networks. Unfortunately, others are self-destructive, such as the use of alcohol or drugs.

In addition, incarceration is an event that those in poverty are much more likely to encounter than are the nonpoor. Over 40 years ago, Jeffrey Reiman entitled the first edition of his book on the subject *The Rich Get Richer and the Poor Get Prison: Ideology, Class and Criminal Justice* (1979). Unfortunately, it still remains the case that poverty significantly elevates the risk of incarceration. Furthermore, African American youth face a significantly higher risk of experiencing the criminal justice system than their white counterparts (Alexander 2020). In one influential study, it was found that by the time black males reached their early 30s, one out of five would have spent time in the correctional system (Pettit and Western 2004). This, in turn, serves to reduce one's employability, dramatically stunting an individual's development and potential.

Suffice it to say that a third bitter taste of poverty involves not being able to achieve the full development of one's potential and one's children's potential. This is perhaps the most painful pill to swallow. It is poverty's knack of being able to undercut the capabilities that are found in all of us. It is not an exaggeration to call this a tragedy, for that is precisely what the loss of such human potential is.

I have chosen in this section to focus on what in my view is the essence of the poverty experience in people's lives—having to make major compromises concerning the daily necessities that most of us take for granted; enduring significant levels of stress as a result of such insufficiencies; and experiencing the stunting of one's own development and children's development as a result of impoverishment. These can be summarized in Alexander Chase's observation that "The rich man may never get into heaven, but the pauper is already serving his term in hell." This is the painful and all too human cost of what it means to be poor in a land of plenty.

What Impact Does Poverty Have Upon Family Dynamics?

Just as poverty impacts upon individual development and growth, impoverishment can also influence family dynamics and relationships. This is particularly true for those experiencing long-term bouts of poverty. Several of these effects are discussed below.

Extended Kinship

Various anthropological studies have indicated that those in poverty often utilize a larger network of kinship (than the nonpoor) in order to exchange resources and services. This extended network serves as a coping mechanism for dealing with the uncertainties and hardships of poverty that were discussed earlier (e.g., Edin and Lein 1997; Furstenberg 2020).

For example, in Carol Stack's study of a poor, black community called The Flats, she found that it was virtually impossible for families to cover their various expenses and needs completely on their own. Consequently, a system of collective sharing arose within The Flats as an adaptive strategy to survive the daily uncertainties and depravation of poverty. As Stack writes,

> *In the final months of my life in The Flats, I learned that poverty creates a necessity for this exchange of goods and services. The needs of families living at bare subsistence are so large compared to their average daily income that it is impossible for families to provide independently for fixed expenses and daily needs. Lacking any surplus of funds, they are forced to use most of their resources for major monthly bills: rent, utilities, and foods. After a family pays these bills they are penniless.* (1974, 29)

This system of exchange encompassed a wide network of kin and friends within The Flats. Only through such a collective response were families able to get through the daily trials and tribulations of long-term poverty.

Likewise, in Harvey's (1993) ethnographic study of a white, displaced farming population that had located in a community called Potter Addition, a similar process of mutual sharing and obligation developed across a wide network of kin. Family and kin members could be counted on to help in various situations, just as they themselves would be counted on for mutual assistance by others.

Likelihood of Marriage

A long line of ethnographic, sociological, and demographic studies have indicated that the likelihood of marriage is substantially reduced among the poverty stricken when compared with the nonpoor (Cherlin 2020). The fundamental reason behind this association is that individuals contemplating marriage are generally seeking (or desire to be) an economically secure partner (Sassler and Lichter 2020). Poverty undermines the availability of such partners. Hence individuals in these situations are more likely to delay or forego marriage.

Well known within this vein of research has been the work of William Julius Wilson (1987, 1996, 2016). His analyses have focused on the increasing problems found within the inner city among African Americans and the reasons why such problems appear to have worsened over the last three decades. A critical factor in understanding the falling rate of marriage within the inner-city population has been the economic restructuring that has resulted in the movement of capital and job opportunities out of central city areas. As Wilson writes,

> *The black delay in marriage and the lower rate of remarriage, each associated with high percentages of out-of-wedlock births and female-headed households, can be directly tied to the employment status of black males. Indeed, black women, especially young black women, are confronting a shrinking pool of "marriageable" (that is economically stable) men.* (1987, 145)

As a result, the rate of marriage within poverty-stricken inner cities is considerably lower than that within the general population.

Childbearing

Demographic data indicate that there is an association between lower levels of income and somewhat higher rates of fertility. For example, if we examine the total number of births per 1,000 women aged 15–44 years in 2017, women residing in a family with incomes below $10,000 had a rate of 66.4, for those with a family income between $75,000 and $99,999 it was 51.7, and for those with a family income over $200,000 the number was 43.9 (U.S. Census Bureau 2019d). In addition, women at lower income and educational levels tend to have children at earlier ages and are more likely to bear children out of wedlock. For example, in 2016, 62 percent of all births were outside of marriage for women with less than a high school degree, while for women with a college degree the percentage was 10 percent (Wildsmith, Manlove, and Cook 2018).

Two factors appear critical in understanding why poverty is associated with these patterns. First, research indicates that the poor have less access and information regarding birth control (Luker 1996). In addition, the poor are least able to afford contraception (and specifically abortion). As a result, survey research indicates that poor women are more likely than nonpoor women to report that they have experienced an unwanted or unintended birth (Maynard 1997).

A second reason for higher fertility rates, particularly among teenagers in dire poverty, is the perception of a lack of future opportunities. In a world of negatives, having a child may be seen as one of the few positive actions one can take. The Children's Defense Fund puts this idea aptly by stating, "In many ways, the best contraceptive is a real future."

Marital Dissatisfaction, Violence, and Dissolution

Research has consistently found that poverty and lower income are associated with a greater risk of separation and divorce, as well as spousal and child violence (Jonson-Reid et al. 2020). When unemployment precipitates a fall into poverty (as discussed earlier), it can place a tremendous strain upon a marriage.

Married couples in poverty tend to face significant economic stress, which negatively affects their levels of marital happiness and well-being (Karney and Bradbury 2020). This, in turn, increases the likelihood that couples will attempt to resolve such dissatisfaction through physical violence or divorce. Indeed, poverty is strongly associated with an increased risk of physical and mental violence within families (Jonson-Reid et al. 2020; Kim and Drake 2018; Landers, Carrese, and Spath 2019). This is reflective of the enormous stress and strain upon individuals that we discussed earlier.

Concluding Thoughts

Poverty places a heavy burden upon all who walk in its ranks. This is particularly the case for those experiencing long-term poverty. The daily struggle of trying to make ends meet produces anxiety and stress in the lives of individuals. It also stunts development, particularly for children.

Likewise, the conditions of poverty place a tremendous strain upon family relationships. It acts to magnify and intensify the everyday problems found in most relationships. The result is often emotional and physical pain.

The concern throughout this section of the book is with the condition of poverty and its impact upon individuals, families, and society. It is therefore important to highlight the distinction between the condition of poverty and the poor themselves. Too often we look at the issues discussed in this chapter and blame the poor for bringing these on themselves, while losing sight of the fact that it is the condition of poverty that results in much of the stress and frustrations that we have seen. As stated earlier, poverty represents a state of extreme economic and social deprivation. The poor, on the other hand, are individuals and families who for some period of time occupy such a state. The condition of poverty, and ameliorating its deleterious effects, is where our concern and efforts should lie.

Finally, it must be emphasized that in spite of these very serious components of poverty, research has repeatedly demonstrated that those who fall below the poverty line essentially hold the same fundamental aspirations, beliefs, and hopes as most other Americans (Duina 2018). They have also been shown to have a number of strengths and sources of resilience (Fankenhuis and Nettle 2019). For example, throughout my *Living on the Edge* book, it was clear that those in poverty and on public assistance repeatedly expressed support for and tried to fulfill the mainstream goals of wanting to get ahead in life, working hard, struggling to provide the best for their children, and persevering despite the many obstacles laid in their path.

ONLINE ACTIVITIES

confrontingpoverty.org

Visual images and photography are particularly powerful ways to convey the pain of poverty. Jacob Riis's 1890 book *How the Other Half Lives* documented the wretched conditions of tenement dwellers in an area known as "the Bend" in New York City during the 1880s. Riis used his vast knowledge as a police reporter to chronicle the situations that impoverished families found themselves languishing in. Equally important, Riis relied upon the relatively new technology of photography to visually document the conditions he wrote so provocatively about. Looking at his photographs today, they continue to stand as a powerful statement against the horrific conditions he had found in the city of New York.

During the Great Depression of the 1930s, photography was once again used to provide a lens into the suffering brought about by the economic collapse and the Dust Bowl conditions in America's heartland. Photographers such as Walker Evans and Dorothea Lange vividly recorded these conditions as part of the Farm Security Administration's photography program.

More recently, the Danish photographer Jacob Holdt captured the pain of poverty in his 1985 book, *American Pictures*. During the late 1970s and 1980s, he presented his slideshow across many U.S. and Canadian college campuses, having a profound effect on those who saw it.

For our online activity, we follow in this photographic tradition by visiting a visual and written exposé of poverty across America. Begin by going to the *Confronting Poverty* website and click on the "Discussion Guide." Now click on Module 2, and then click on the sidebar link, "Geography of Poverty." This will take you to an innovative website that follows a photographer and writer in what they label "A journey through forgotten America."

The website is divided into different regions of the country. Begin with the introduction. This will give you some background into the project. You can then look at the different sections of the country in order, or pick and choose the regions that you would like to learn more about.

What each of these sections demonstrates is a major theme we will explore in the next chapter—that poverty exerts a powerful influence upon the health of a community. All of the regions in this exposé have been devastated by poverty and economic blight. This has included massive job loss, exposure to toxic pollutants, a collapse of social services, and much more. These, in turn, profoundly diminish the lives of families struggling to survive under such conditions. As you explore the different regions of the country, take time to contemplate and consider the meaning behind the visual images that you encounter.

CHAPTER 8 Communities

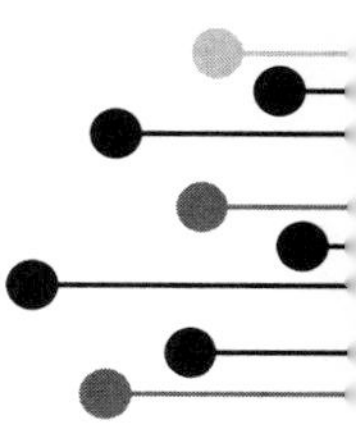

Just as individuals and families are negatively impacted by poverty, so too are neighborhoods and communities. Poverty-stricken communities tend to be exposed to a host of daunting challenges. These include a lack of basic services and infrastructure, an unhealthy physical environment, issues of crime and safety, lack of employment opportunities, and schools strapped for resources. We touch upon each of these in this chapter.

Over the past 30 years, considerable research has focused on the economic well-being of the neighborhoods that individuals reside in as one way in which to describe and understand the nature of American poverty. The argument is that neighborhoods mired in poverty detrimentally affect all who reside in such communities (including the nonpoor) and are particularly harmful to children. For example, Paul Jargowsky poses the question, "Why should we be concerned with the spatial organization of poverty?" His answer is the following:

> *The concentration of poor families and children in high-poverty ghettos, barrios, and slums magnifies the problems faced by the poor. Concentrations of poor people lead to a concentration of the social ills that cause or are caused by poverty. Poor children in these neighborhoods not only lack basic necessities in their own homes, but also they must contend with a hostile environment that holds many temptations and few positive role models. Equally important, school districts and attendance zones are generally organized geographically, so that the residential concentration of the poor frequently results in low-performing schools.* (2003, 2)

As we discussed in Chapter 3, most individuals in poverty do not live in highly impoverished communities. However, for those who do, residing in such an environment constitutes an additional burden to bear. It results in a diminished quality of life above and beyond their individual poverty status.

Physical Environment and Infrastructure

Where you grow up and live can have a profound influence upon your overall well-being. One of the most striking illustrations of this pertains to the physical environment found in neighborhoods and communities. A vast body of research has shown that those in high-poverty and nonwhite neighborhoods are much more likely to be exposed to a wide range of toxic pollutants.

The field of environmental justice has shed light on these disparities over the last three decades (Bullard 2000). Those living in low-income or poverty-stricken neighborhoods are much more likely to be exposed to higher levels of environmental toxins (Kravitz-Wirtz et al. 2018; Muller, Sampson, and Winter 2018), including elevated rates of air, water, and soil pollution. These, in turn, result in a higher incidence of various diseases including cancer and cardiovascular disease.

The recent case of the tainted water supply in Flint, Michigan, is but one in a long line of tragedies showing the detrimental environmental impact of living in low-income neighborhoods. Other well-known cases in which the poor were disproportionally impacted by an environmental catastrophe include the 1995 heat wave in Chicago killing 739 mostly elderly and black residents; Hurricane Katrina, which decimated low-income neighborhoods in New Orleans; and the recent coronavirus pandemic, which has disproportionally affected low-income and populations of color.

These environmental effects are particularly pernicious for children. Children residing in poverty-stricken neighborhoods are much more likely to be exposed to lead poisoning, asthma, and a host of environmentally induced illnesses, compared with their counterparts in more affluent communities.

As one travels across the country, startling contrasts come into view that are more typically thought of as found only in extremely poor countries. The life expectancy in some inner-city neighborhoods is lower than that in countries such as Bangladesh (McCord and Freeman 1990). Likewise, some of the rural communities in Appalachia or the Deep South are reminiscent of conditions found in developing countries (Abramsky 2013). American Indian reservations, in particular, are often marked by debilitating conditions (Mauer 2016).

Poor neighborhoods also tend to be plagued by a failing infrastructure. This includes a deterioration in the quality of roads and sidewalks, systems of drainage and sewage, street lighting, and housing stock. All of these have a detrimental impact upon the quality of life.

An example of this can be found in what may be the poorest town in the United States—Centreville, Illinois. Located just 10 minutes from downtown St. Louis, the town once had a number of manufacturing jobs. However, as has been the case across the country, such jobs have long since disappeared, leaving behind an impoverished community where 95 percent of its residents are African American. The town sits on a flood plain, and for the past 20 years whenever there are heavy rains, raw sewage flows across the yards of most homes, and at times backs up into these homes. The current infrastructure of pumps and sewer lines to handle such flooding has deteriorated to such a degree that it can no longer do the job it was intended to do. The town simply does not have the resources to make the necessary repairs, while its residents are trapped in their homes, unable to move because no buyers are interested in moving into such a community. As one resident put it,

> *People don't realize the toll it all takes—not being able to flush your toilet, embarrassment when friends visit, the constant smell, the dirt and rust on*

your car, watching where you step when you walk, having all the money you've invested in your house disappear, feeling trapped, feeling like you let down your family, trying to encourage your children to see a bright future. (St. Louis Post Dispatch, *February 23, 2020)*

Another example of how the physical environment and infrastructure affect health and well-being is the fact that not having adequate and safe sidewalks can negatively impact the ability of city residents to get out of their homes and exercise. When combined with a lack of parks and green spaces, and a fear of crime, the physical environment can shape the level of activity that individuals are able to engage in (Sharifi et al. 2016). This, in turn, can result in higher rates of diseases associated with a sedentary lifestyle.

Isolation and Segregation

Poor neighborhoods are often isolated and segregated from the surrounding region. These are areas frequently shunned and avoided by those residing outside of these communities. Whether it be inner-city blighted neighborhoods or remote rural economically depressed localities, isolation and segregation are frequently the norm.

This is particularly the case for those poor neighborhoods in which a majority of the residents are nonwhite. Residential segregation on the basis of race remains a highly salient feature of American society. This segregation has remained at elevated levels during the first part of the twenty-first century, while segregation on the basis of income has in fact increased (Reardon and Bischoff 2011). The result is that these neighborhoods are increasingly isolated from the rest of the wider regions.

This neighborhood context of isolation has been particularly significant in the seminal work of William Julius Wilson (Wilson 1987, 1996, 2009, 2016), Douglas Massey (Massey and Denton 1993; Massey 2007, 2016), and Robert Sampson (Sampson 2012; Sampson, Raudenbush, and Earls 1997; Morelli and Sampson 2020). As discussed in Chapter 4, Wilson's work has focused on the pattern of inner-city impoverished neighborhoods becoming increasingly isolated from the surrounding metropolitan regions. This has resulted in accentuating the feelings of alienation and despair often found in those communities.

One consequence of the increasing bifurcation of our society is what has been labeled the Brazilianization effect. The prosperous have been progressively isolating themselves from the poor and disadvantaged in society (Massey 1996). Gated and walled communities have been growing at a rapid rate, as has the percentage of Americans in prison. Both of these trends have the effect of isolating and physically separating the haves from the have nots. As Allan Hanson (1997a, 1997b) has argued, this has become the modern way in which more and more of the affluent deal with the social problem of poverty—that is, refusing to even see it. It is no coincidence that private security and prison construction are two of the top growth industries in the United States.

One community in California literally resembled the Middle Ages with a wall, a moat, a drawbridge, and a device called a bollard that fires a three-foot metal cylinder into the bottom of unauthorized cars (Thurow 1996). Large-scale walled and gated building projects have been going up across the country, particularly in Florida, California, Arizona, and Nevada. These developments are often broken into various "villages," with each village having its own gated entrance and walled perimeter. Mario Ruiu (2014) reports that approximately 30 million Americans live in such communities, with substantial increases expected in the years ahead. The bottom line is that both poverty-stricken and affluent communities are becoming increasingly isolated. In this sense, the geographical divide in America has been getting wider.

Basic Social Services and Cost of Living

Connected to the isolation, segregation, and deteriorating physical environment in poverty-stricken neighborhoods is a lack of basic social services. This encompasses a wide range of amenities, from not having parks and places for recreation, to inadequate police and fire protection.

One of the most noticeable shortages in low-income communities is the lack of good-quality, affordable, and healthy food (Hossfeld, Kelly, and Waity 2018). These areas are often described as food deserts. Large supermarkets generally avoid impoverished neighborhoods in deciding where to locate their stores. What is often left are convenience shops, gas stations, and fast-food outlets, resulting in a dearth of healthy food choices.

Access to affordable, reliable transportation is also in short supply. Being confined to a low-income neighborhood when coupled with transportation problems often results in the poor paying more and spending more time acquiring basic necessities (Silber 2017). This includes paying higher prices for food at the local grocery store, not being able to buy in bulk or take advantage of items on sales, a scarcity of neighborhood retail outlets, and limited access to financial institutions, resulting in being exposed to predatory lending practices such as check-cashing stores and pawnshops (Squires 2004).

Many other social services are often in short supply as well. These include the presence of affordable, accessible, and good-quality childcare. Similarly, health-care providers, social service agencies, and basic retail outlets are often hard to come by. Accentuating these shortcomings is the fact that the quality of the housing stock in impoverished communities is often of substandard quality. The result is, again, a diminished quality of life.

Crime and Safety

Just as good health is often compromised as a result of living in high-poverty neighborhoods, so too is living in a safe and crime-free environment. Those living in poverty-stricken neighborhoods are much more likely to be victims of various crimes compared to those living in nonpoor communities. They include robbery, assault, murder, sexual assault, gang violence, and vandalism. As a recent Housing and Urban Development (HUD) report notes, such crime "wreaks a terrible impact not only on individual victims, their families, and friends but also on nearby residents and the fabric of their neighborhoods. Exposure to violent crime can damage people's health and development, and violence can push communities into vicious circles of decay" (HUD 2016, 1).

Communities characterized by high levels of racial residential segregation and concentrated disadvantage are also plagued by higher levels of crime, including violent crime. A Bureau of Justice study finds that persons in poverty had over double the rate of violent victimization compared to those in upper income households (Harrell et al. 2014). As the HUD report goes on to observe, "Poverty, segregation, and inequality are related to neighborhoods' access to resources and ability to solve problems, including problems that foster crime. These resources include access to institutions, particularly effective community policing and the swift prosecuting of violent crime" (HUD 2016, 1).

In addition, high levels of distrust exist between poor neighborhoods of color and the police (Braga, Brunson, and Drakulich 2019). As the Black Lives Matter movement has repeatedly demonstrated, Americans of color are much more likely to "be stopped, searched, frisked, and arrested by police than similarly situated whites" (Brage, Brunson, and Drakulich 2019, 539).

Education

One of the most significant consequences of living in a lower-income or poverty-stricken neighborhood is that the education a child receives is likely to be of substandard quality (Morrissey and Vinopal 2017). A report by the Department of Education begins with the following statement: "While some young Americans—most of them white and affluent—are getting a truly world-class education, those who attend school in high poverty neighborhoods are getting an education that more closely approximates schools in developing countries" (U.S. Department of Education and Equity and Excellence Commission 2013, 12).

One reason for this is the way that public education is funded in this county. The United States is one of the very few industrialized countries where the bulk of funding for public schools comes from state and local tax dollars rather than from the federal government. In particular, the overall value of real estate in a school district is a key determinant of the amount of resources that the district will have available. Consequently, children living in lower-income neighborhoods tend to be enrolled in schools with far fewer resources and, as a result, a lower quality of instruction and materials than children living in well-to-do neighborhoods.

In their book *The American Dream and the Public Schools*, Jennifer Hochschild and Nathan Scovronick note,

> *School district boundaries help to provide such an advantage when they follow neighborhood lines that separate wealthy children from those who are poor and often nonwhite; school financing schemes have this effect when they are based on local property value and thereby create or maintain a privileged competitive position for wealthier children at the expense of the others. Tracking provides advantages when the best teachers or the most resources are devoted to a high track disproportionately filled with wealthier students. (2003, 12–13)*

Research also indicates that since the mid-1970s, schools have actually become more segregated on the basis of race and income. As Erica Frankenberg and colleagues note, "Segregation for black students is rising in all parts of the U.S. Black students, who account for 15% of enrollment, as they did in 1970, are in schools that average 47% black students" (2019, 4). Furthermore, Latino students are even more segregated. The authors find that "the segregation of Latino students is now the most severe of any group and typically involves a very high concentration of poverty" (9).

Schools that are predominately minority are also highly skewed in the direction of poverty and low income (Frankenberg et al. 2019). Rather than reducing the differences and disadvantages that some children face, the structure of schooling in the United States further increases and exacerbates those differences. As Hochschild and Scovronick state,

> *Public schools are essential to make the American dream work, but schools are also the arena in which many Americans first fail. Failure there almost certainly guarantees failure from then on. In the dream, failure results from lack of individual merit and effort; in reality, failure in school too closely tracks structures of racial and class inequality. Schools too often reinforce rather than contend against the intergenerational paradox at the heart of the American dream. (2003, 5)*

The intergenerational paradox that the authors refer to is that "Inequalities in family wealth are a major cause of inequality in schooling, and inequalities of schooling do much to reinforce inequalities of wealth among families in the next generation—that is the intergenerational paradox" (23). Indeed, research has shown that the amount of education and wealth of parents is highly correlated with the educational levels achieved by their children (Ermisch, Jantti, and Smeeding 2012; DiPrete 2020) and that schools serve as sorting machines that reinforce and accentuate inequalities (Domina, Penner, and Penner 2017).

In my interviews in the *Chasing the American Dream* book, I observed this process repeatedly. Those who had done very well professionally had often graduated from a rather small range of outstanding secondary schools and universities that their parents had the financial resources to send them to. They in turn were able to pass on such educational advantages to their children.

On the other hand, the experiences of Darlene Taylor stand in sharp contrast. Darlene, 54 years old at the time of our interview, shared her recollections of attending an inner-city school and growing up in a neighborhood that was becoming increasingly impoverished.

> *There was this emergence of increasing violence in our community. I witnessed and experienced this violence in the community and the home. It was a very turbulent time for me and my siblings and the environment that we were being exposed to.*
>
> *I would see and be exposed to acts of school violence. One of my good friends got shot in the face probably in the 7th almost going to 8th grade. This guy was really a nice kid. You know, he wouldn't bother anybody.*
>
> *I went to Southeast [a high school] from '71 to '75. I graduated from there, but many acts of violence in the community. I was getting older, so I was starting to recognize things and seeing things on the news. We had several stabbings and shootings. We had police in our school. That was the days before the metal detectors. Then I think at some point, it's a little foggy, but I think we did end up having metal detectors before I graduated from high school, which felt weird and confining and strange. Southeast was in one of the most violent neighborhoods later in the history of the city, and became one of the most crime ridden neighborhoods that you would have. (Rank, Hirschl, and Foster 2014, 118)*

In recalling some of her classes in school, Darlene remarked,

> *There were classes on this ground level, and the guys would pass the weapons or whatever outside to somebody sitting near the windows, you know, if the teacher had stepped out or whatever. I remember, I think a couple times, there were victims laying on the ground. And they would cover them up. So it was like, "What is happening in our world and in our community?" (Rank, Hirschl, and Foster 2014, 118)*

In summarizing the research on education, neighborhood, and income, Greg Duncan and Richard Marnane state, "As the incomes of affluent and poor American families have diverged over the past three decades, so too has the educational performance of the children in these families. Test score differences between rich and poor children are much larger now than thirty years ago, as are differences in rates of college attendance and college graduation" (2011, 15). Unfortunately, it appears that we may be moving even further afield of a level playing surface.

Employment and Jobs

A final consequence of living in a poverty-stricken community is the scarcity of decent-paying jobs that can support a family. Many researchers have pointed out the applicability of spatial mismatch to describe this situation

(Andersson et al. 2018). This refers to the condition that there is a mismatch between the number of people needing good-paying jobs and the actual number of such jobs. These communities are nearly always defined as being economically depressed areas. Whether found in Appalachia, inner cities across the Rust Belt, the Mississippi Delta, or American Indian reservations, these are communities marked by a lack of decent-paying jobs.

Many of these areas have been hard hit by the deindustrialization that has been occurring across all of America. This deindustrialization has devastated a number of communities and has particularly hit hard nonwhites. As Arne Kalleberg notes,

> *The expansion of bad jobs has made things worse for minority group members (such as blacks and Hispanics) in particular, who tend to be concentrated in these jobs. Jobs that pay very low wages and not valued very highly by employers, customers, or employees. When jobs require few skills and workers can be easily substituted and replaced, employers have few incentives to train workers and to develop compensation strategies designed to retain them, a pattern that leads to high turnover. Low wages also leave many Americans at or below the poverty line, even in periods of high employment. (2011, 181–182)*

Concluding Thoughts

As we saw in the previous chapter, poverty exerts a detrimental impact upon the health of individuals and their families. The same is true for the neighborhoods and communities that are left in the wake of poverty. Such communities are often plagued by higher levels of environmental toxins, deteriorating infrastructure, lack of social and human services, elevated rates of crime, struggling school systems, and a shortage of good-paying jobs. These conditions affect all who are residing in such communities, poor and nonpoor alike.

Consequently, just as poverty undermines the quality of life for individuals, so too does it undermine the health and well-being of communities. Poverty-stricken neighborhoods place additional burdens upon individuals who are already struggling to make ends meet.

But they also place a burden upon the wider geographical area in which they are located. Regions marked by high levels of inequality across wider geographic areas are characterized as having less trust, social cohesion, racial harmony, and community participation. They also tend to score lower on a range of quality of life and happiness indicators (Wilkinson and Pickett 2010). In this way, they undermine the well-being of entire regions. As the Roman poet Horace wrote 2,000 years ago, "Your own property is at stake when your neighbor's house is on fire."

ONLINE ACTIVITIES

confrontingpoverty.org

One of the most striking aspects of where Americans live is the degree of racial residential segregation found across the country. Although the levels of segregation have declined over the past 50 years, they nevertheless remain quite high. Throughout the United States, there is a strong tendency for neighborhoods to be relatively homogeneous with respect to their racial and ethnic composition.

In order to examine these patterns in greater detail, we will explore a highly innovative website developed by the *Washington Post*. On the *Confronting Poverty* website, go to Fact 2 on the "Facts and Myths" page, and click on the *Washington Post* link on the sidebar.

You can begin by reading the introductory comments on the homepage. The *Post* uses Census data from 1990, 2000, 2010, and 2016 to construct its interactive mapping program of racial residential segregation.

As you scroll down, you will see a link stating "Jump to explore your city." Click on this (you can also just read all the way down to the bottom and this will appear as well). I would suggest that we start by looking at a major metropolitan area that is highly segregated by race. Choose to enter either Detroit, Chicago, Milwaukee, or St. Louis. All of these cities are highly segregated.

Once you enter one of these cities, you will see the screen color coded where different racial groups are residing. In these four cities, the two major groups in terms of residence are whites and blacks. Whites are coded in red and blacks are coded in blue. First zoom out until you can see the entire metropolitan area. You will notice that in each of these cities, we can graphically observe the degree of racial segregation through this color coding. Each of these cities is marked by areas that are almost entirely red or blue, showing dramatically the level of residential segregation.

The left side menu box allows us to see how these patterns have changed over time. First choose the year 1990. Then click on 2000, 2010, and 2016 to observe how the map changes. Although there are some differences, the color coding largely remains the same.

Next, you can zero into much smaller areas in these cities by clicking the zoom button on the upper right-hand portion of the screen. This allows you to look in more detail at particular neighborhoods within these metropolitan regions.

Finally, try entering your current location to see how segregated your own community compares. Type in your city or address to begin exploring the patterns of residence by race in your locale. Repeat the steps that you took earlier. To what extent are these patterns of residence similar to what you were looking at earlier?

The dynamic of racial residential segregation is one that hits minorities particularly hard. Metropolitan residents in central city neighborhoods find it much more difficult to access better paying jobs in the surrounding suburban neighborhoods. The result is often high levels of unemployment in these areas, a noticeable lack of public and social services, and high rates of poverty.

CHAPTER 9 The Nation

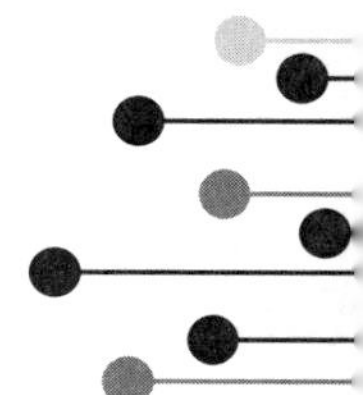

Clearly the cost of poverty for those impoverished is high. As we discussed in Chapter 7, substantial research has documented that poverty exacts a heavy toll from those who fall within its grasp. To take but one example, poverty has been shown to exert a powerful influence upon an individual's physical and mental health. Those living in poverty tend to have significantly worse health as measured by a variety of indicators when compared to the nonpoor.

As we have seen, the effect of poverty upon children is particularly destructive. Poverty serves to stunt children's physical and mental development. Poor infants and young children in the United States are far more likely to have lower levels of physical and mental growth (as measured in a variety of ways) than their nonpoor counterparts. As children grow older, and if they continue to reside in poverty, the disadvantages of growing up poor multiply. These disadvantages include attendance at inferior schools, environmental hazards associated with poverty-stricken neighborhoods, unmet health needs, and a host of other hardships.

Furthermore, as discussed in Chapter 8, poverty takes a heavy toll upon communities. Neighborhoods mired in poverty are much more likely to be plagued by a wide variety of problems. These include higher rates of crime, fewer services, greater toxins and pollutants, lower quality schools, fewer job opportunities, and so on.

What are perhaps less obvious are the costs of poverty to the nation as a whole. To a large extent, we have failed to recognize that poverty places enormous economic, social, and psychological costs on the nonpoor as well as the poor. These costs affect us both individually and as a nation, although we have been slow to recognize them. Too often the attitude has been, "I don't see how I'm affected, so why worry about it?"

Yet the issues that many Americans are in fact deeply concerned about, such as crime, access and affordability of health care, race relations, or economic productivity, to name but a few, are directly affected and exacerbated by the condition of poverty. As a result, the general public winds up paying a heavy price for allowing poverty to walk in our midst. A report by the Children's Defense Fund on the costs of childhood poverty makes this strikingly clear.

> *The children who suffer poverty's effects are not its only victims. When children do not succeed as adults, all of society pays the price: businesses are able to find fewer good workers, consumers pay more for their goods, hospitals and health insurers spend more treating preventable illnesses, teachers spend more time on remediation and special education, private citizens feel less safe on the streets, governors hire more prison guards,*

> *mayors must pay to shelter homeless families, judges must hear more criminal, domestic, and other cases, taxpayers pay for problems that could have been prevented, fire and medical workers must respond to emergencies that never should have happened, and funeral directors must bury children who never should have died.* (Sherman 1994, 99)

This sense of a broad awareness of the costs of poverty can be referred to as enlightened self-interest. In other words, by becoming aware of the various costs associated with poverty, or conversely, the various benefits associated with the reduction of poverty, we begin to realize that it is in our own self-interest to combat the condition of poverty.

Alexis de Tocqueville referred to this in his 1840 treatise on America as self-interest properly understood. In fact, the full title of the chapter from his *Democracy in America* book is "How the Americans Combat Individualism by the Doctrine of Self-Interest Properly Understood." His basic premise was that "one sees that by serving his fellows, man serves himself and that doing good is to his private advantage."

This awareness is often accomplished through education since such connections are frequently not self-evident. The case of poverty is a good example. For most Americans, poverty is seen as an individualized condition that impacts exclusively upon that person, their family, and perhaps their neighborhood. Rarely do we conceptualize a stranger's poverty as having a direct or indirect effect upon our own well-being. By becoming aware of such impacts through informed knowledge, we begin to understand that reducing poverty is very much in our enlightened self-interest.

The Economic Cost of Childhood Poverty

One question then is what might be the economic cost of poverty to the nation? An analysis by Michael McLaughlin and Mark Rank (2018) sought to estimate this through calculating the annual cost of childhood poverty in the United States. In order to do so, the authors relied on the latest government data and social science research in order to calculate the societal impact that childhood poverty exerted upon the country as a whole. In particular, they examined the direct effect that childhood poverty has upon lowering future economic productivity, higher health care and criminal justice costs, and increased expenses as a result of child homelessness and maltreatment.

In Table 9.1 we can see the annual estimated costs of childhood poverty for seven broad areas. Childhood poverty results in an annual loss of 294 billion dollars due to lowered economic productivity through reduced earnings. In addition, increased health costs amount to 192 billion, whereas costs associated with increased crime and incarceration (increased victimization costs of street crime; increased corrections and crime deterrence; increased social costs of incarceration) total 406 billion dollars.

As we can see, child poverty represents an enormous economic burden to the United States. This is largely because living in poverty stunts the

Table 9.1 The Costs of Childhood Poverty

Type of Cost	Dollar Amount (in Billions)
Reduced earnings	294.0
Increased victimization costs of street crime	200.6
Increased health costs	192.1
Increased corrections and crime deterrence costs	122.5
Increased child homelessness costs	96.9
Increased social costs of incarceration	83.2
Increased child maltreatment costs	40.5
Total cost of child poverty	1,029.8

Source: McLaughlin and Rank (2018).

growth and undermines the potential of children. As Martin Ravallion notes, "Children growing up in poorer families tend to suffer greater human development gaps, with lasting consequences for their adult lives" (2016, 595). Impoverished children grow up with fewer skills and are less able to contribute to the economy. They are more likely to engage in crime and experience more frequent health-care problems. These costs are ultimately borne not only by the children themselves but also by the wider society as well.

By summing together these costs, the overall estimate is that in 2015, childhood poverty in the United States was costing the nation $1.03 trillion dollars a year. This number represented 5.4 percent of the U.S. annual GDP.

Perhaps a better way of gauging the magnitude of the costs of childhood poverty is to compare it with the total amount of federal spending in 2015. The federal government spent a total of $3.7 trillion dollars in 2015. This included the entire range of programs and agencies supported by the government, including defense spending, Social Security, infrastructure, and so on. The annual cost of childhood poverty—$1.03 trillion—therefore represented 28 percent of the entire budget spent by the federal government in 2015.

Consequently, to argue that we pay a large economic price for having the highest rates of poverty in the industrialized world is actually an understatement. Childhood poverty represents an enormous drain on both the U.S. economy and society as a whole. It results in sizeable losses in economic productivity, higher health care and criminal justice costs, and significant costs associated with remedial efforts to address the fallout of childhood poverty.

One question that naturally arises in a study such as this is what would it cost to reduce poverty in the United States? Moreover, might it be more cost-effective to simply accept the high levels of U.S. childhood poverty rather than pay the price of reducing poverty?

With these questions in mind, two analyses have indicated that the cost of reducing childhood poverty is a fraction of what such poverty is costing us. The Children's Defense Fund (2015), in conjunction with the Urban Institute, has estimated that childhood poverty could be reduced by 60 percent at a cost of 77 billion dollars. This would be accomplished through expanding an array of programs that have been shown to be effective in reducing poverty such as the Earned Income Tax Credit, a higher minimum wage, childcare subsidies, and so on. Similarly, Luke Shaefer and colleagues (2018) have estimated that by transforming the Child Tax Credit into a Universal Child Allowance, childhood poverty could be reduced by 40–50 percent, with extreme poverty eradicated, at a cost of approximately 70 billion dollars.

Taking these studies into account, if we assume that childhood poverty could be roughly cut in half through an annual expenditure of 70 billion dollars, that 70 billion dollars would save us approximately half of the 1.03 trillion dollars that we project poverty costs us, or 515 billion dollars. The bottom line is that according to these studies, the ratio of savings to cost is slightly more than 7 to 1. For every dollar spent in poverty reduction, we would save over 7 dollars in terms of the economic fallout from poverty.

However, there is a second way of estimating the difference between the price of ending poverty and what it is costing us. It is through a measure known as the poverty gap or the poverty income deficit. This measures what it would cost to lift all poor households with children under the age of 18 years to the level of the poverty line. In other words, how much total income is needed to pull every American child out of poverty? According to the U.S. Census Bureau (2016), that figure for 2015 was 86.9 billion dollars. For 86.9 billion dollars, every American household with children under 18 years of age in poverty could be raised out of poverty.

We can then compare this figure to our overall estimate of the costs of childhood poverty, which is 1.03 trillion dollars. Combining these two figures results in a ratio of savings to cost of approximately 12 to 1. Consequently, when using the Census measurement of the costs associated with eliminating poverty, the result is an even higher rate of savings than when using the two earlier mentioned studies.

The bottom line is that reducing poverty is clearly justified from a cost–benefit perspective. Investing in programs that reduce childhood poverty is both a smart and effective economic policy.

It should be noted that there were many additional costs that were clearly not accounted for in the McLaughlin and Rank analysis. For example, poverty has been shown to be strongly related to teenage childbearing. In turn, research suggests that the economic cost of teenagers bearing children is high. By reducing childhood poverty, which would lower teenage childbearing, we would bring down these economic and societal costs. Consequently, the estimates should be seen as a lower bound with respect to the costs of childhood poverty.

In addition, there are significant costs associated with poverty during adulthood that were not at all taken into account. The analysis focused only on the costs of childhood poverty. However, as we have seen in Chapter 2, poverty also strikes individuals at various points throughout their lives. In fact, as noted earlier, poverty will reach a majority of Americans at some point during their adulthood. As such, the overall figure of $1.03 trillion dollars a year is undoubtedly a significant underestimate of the true costs of American poverty.

Furthermore, it is important to point out that this analysis has calculated an overall annual cost to the United States. Rather than a one-time cost, the economic cost of childhood poverty is approximately 1 trillion dollars per year. This clearly constitutes a significant ongoing drag upon the overall U.S. economy.

Finally, it is pertinent to note that since the early 1980s, the overall rate of poverty for children has ranged between 16 and 23 percent. It has thus remained stubbornly high during this period of time. In fact, as we saw in Chapter 3, children are currently the age group at the highest risk of poverty, and that risk is particularly extreme for younger aged children. If these trends and patterns continue, the cost of childhood poverty in the future will likely remain large indeed.

Equality Versus Efficiency?

There is, however, an argument often made with respect to not fully addressing poverty and inequality on a national level. It is based on the assumption that there is a necessary trade-off between having a strong economy and a robust social welfare state. The recent origins of this argument can be traced back to an influential book entitled *Equality and Efficiency: The Big Tradeoff* by the economist Arthur Okun.

Okun makes the case that the social policy goals of equality and efficiency are generally in opposition to each other. As he states,

> *But in this essay I… discuss a… nagging and pervasive tradeoff, that between equality and efficiency. It is, in my view, our biggest socioeconomic tradeoff, and it plagues us in dozens of dimensions of social policy. We can't have our cake of market efficiency and share it equally. (1975, 2)*

For example, according to this argument a society that strives to create a more egalitarian society through a strong welfare state and redistributive policies tends to reduce economic efficiency because the incentives for entrepreneurship and economic productivity are reduced—higher taxes and more regulation result in a less efficient and productive economy. On the other hand, a society that seeks to increase its economic efficiency through the lowering of taxes and regulations results in greater levels of inequality and poverty because more laissez faire capitalism tends to produce bigger winners and losers if left on its own. As Okun states, "We can't have our cake of market efficiency and share it equally."

Based on this, the argument is often made that in order for the United States to have a strong economy, it must have a very limited social welfare state. Yet is this argument true? It turns out that the past 20 years have put this idea to rest. Some of the most robust economies during this time period have also had very comprehensive social safety nets. The countries of Norway, Germany, Sweden, and the Netherlands quickly come to mind as examples of countries that have been able to achieve both economic efficiency and greater social equality.

Investing in human resources through a social welfare state turns out to be smart economic policy. As Monica Prasad explains,

> *There are aspects of the welfare state that can benefit economic growth. Health care and education are the most obvious examples: well-educated citizens are more capable of making innovations that lead to productivity gains, and healthy workers lose fewer workdays to illness. More recently, researchers have shown that other kinds of programs, such as food stamps and unemployment insurance, have positive economic effects. The welfare state contributes to productivity and economic growth by avoiding the underutilization of the human capital of the poor. A welfare state can also benefit the economy by providing Keynesian stimulus during slumps. The welfare state, Walter Korpi argues, is not a leaky bucket, taking away from productivity, but an irrigation system, ensuring that the economy continues to grow by nurturing the ground from which productivity blooms. (2018, 219)*

Furthermore, recent research has indicated that high levels of inequality may actually dampen economic growth (Cynamon and Fazzari 2015). One reason for this is that by underinvesting in a segment of the population, the economy loses some of its potential human capital, as argued above. On the other hand, social policies that invest in educational, health, and skill development are rewarded with a more dynamic and innovative workforce. This, in turn, helps to create greater economic growth and productivity for the society as a whole. Consequently, one can make a further argument for why the societal cost of poverty is high—it potentially serves as an overall drag on economic productivity.

The Cost to American Principles

A second way to consider the impact of poverty upon the nation is to weigh its negative effect upon the principles that it upholds. As argued in my *One Nation, Underprivileged* and *Chasing the American Dream* books, America has been defined by a set of core values and principles. These have included the guaranteeing of various freedoms and rights to all, an emphasis upon the importance of equality of opportunity, and the belief that America represents a fair and just society. The existence of widespread poverty seriously undermines each of these values.

Guaranteed Rights

With respect to the guaranteeing of various rights to everyone, the federal and state governments along with our judicial systems have traditionally been viewed as the guardians and protectors of specific freedoms that are the entitlements of all citizens. The Bill of Rights, for example, specifies what some of these are, such as freedom of speech, freedom to peaceably assemble, and so on. Liberty is often interpreted as the freedom to engage in such activities and behaviors. And yet if poverty reduces an individual's ability to fully partake in those rights, liberty has been curtailed, even though they are still guaranteed under the law.

Take the judicial right that citizens are assumed innocent until proven guilty. A strong argument can be made that the ability to fully benefit from this right is directly affected by the amount of financial resources one is able to bring to bear upon the legal system. Derek Bok uses the right to an attorney to illustrate how economic reality infringes upon this guaranteed right:

> *Surely there is no other nation where the nature of individual freedom has been elaborated in such detail, or any other society that is so well organized to ensure that essential liberties are defended and preserved. At the same time, freedom in the United States may be more limited by other forces than it is abroad. For example, the government in America often makes less effort than others to make sure that all or most Americans have the means to exercise important rights they formally possess. To choose but one example, it is impressive to grant everyone accused of a serious crime the right to qualified counsel, but the right may not be worth much in practice if the lawyers assigned turn out to have so little time that they can scarcely do more than hastily agree to exchange a guilty plea for a slightly reduced sentence. Yet this is the situation that exists in many jurisdictions of this country.* (1996, 311)

Many other rights can also be seen in this light as well. For example, take the basic right to vote. Although all citizens have the right to vote, in reality, economics plays a key role in influencing overall voter participation rates. The fact that the United States conducts its elections on Tuesdays rather than on weekends or a holiday, combined with our cumbersome registration procedures, tends to create barriers for the poor. Leonard Beeghley writes,

> *In sum, while any individual can presumably go to the polls, the structure of voting means that middle-class and rich people dominate this form of participation. The poor and working class are least capable of voting on a working day, getting registered, coping with voting procedures, and overcoming the problem posed by separate and frequent elections. These facts exist externally to individuals, decisively influencing rates of participation. Thus, for those at the lower end of the stratification hierarchy, the pluralist system may seem open but it is closed in fact.* (2000, 143)

These examples illustrate the more general point I am making regarding liberty and the sense of rights guaranteed under the law. Although in principle such rights apply to all, in reality, economics, and particularly poverty, infringes upon the full realization of those rights.

Equality of Opportunity

A second fundamental American value has been the importance of equality of opportunity. There is the strong belief in equality with respect to access of opportunities. For example, every citizen has the right to an education and a means to a livelihood. No one should be denied these on the basis of their race, gender, class, religion, or other extraneous factors.

Furthermore, equality of opportunity conveys the notion that individuals should be judged and rewarded on the basis of their abilities. Robert Haveman notes in his book *Starting Even* that "it has to do with having the same chance to run the race for economic success as others with similar talents and drives. Equality of opportunity exists if a black youth and a white youth have the same access to education, training, jobs, earnings, and incomes, according to their abilities" (1988, 30).

It turns out that poverty dramatically infringes upon this concept of equal access to opportunity. For example, education has long been viewed in the United States as an important means for achieving opportunities such as economic success. Public education began in the nineteenth century as a way of ensuring that all children would have an entry to this important tool.

Yet in order to effectively compete for economic opportunities, the quality and quantity of education are critical. On both counts, poverty stunts the educational process. Public education is largely funded through local real estate taxes. Those who grow up in poor households are likely to be living in lower-income areas. These communities, in turn, are limited in the amount of financial resources that they can acquire and devote to their school system (as a result of a small tax base). Consequently, the ability of a poor school district to purchase state-of-the-art educational resources (e.g., computers, lab equipment, library materials, etc.), and to attract highly qualified teachers (by paying competitive salaries) is fundamentally compromised. This, in turn, results in a reduction in the quality of education that each pupil receives. One has only to compare the physical facilities of any inner-city public school with that of an affluent public suburban school or private school to visually observe the process I am describing. Furthermore, the ability to go on to college, let alone a prestigious college, is severely constrained by poverty. Low-income 18-year-olds often do not have the resources, time, expectations, or educational preparation (as a result of the above mechanisms) to pursue such a goal.

These realities illustrate that while all children have access to education, the type of education they wind up with is strongly influenced by their family's socioeconomic standing. This, in turn, constrains their ability to compete for future opportunities in the marketplace. Seen in this light, equal access to opportunities becomes less fact than fiction (Putnam 2015).

The manner in which poverty restricts access to opportunities can be witnessed in other areas as well. Take the case of health. In order to effectively compete in the labor market, one must have reasonably good health. Yet as we saw in Chapter 7, poverty has a disproportionally negative impact on health status. Adults who are poor are more likely to have higher rates of heart disease, cancer, diabetes, and virtually every other major illness and cause of death. Children in poverty are also more likely to suffer from various health aliments such as lead poisoning, asthma, injury from accidents, and violence. In addition, these illnesses are less likely to be attended to through the health-care system, further exacerbating the conditions. As a result, health deteriorates, again leading to reduced opportunities.

In short, the American ideal of equal access to opportunities is undermined by the existence of poverty. As illustrated in the examples above, the poor simply do not have the same chances to compete for the same opportunities as others in our society do. This is particularly troubling in that America has prided itself on being the land of the American Dream, where individuals can freely travel from "rags-to-riches" upon a ladder of opportunity.

Justice

A third core American ideal and value is the principle of fairness or justice. Americans like to think of their country as a place where people are able to get out of life what they have put into life. This implies that individuals receive in life what they deserve—those who do well deserve it, and those who fail to do well also deserve it. From this perspective then, those in poverty are largely deserving of their economic fate.

In contrast to this, the argument made here is that the vast majority of the poor are not deserving of their fate. A relatively straightforward way to see this is if we simply examine the demographic composition of the poverty population. We can see in Table 9.2 that 30.8 percent of those in poverty in 2019 were children under the age of 18 years. I would challenge anyone to make the argument that a five-year-old child deserves to live in poverty as a result of their prior actions. That argument simply cannot be made.

An additional 14.3 percent of the poor are age 65 years or over, a category that many people feel is deserving of assistance. A further 9.6 percent of the poor are between the ages of 18 and 64 years and suffer from some type of disability. Again, this is a category that most of us would say deserves some help. Therefore, simply looking at the demographics, we see that over half (54.7 percent) of the poverty-stricken population fall into categories that many people would agree are not deserving of impoverishment.

For the remainder of the poor, as I have argued in Chapter 6, research has shown that much of their poverty is the result of failings at the economic and political levels, such as the lack of enough decent-paying jobs to support a family. Elise Gould (2015) found that for those between the ages of 18 and

Table 9.2 Composition of the Poverty Population	
Demographic Characteristic	**Percent (%)**
Children (under 18 years)	30.8
Elderly (65 years and over)	14.3
Disability (age 18–64 years)	9.6
18–64 years (no disability)	45.2
Total	100.0

Source: U.S. Census Bureau (2019).

64 years and who were eligible for work (i.e., not in school, retired, or disabled), 63 percent were employed. However, because of the nature of low-wage jobs, they were not able to work themselves out of poverty. And for those out of work, research has shown that they have worked in the past and will continue to work in the future.

Ethnographic research has also shown that with respect to work attitudes and motivation, those in poverty exhibit similar behaviors and attitudes as the overall population (Duina 2018). Consequently, the basic conclusion is that for the vast majority of the poor, impoverishment cannot be justified in terms of prior negative actions.

However, what makes poverty particularly grievous is the stark contrast between the wealth, abundance, and resources of America on the one hand, and its levels of destitution on the other. Something is seriously wrong when we find that in a country with the most abundant resources in the world, there are children without enough to eat, families who cannot afford health care, and people who are sleeping on the streets for lack of shelter.

This was precisely the contrast that President Johnson was referring to in his inaugural address of 1965, when he spoke about the meaning of America,

> *Conceived in justice, written in liberty, bound in union, it was meant one day to inspire the hopes of all mankind; and it binds us still. If we keep its terms, we shall flourish. First, justice was the promise that all who made the journey would share in the fruits of the land. In a land of great wealth, families must not live in hopeless poverty. In a land rich in harvest, children just must not go hungry. In a land of healing miracles, neighbors must not suffer and die unattended. In a great land of learning and scholars, young people must be taught to read and write. (Johnson 1965)*

It should also be noted that the gap between extreme prosperity and economic vulnerability has never been wider (Atkinson 2015; Stiglitz 2012). The venerable economist Paul Samuelson, writing in the first edition of his introductory economics textbook in 1948, observed that if we were to make an income pyramid out of a child's play blocks, with each layer representing $1,000 of income, the peak would be somewhat higher than the Eiffel Tower, but almost all of us would be within a yard or so of the ground. By the time of Samuelson's 2001 edition of the textbook, most of us would still be within a yard or two of the ground, but the Eiffel Tower would now have to be replaced with Mount Everest to represent those at the top.

Or take what has happened with respect to the distance between the average worker's salary and the average CEO's salary. In 1980, the average CEO of a major corporation earned 42 times that of the average worker's pay. Today it is close to 300 times (Mishel and Wolfe 2019). Adding insult to injury, during the past 40 years, an increasing number of companies have demanded concessions from their workers, including pay cuts and the elimination of health benefits in order to keep their labor costs down, while those at the top have prospered beyond any sense of decency.

Patterns of wealth accumulation have become even more skewed. Today in America, we find that the top 1 percent of the U.S. population currently own 46 percent of the entire financial wealth in the country, while the bottom 60 percent of Americans are in possession of less than 1 percent of the country's financial wealth (Wolff 2017). And while all of these trends have been happening, our social policies have continued to give more to the well-to-do and less to the economically vulnerable, with the argument that these policies have been helping all Americans.

A new way of thinking recognizes this as a moral outrage. Injustice, rather than blame, becomes the moral compass on which to view poverty amidst abundance. This type of injustice constitutes a strong impetus for change. It signals that a wrong is being committed that cries out for a remedy. A shift in thinking recognizes this and is premised upon the idea that social change is essential in addressing the injustices of poverty.

Concluding Thoughts

The bottom line is that the price of poverty to the country is exceedingly high. By allowing poverty to persist at such levels, we wind up spending considerably more in many areas than if poverty were substantially reduced. Impoverishment breeds serious health problems, inadequately educated children, and higher rates of criminal activity. As a result, we pay more for health care, we produce less productive workers, and we divert needed resources into the building and maintaining of correctional facilities. In each of these cases, we are spending our money on the back end of the problem of poverty rather than on the front end, which is almost always a more expensive approach to take.

The old saying "An ounce of prevention is worth a pound of cure" is certainly apropos. As has been demonstrated, it is not a question of paying or not paying. Rather, it is a question of how we want to pay, which then affects the amount we end up spending. I assume that most of us would prefer to spend our money in a smart and efficient way. That is precisely what I am advocating for in targeting poverty as a priority issue. By making an investment up front to alleviate poverty, the evidence suggests that we will be repaid many times over in the lower costs associated with a host of social problems.

Yet it is also true that we will not recoup these lower costs overnight. It will take time in order for these savings to become apparent. And therein lies part of the problem. Too often we base our policy decisions upon the short-term rather than the long-term gains. Congressional and presidential terms of two or four years tend to drive the policy process. Nevertheless, it is the long-term savings that can produce the greatest benefits over time.

Poverty also extracts a high cost with respect to our values and principles. The existence of widespread poverty calls into question the legitimacy of our adherence to everyone being entitled to certain rights, opportunities, and a sense of fairness. This undermines the very essence of what America stands for.

Finally, I believe that there is an important psychological benefit to investing our resources in ways that avoid or substantially reduce social problems in the first place, rather than spending our resources upon the negative fallout from such problems. Such a benefit is difficult to measure financially, but ask yourself what kind of community you would prefer to live in—one in which we spend our money on building prisons, or one in which we invest in people and their neighborhoods so that they do not eventually wind up in prisons? I believe that most people intrinsically feel better about communities that are characterized by the latter rather than the former. In short, reducing poverty is in our psychological self-interest, as well as in our economic and social self-interest.

ONLINE ACTIVITIES

confrontingpoverty.org

In this chapter, we have examined the costs of poverty upon the nation as a whole. We have seen that such costs are substantial. But there is another area where we might also consider the national costs, and that is with respect to the extent and severity of economic inequality.

Economic inequality refers to how wide or narrow the distributions of income and wealth are within a country. As we saw in our online activity for Chapter 2, the United States tends to be on the high end of inequality compared to other OECD countries.

Why might this concern us? One researcher who has been interested in answering this question is the British social epidemiologist Richard Wilkinson. Over the past few decades, Wilkinson has been at the forefront of examining the question "Does inequality matter?" To hear Wilkinson's answer to this question, go the *Confronting Poverty* website, and click on the Discussion Guide. Next, click on Module 8, and click on the TED talk on the sidebar.

In responding to the question of does inequality matter, Wilkinson's answer is a resounding yes. In his talk, he provides data to show that countries with a wider degree of economic inequality tend to have many more problems than countries with a narrower distribution.

After you have finished watching the TED talk, consider what might be some of the implications of these findings. Given that rising levels of inequality appear to be associated with a range of social problems, what can be done to reverse this trend? Consider the types of policies that might be put in place to address and alleviate the high levels of U.S. inequality. Do you think that such policies are politically feasible? Why or why not?

PART

IV

Addressing and Alleviating Poverty

Having examined the scope, reasons, and consequences of poverty, we are now in a position to explore our final question—How best to address and alleviate poverty? Effective strategies for reducing poverty must be based upon a clear understanding of who is at risk, why poverty exists, and the effects and consequences of poverty.

In Chapter 6, we discussed the structural vulnerability perspective as an important way to understand poverty. We can summarize that approach as follows. First, although a majority of Americans will experience poverty at some point in their lives, those who have less human capital (education, skills, etc.) are more prone to encountering poverty. This poverty is often triggered by events related to job loss, family change, or medical problems. Those lacking in human capital are less protected from the economic damage of these events. Second, the amount of human capital that individuals have acquired is largely the result of differences in social class and cumulative inequality. Those coming from a lower income and/or nonwhite background will tend to have acquired less valuable human capital. Third, while the lack of human capital helps to identify who loses out at the economic game, the fact that there are losers in the first place has to do with failings at a structural level resulting in a lack of opportunities for all who need them.

Based on this understanding, we can now detail several strategies and policies that will effectively reduce the amount and severity of poverty. We begin by looking at strengthening the social safety net. As we have seen, individuals tend to fall into poverty sporadically, often as the result of detrimental events occurring. A strong and effective safety net can serve to mitigate the extent of such a fall, while allowing individuals time to get back on their feet.

Next we will focus on increasing access to key public resources and services that enable people to thrive during their lives. These include a good education, access to health care, affordable housing, and quality childcare. These are the building blocks that allow individuals to live a livable life. We will also examine policies designed to support single-parent families specifically, including child support enforcement.

Our last two chapters are designed to provide more overall opportunities or chairs in the musical chairs analogy. We discuss ways in which to create more jobs that provide a livable wage. In addition, we will explore the idea of a universal basic income as an alternative source of economic means. Finally, we will look at the role of organizing in creating changes at the grassroots, community, and national level which can then lead to policy changes at the political level.

CHAPTER

10 Strengthening the Social Safety Net

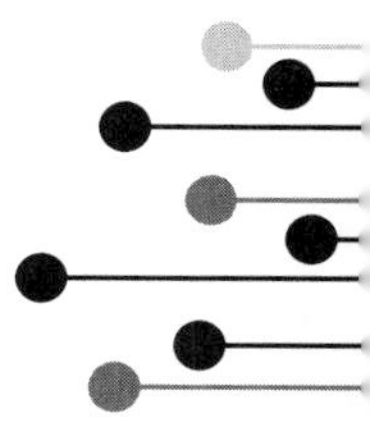

We begin our exploration of ways to reduce and mitigate poverty with the importance of a strong and effective social safety net. No matter how robust economic growth may be, some individuals and families will invariably fall between the cracks. Whether through the loss of a job, a sudden disability, or some other unanticipated event, there are times and situations in people's lives when a social safety net is needed. Indeed, we saw in Chapter 2 that three-quarters of the U.S. population would experience at least one year in poverty or near poverty. In the industrialized countries, the safety net has taken the form of various programs and policies encompassed under the social welfare state, while in the less industrialized countries the role of the social safety net has more typically been fulfilled by the extended family.

Hyman Minsky (1986) pointed out that free-market economies are prone to periods of instability, such as periodic recessions and economic downturns. Safety net programs help to serve as automatic stabilizers for the economy during these periods. That is, they grow during times of need and diminish during more prosperous times. For example, as rates of unemployment rise, more individuals draw on unemployment insurance to weather the temporary economic problems caused by the lack of jobs. As economic conditions improve, more people are able to find jobs and so no longer need unemployment insurance. In this fashion, safety net programs help to automatically stabilize the instability inherent within the economy.

A social safety net is therefore important in assisting individuals and families during times of need and in alleviating the economic instability associated with recessionary periods. One of the reasons that the U.S. rate of poverty is so high, and the Scandinavian nations' rates are so low, is a result of differences in the extent and depth of their social safety nets. Compared to other Western industrialized countries, the United States devotes far fewer resources to programs aimed at assisting the economically vulnerable (Alesina and Glaeser 2004; Brady, Blome, and Kleider 2016). In fact, the United States allocates a smaller proportion of its GDP to social welfare programs than virtually any other industrialized country (Lee and Koo 2016). As Charles Noble writes, "The U.S. welfare state is striking precisely because it is so limited in scope and ambition" (1997, 3).

In addition, the U.S. social safety net might be thought of as a crazy quilt stitched rather haphazardly over the decades. Specific programs are administered and funded by different federal and state departments, benefits in the same program can vary widely by states, and eligibility criteria differ across programs (Gilbert 2017; Kenworthy 2014).

In contrast, most European countries provide a wide range of universal social and insurance programs that largely prevent families from falling into poverty (Kenworthy 2019). These include substantial family or children's allowances, which are designed to transfer cash assistance to families with children. Unemployment assistance is far more generous in these countries than in the United States, often providing support for more than a year following the loss of a job. Furthermore, health coverage is routinely provided, along with considerable support for childcare.

The result of these social policy differences is that they substantially reduce the extent of poverty in Europe and Canada, while U.S. social policy exerts only a small impact upon poverty reduction. As Rebecca Blank (1997) notes, "The national choice in the United States to provide relatively less generous transfers to low-income families has meant higher relative poverty rates in the country. While low-income families in the United States work more than in many other countries, they are not able to make up for lower governmental income support relative to their European counterparts" (pp. 141–42).

Consequently, a key reason behind why the United States has such high levels of poverty is a result of the nature and scope of its social safety net. The Scandinavian countries are able to lift a significant percentage of their economically vulnerable above the threshold of poverty through governmental transfer and assistance policies. In contrast, the United States provides substantially less support through its social safety net, resulting in poverty rates that are currently among the highest in the industrialized world. As Lane Kenworthy argues,

> *The United States has done less well by its poor than a number of other affluent nations. The reason is straightforward. Like their counterparts abroad, America's least well-off have been hit hard by shifts in the economy since the 1970s, but whereas some countries have ensured that government supports rise as the economy grows, the U.S. hasn't. (2019, 121)*

Modifying and Strengthening the Safety Net

A social safety net is therefore important in assisting individuals and families during times of need, as well as buttressing the economic instability associated with recessionary periods. Safety net programs in the United States are considered those in which an individual must be below a certain income and asset level to qualify. In addition, particular programs are sometimes aimed at specific population groups. For example, the Supplemental Security Income (SSI) program is designed to provide cash assistance to those with a physical or mental disability. Other programs, such as the Supplemental Nutrition Assistance Program (SNAP), have a much broader reach.

The U.S. social safety net has become noticeably weaker over the past 40 years. Cash welfare programs have lost much of their purchasing power during the past three decades (Shaefer et al. 2020). The 1996 welfare reform changes transformed the entitlement status of AFDC into the nonentitlement Temporary Assistance to Needy Families (TANF) program. Other programs have lost considerable ground in terms of their coverage of the population. These include housing assistance, nutritional programs, and unemployment insurance. The one exception has been an increase in low-income children qualifying for either Medicaid or the CHIP program, as well as the Affordable Care Act. Overall though, the already weak U.S. safety net has gotten considerably weaker over the past 40 years.

One of the reasons for this can be found in the tension between providing help to the needy on one hand, and not wanting to create disincentives to work or marriage on the other hand. The idea goes back hundreds of years. If a safety net is too generous, the fear is that it will undermine the work ethic within the population, particularly for those at the lower end of the income distribution—why seek employment in a low-paying and difficult job if decent benefits are available from the social welfare state? Likewise, if benefits are made available to all, the necessity of marriage is viewed as weakened, as are the disincentives to out-of-wedlock childbearing.

A substantial body of research has examined the extent to which current U.S. welfare programs create work or family disincentives. The vast majority of these studies indicate little effect of welfare programs upon behavior. As economist Robert Moffitt summarizes,

> *A traditional issue with examining how safety net programs affect low-income families is whether those programs discourage work and hence increase the proportion of families with very low or zero earnings, and whether those programs encourage the formation of single-parent families.... The existing evidence show that neither work disincentives nor family structure incentives are large in magnitude, especially in the aggregate.* (2015, 744–45)

Nevertheless, the recent emphasis in U.S. policy toward its social safety net has focused heavily on the concept of not creating work or marriage disincentives. This has become more pronounced in recent years as a result of the reduced attractiveness of work over the past four decades. Wages have stagnated, jobs are providing fewer benefits, and so on. Therefore, in order to ensure that welfare is not a viable alternative, a safety net that was weak in the first place has been made even weaker. Public assistance benefits have been allowed to erode over recent years, time limits have been imposed on receiving welfare, work requirements have been made more stringent, financial disincentives have been put in place to discourage childbearing while on welfare, and so on. The major thrust of recent American policy has emphasized work and marriage incentives, while largely ignoring the equally important issue of providing adequate assistance to the needy.

The approach taken here is quite different. Rather than making the social safety net less attractive, the strategies discussed in the next chapters focus on making work considerably more attractive, particularly at the bottom end of the income distribution. We will discuss the importance of ensuring that workers are paid a decent, livable wage. We will also review policies to increase the accessibility of quality education, health care, affordable housing, and childcare, all of which contribute to the ability and attractiveness of working within the economy. Also discussed is the concept of building assets through one's own contributions along with a government match, which again furthers the appeal and rewards of work.

Given this, an effective safety net that provides adequate protection against economic hardships is called for. By making work a more attractive option, the danger of creating work disincentives through the strengthening of the safety net is substantially reduced. Rather, those who must turn to a social safety net program under our new set of policies would be provided with adequate protection. They would include individuals who have temporarily lost a job, men or women suffering from a physical or mental disability, or older individuals who have depleted their resources. In these cases, a viable safety net is essential.

Two approaches could be taken toward achieving this goal. The first would be to strengthen the current array of programs that are directed to those in economic need. The major programs include unemployment insurance, workman's compensation, SSI, TANF, SNAP (or better known as food stamps), and the Medicaid program. Each of these programs could be evaluated to determine whether the amount of resources and eligibility requirements are adequate to meet the current needs.

In fact, simply achieving greater participation levels in the current array of safety net programs would reduce the overall rate of poverty. For example, Sheila Zedlewski and colleagues (2002) estimated that for those under age 65 years, full participation in the Food Stamp, SSI, EITC, and TANF programs could lift 3.8 million people out of poverty. In addition, full participation would reduce the rate of extreme poverty (those below 50 percent of the poverty line) by 70 percent. As in the case with Medicaid and CHIP, simplifying and streamlining the enrollment process, along with increased outreach and educational efforts, have the potential to substantially raise safety net participation levels.

A second approach would be to consolidate the vast number of U.S. social safety net programs into an overall program that would be directed to the needy. Eligibility would be guided by a series of criteria depending on the individual's circumstances. These would include the existence of conditions such as ill health or disability, unemployment, and so on. If individuals were to qualify, they would then be given a stipend to cover their basic needs. Periodic updates would allow for any needed changes in eligibility status.

There is an underlying recognition here that there will always be individuals who fall through the cracks. A wise society makes sure that the need is genuine, but a decent society also makes sure that they are provided with enough resources to humanely exist. Putting in place an effective yet compassionate social safety net ensures that such values are supported.

Asset-Building Policies

Social safety net policies are designed to alleviate the current conditions of poverty. This is understandable given that poverty impacts upon children and adults in the here and now. Yet approaches to poverty alleviation must also pay attention to longer run processes and solutions. In particular, the accumulation of assets is crucial. The acquisition of such assets allows individuals to more effectively function, and for our purposes, to reduce their risk of poverty. These assets enable individuals to ride out periods of economic vulnerability. In addition, assets can build a stake in the future that income by itself often cannot provide. Unfortunately, the opportunities to acquire such assets have been in short supply for lower-income individuals.

In addition, the asset policies discussed here are guided by a question of justice. A number of policies are in place that encourage asset accumulation for the middle and upper class. It is only fair that comparable policies are developed for those with less resources. As Thomas Shapiro and Edward Wolff observe, "Current public policy offers substantial, highly regressive subsidies for wealth and property accumulation for relatively well-off individuals. In contrast, poverty policy has ignored asset building for resource-poor families" (2001, 6). The policies suggested here are an attempt to redress this imbalance. We might think of such asset-building policies as part of a long-term safety net.

There have been periods in our history when social policy was explicitly designed to foster asset accumulation for a large number of Americans, including those at the lower end of the income distribution (although racial groups such as African Americans and American Indians have often been excluded). For example, the Homestead Act of 1862 allowed pioneers to lay their stake on 160 acres of land. As long as they remained and worked the land for five years, they became its owners. This policy enabled many families to build their future and their children's future. During the 75-year duration of the Homestead program, 1.5 million households were given title to 246 million acres of land (Williams 2000). In addition, the homestead itself represented a very tangible asset that could then be handed down to the next generation. By the time of the fourth generation, it is estimated that approximately 46 million Americans were descendants and beneficiaries of those who had homesteaded (Williams 2000). The Homestead Act constituted a major asset-based policy in U.S. history that improved the lives of millions and played an important role in the economic development of the United States.

Another large-scale asset-based policy was the GI Bill. Initiated in 1944, the original GI Bill provided 500 dollars per year for college tuition and 50 dollars a month for living expenses to veterans of World War II. This policy had a profound impact on opening the doors of higher education to those who were without such help. At its peak in 1947, 49 percent of all students enrolled in higher education were supported by the GI Bill. Nearly 8 million

World War II veterans received educational benefits provided by the bill. In addition, approximately 10 million veterans of World War II and the Korean War were able to use the GI loan program to purchase homes or start businesses (Mettler 2005). Once again, not only did this policy help millions of Americans, but it also was a sound investment in the country as a whole (Mettler 2002, 2005).

Although not as dramatic as the above examples, policies continue to exist that encourage the development of assets. These policies are primarily delivered through the tax code (known as tax expenditures). For example, the ability to deduct the interest paid on a home mortgage when filing one's income tax returns has enabled millions of Americans to lower their costs of owning a home. Partially as a result of this, the home has come to represent the major asset held by most Americans (U.S. Census Bureau 2019e). Clearly, governmental policy has encouraged the accumulation and growth of home ownership. Other examples of asset-building policies through the tax code include the lower tax rate on capital gains, the deduction allowed for contributions to individual retirement accounts (IRAs), and the exclusion of employer contributions to pension funds. However, each of these types of asset policies primarily benefits the middle and upper classes. It is estimated that 75 percent of such tax expenditures go to families in the top 40 percent of the income distribution, while 24 percent go the top 1 percent (Center on Budget and Priorities 2019a).

In contrast, there is a significant percentage of the population lacking in assets, particularly financial assets such as savings or stocks. For example, in earlier work I have shown that a majority of Americans will experience at least one year in which they are considered asset poor, and that the risk has been rising in more recent times (Rank, Hirschl, and Foster 2014). Indicative of this is the fact that 37 percent of Americans report that they do not have enough savings to cover a $400 emergency (Federal Reserve Bank 2020). The familiar expression of living paycheck to paycheck unfortunately applies to many, if not most, Americans.

As many scholars have demonstrated, the accumulation of assets is largely dependent upon having an income surplus, along with the belief and faith that one's income will remain relatively stable from one month to the next (Edin 2005). Given the nature of poverty and lower-income jobs, both of these requirements are often in short supply.

What then can be done to build the financial assets of those who have been left out? One idea is expanding programs that enable Americans to build up their personal savings, so they can provide rainy-day protection. Many states around the country have been experimenting with such policies. They allow individuals to put aside a percentage of their monthly income with a generous match from the state, in much the same way that employers contribute to employees' 401(k) accounts. These funds can then be used to address future concerns and expenses. Ramping up such a policy on a federal level could provide an important reservoir for families in need.

The rising tide of children's development accounts (CDAs) is another asset-building policy. These accounts are designed to build the savings of children such that they can be used for educational or other expenses when they turn 18 years of age. They are generally started with an initial deposit by the government when the child is born, and then later deposits by parents are frequently matched by state governments. These programs are found in a majority of U.S. states as well as in a number of other countries.

Another means of developing assets and broadening the base of wealth is through employee ownership plans. These include Employee Stock Ownership Plans, 401(k) plans, and broad-based stock option plans. Data from the General Social Survey indicate that as of 2014, 19.5 percent of all employees working in the private sector reported owning stock or stock options in their companies (National Center for Employee Ownership 2019). Employee ownership plans represent yet another potential means for individuals to build their assets, while at the same time raising the productivity of workers. An example of a country that has invested heavily in the concept of asset building has been that of Singapore, with its Central Provident Fund (CPF). Introduced in 1955, the CPF is a mandatory pension fund in which its members are able to use their savings for housing, medical expenses, and education.

Concluding Thoughts

Building a strong and effective social safety net is a first line of defense against poverty (Marx, Nolan, and Olivera 2015). As we have seen in earlier chapters, many Americans will at some point experience periods of economic turmoil and poverty. Having a robust safety net in place can provide immediate protection against these economic downturns.

In addition, policies that enable individuals to build their economic assets provide households with an emergency reservoir to tap into during times of economic hardship. Such a reservoir can provide an important source of financial assistance to help weather periods of rainy days.

The ability to protect households from experiencing poverty should be one of the prime objectives of government policy. As we saw throughout the prior section, poverty extracts a high price upon individuals, families, communities, and the nation as a whole. Alleviating such effects through a strong safety net needs to be supported and strengthened.

ONLINE ACTIVITIES

confrontingpoverty.org

Our online activity for this chapter consists of getting the chance to read the thoughts of a handful of key poverty scholars brought together in one piece. Begin by going to the *Confronting Poverty* website. Next, click on the research page, and then click on the *Rugged Individualism* book link. There you will find on the sidebar, Chapter 4, which you can now open.

This chapter contains the thoughts of a number of important poverty scholars. Separate interviews were conducted with each researcher, and then parts of those interviews were put together to form this chapter. It gives you the opportunity to hear in a relatively few pages from a range of scholars regarding their thoughts on poverty and inequality.

In particular, there is considerable discussion centering on the United States and its lack of a strong safety net. Many explanations exist for why the social welfare state in the United States is minimal. You will read a number of important insights in this chapter around this question. There is also considerable discussion on the topic of inequality. The chapter should provide you with an important supplement to the issues discussed in Chapter 10.

CHAPTER 11 Increasing Access to Key Public Goods and Services

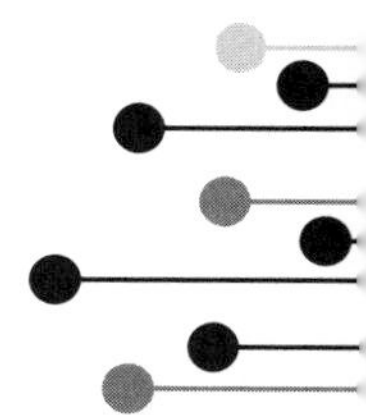

In some respects, the conditions of poverty and near poverty in the United States are worse than the actual dollar amounts would indicate. The reason is that several key social and public goods have become increasingly inaccessible for a number of American households. In particular, a quality education, health care, and affordable housing are either out of reach or are obtained only through considerable economic expenditure and hardship. Yet these social goods are vital in building and maintaining healthy and productive citizens.

Virtually every other Western industrial society provides greater access and coverage to health care and affordable housing than does the United States. They also do not display the wide fluctuations in educational quality that American children are subjected to at the primary and secondary levels. Why? The underlying reason is the belief that there are certain social and public goods that all individuals have a right to, and that making such resources accessible results in more productive citizens and societies in both the short and long run. In addition, there is the recognition that they reduce the harshness of poverty and inequality.

Each of these areas is complex and wide in their scope. Countless books and articles have been written on these subjects, as well as ongoing legislative debates. I touch upon only several key points and ideas on these topics, leaving it to my readers to further explore the specifics and nuances.

Quality Education

The ability to receive a quality education is one of the most vital assets that an individual can acquire. Indeed, a key motivation behind the introduction of public education in the mid-1800s was the importance of making education accessible to the general public, rather than to only the wealthy and privileged. Horace Mann, the well-known nineteenth-century educator, spoke of public education as the "great equalizer" and as a place where both disadvantaged and advantaged children would be taught under one roof. The expansion and access to public education has had a profound impact upon the well-being of Americans and American society. It has contributed to an effective and productive workforce, a more informed citizenry, and countless other benefits.

Public education remains the avenue through which most Americans acquire their educational training. The vast majority of today's students attend public schools. In 2019, 90 percent of all primary and secondary students were enrolled in public schools, while 74 percent of students going on to college attended public institutions (National Center for Education Statistics 2020). As a result, public education remains the dominant vehicle for the vast majority of American students.

Unfortunately, as a result of the way that public education is funded at the primary and secondary levels, the quality of that education varies widely depending on the wealth of the community that one resides in. A report by the U.S. Department of Education and Equity and Excellence Commission begins with the following statement: "While some young Americans—most of them white and affluent—are getting a truly world-class education, those who attend school in high poverty neighborhoods are getting an education that more closely approximates schools in developing countries" (2013, 12).

The bulk of U.S. school funding for elementary, middle, and high schools comes from the local tax base, primarily property taxes. Well-to-do school districts with a richly endowed property tax base will generally have ample funding to operate quality public schools. This involves paying teachers competitive salaries, keeping student/teacher ratios relatively low, purchasing the necessary educational resources such as books for libraries or computer equipment for instruction, and so on.

On the other hand, residing in a poor community with a diminished tax base often results in schools that are financially strapped. Teachers are frequently underpaid and overstressed, the physical facilities may be severely deteriorated and outdated, and class sizes are often quite large, along with a host of other disadvantages. These children, who are predominately low-income and frequently of color, wind up being denied a quality education as a result. Linda Darling-Hammond and Laura Post write,

> *Few Americans realize that the U.S. educational system is one of the most unequal in the industrialized world, and students routinely receive dramatically different learning opportunities based on their social status. In contrast to most European and Asian nations that fund schools centrally and equally, the wealthiest 10 percent of school districts in the United States spend nearly ten times more than the poorest 10 percent, and spending ratios of three to one are common within states. Poor and minority students are concentrated in the less well funded schools, most of them located in central cities and funded at levels substantially below those of neighboring suburban districts. (2000, 127)*

As a result, many of these children receive an inferior education, which, in turn, will dramatically reduce their ability to effectively compete in the labor market.

To deny children the fundamental right to a decent education is both morally wrong and bad social policy. It flies in the face of the American concept of equality of opportunity. Countless studies have documented the immediate and lingering effects of high-quality versus inferior-quality education upon later life outcomes. Improving public education for low-income children is absolutely essential.

Several steps are warranted. First, it is clear that although money in and of itself is not the complete answer, it nevertheless represents a large part of the solution. This is particularly the case for school districts unable to provide the necessary educational tools for its students (qualified teachers, educational materials, etc.). Evening out the vast financial differences currently found across school districts, and then spending the additional money wisely by hiring qualified teachers and building strong curricula can make a significant difference. As Craig Jerald, a senior policy analyst at the Education Trust put it, "The picture has become crystal clear. If you do both of those things you can really solve the problems" (*New York Times*, August 9, 2002).

Emphasis should be placed upon the federal and state governments to even out the gaping disparities in school financing. Several states have begun to move in this direction, but many more need to follow their lead. As noted above, differences in spending per pupil can vary by thousands of dollars, with wealthy students who are blessed by a myriad of social and economic advantages enjoying the most in terms of public per-pupil spending, while students from poor backgrounds and possessing the fewest advantages wind up receiving the least in terms of public tax dollars.

Beyond ensuring that all students have sufficient funding for their educations, spending these funds wisely is critical for improving the quality of education for lower-income children. A number of steps should be taken that have been shown to be effective. These include spending money on the classroom (smaller class sizes, teacher development, educational materials) rather than on bureaucracy; hiring well-qualified teachers and principals trained in the subjects they are teaching; developing a challenging curriculum with high expectations; involving parents in the education of their children; and establishing an orderly learning environment (U.S. Department of Education and Equity and Excellence Commission 2013).

Finally, for low-income students to get the most out of their educational experience, there needs to be economic integration within the classroom. That is, schools in which the vast majority of children are in poverty have been shown to have a detrimental effect upon learning (Duncan and Murnane 2011). Poverty puts an enormous strain upon the lives of children, which spills over into their educational environment. This detriment is magnified in schools where most of one's fellow students are also in poverty, and frequently of color. Unfortunately, such schools have been increasing in frequency over the past decades. Research has demonstrated that these students are much more likely to succeed educationally when they are in economically integrated environments, without lowering the performance of middle- or upper-income children (Kahlenberg 2002).

Although economic integration in the classroom can be extremely difficult to achieve given the long-established patterns of residential segregation by race and class, nevertheless it is critical. One approach is to allow parents the ability to choose among a variety of public schools, and then to honor those preferences in a way that would also contribute to economic integration within the particular schools (Willie and Alves 1996). This idea of socioeconomic integration has been gaining ground in a number of communities across the country (see Century Foundation Task Force on the Common School 2002, for examples).

Taken together, the above steps will move us in the direction of improving the educational experience that low-income children are now receiving. Having access to this important resource is essential in competing effectively in the labor market. Although it is vital that there are decent-paying jobs available in the job market, it is also important that individuals have the necessary education and training to compete and succeed at those jobs. It is blatantly wrong that some American children, simply by virtue of their parents' economic standing, must settle for a substandard educational experience, while others receive a well-rounded education. All are American children, and all are entitled to a quality education.

Health Care

As with education, access to quality health care is often dependent upon the size of one's wallet. For those who can afford it, America offers some of the finest medical care in the world. Yet for those unable to absorb the increasing costs, they are frequently left out in the cold without health care. As a result, too many Americans are finding themselves either lacking in health insurance, with insufficient coverage, or with adequate coverage but only at a considerable expense. As Ronald Angel writes, "The United States is unique among developed nations in not providing a basic package of health care to all of its citizens" (2016, 671).

A major reason that the United States has failed to provide universal access to health insurance is that health-care coverage has not been understood as a basic human right. In virtually every other industrialized country, having access to health care is viewed as a basic right. With the exception of the elderly, the United States has not accepted this premise.

In 2019, 26.1 million Americans or 8.0 percent of the population lacked health insurance throughout the year. For those below the poverty line, 15.9 percent had no health coverage in spite of the Medicaid program (U.S. Census Bureau 2020c). Furthermore, if we look across a several year period, we find that many more Americans are without health care at some point (Sohn 2017). And for too many Americans with health insurance, the deductibles may be high and the coverage itself sorely lacking.

The passage of the Affordable Care Act (ACA), and it being signed into law by President Obama in 2010, has had a strong effect on reducing the number of Americans without health coverage. The law's major provisions went into full effect in 2014, and since then the number of uninsured has been cut approximately in half. More Americans are able to access the health system through the ACA than ever before. Nevertheless, the United States still does not offer the kind of universal health-care coverage found in virtually all the other industrialized countries.

One of the reasons that Americans are lacking in health-care coverage, particularly those in or near poverty, is that their place of work does not provide health coverage. Since World War II, the United States has tied health insurance to one's job. Up until the 1970s, this worked reasonably well, but as we discussed earlier, an increasing number of low-wage and part-time jobs have been created during the past 40 years, with many of these jobs lacking in health benefits. Furthermore, for those under age 65 years but out of work, health coverage is unlikely except through the Medicaid program.

Access to health care is important in a variety of ways. Being able to address one's health needs is crucial in maintaining a productive life, both at work and at home. What then can be done to increase the health-care access for those who find themselves left out?

The issue of reforming health care is enormously complex, as was demonstrated in the documentation of the 2010 Affordable Care Act, which ran over 1,000 pages. The legislation reflected the power of various interest groups (e.g., the insurance industry, the American Medical Association, etc.) to shape the particular health-care changes. However, what is now needed is to build a system around the fundamental principle of universal coverage. As noted earlier, the United States is far and away the exception among the industrialized countries in not offering universal coverage for its citizens. The question is not do we have the funds to spend on health care? In fact, we spend more than any country on a per capita basis or as a percentage of GDP (Anderson, Hussey, and Petrosyan 2019). Rather, the question is how best to spend these resources in order to ensure that all Americans will have access to health care, while at the same time maintaining the overall quality of the system?

Universal coverage is essential in reforming the current health-care system. There are at least two ideas for how we might get to such a system. The first is to expand the Medicare program into a "Medicare for All" program. In 1965, President Johnson signed into law the Medicare and Medicaid programs. Medicare was designed to provide health-care coverage for all who were over the age of 65 years. Older Americans were felt to be a vulnerable and deserving population of universal health care.

The idea of converting and expanding the Medicare program has been gaining traction during the past few years, particularly among those in the progressive wing of the Democratic party, such as Senator Bernie Sanders and Representative Alexandria Ocasio-Cortez. The advantage of this approach is that we already have a program in place which is effective in delivering health care to seniors. Expanding this program to include all Americans would be building on the success of the current program, with much of the administration of the program already in place.

The other approach favored by more moderate Democrats has been to expand the ACA to cover more citizens. The argument here is that the ACA has made a good start in covering more Americans and can be refined and fine-tuned to do an even better job. Its supporters argue that it has been hampered during the past 10 years by conservatives working to weaken the program, which has reduced its effectiveness.

Having access to health care is absolutely vital to the well-being of individuals and families (Price, Khubchandani, and Webb 2018). In thinking about the importance of health care, along with education and decent-paying jobs, the late Senator Paul Wellstone noted in a campaign address shortly before his untimely death,

> *If you want real welfare reform, focus on a good education, good health care and a good job. If you want to reduce poverty, you focus on a good education, good health care and a good job. If you want a stable middle class, you focus on a good education, good health care and a good job. If you want to have citizens who can participate in democracy, you focus on a good education, good health care and a good job. And if you want to end the violence, you could build a million new prisons and you could fill them all up, but you will never end this cycle of violence unless you invest in the health and the skill and the intellect and the character of our children—you focus on a good education, good health care and a good job!* (Rank 2004, 213)

In other words, these resources not only allow individuals to reduce their risk of economic vulnerability but also allow them to be productive citizens. Accessibility of health care is essential to this task.

Affordable Housing

Affordable housing represents a third key public good that has become harder to come by in recent years, particularly for low-income households (Desmond 2018). The general rule of thumb is that households should spend no more than 30 percent of their income on housing (which is the standard definition of affordable housing). Yet the Joint Center for Housing Studies at Harvard University (2017) estimates that for low-income renters, slightly over 70 percent were severely burdened by their rental costs, while an additional 10 percent were moderately burdened.

One of the reasons for this has been that the cost of housing over the past 40 years has risen much more steeply than that of worker's wages. For example, the National Low Income Housing Coalition (2019) estimates that in order to afford the fair market rent for an average two-bedroom apartment (that is, paying 30 percent of one's income for rent), a worker needs to be earning $22.96 an hour. Yet as we have seen earlier, many heads of households are earning well below this. Wages have stagnated over the past 50 years and the economy has been producing more jobs at the lower end of the wage scale. For example, the median wage of a janitor or cleaner in 2019 was $12.73 per hour, which is clearly insufficient to afford the rent on a two-bedroom apartment or to purchase a median-priced home in any major metropolitan area (National Low Housing Coalition 2019).

Furthermore, particular areas in the United States are even more severe in their shortage of affordable housing than the above national average. In the state of Massachusetts, one needs to be earning $33.81 an hour to be able to rent an adequate two-bedroom housing unit, while in the city of San Francisco, $60.96 an hour is needed (Glasmeir 2020). As the Millennial Housing Commission noted,

> *...there is simply not enough affordable housing. The inadequacy of supply increases dramatically as one moves down the ladder of family earnings. The challenge is most acute for rental housing in high cost areas, and the most egregious problem is for the very poor.* (2002, iv)

In addition to the proliferation of low-wage work, the private sector's failure to build an adequate stock of lower-end housing units, coupled with the federal government's decreasing expenditures on programs designed to address the housing needs of low-income families, have made affordable housing even scarcer over the past 30 years. The result is that more Americans, particularly those in the bottom quintile of the income distribution, are finding themselves without access to decent quality affordable housing. Given these patterns, it is no wonder that homelessness has become such a visible issue in the past four decades.

The lack of affordable housing affects individuals in several ways. First, households that are already strapped for cash have much less to spend on food, clothing, health care, transportation, and other necessities because they are spending a significant amount of their income on housing. Second, not having decent, affordable, and stable housing has been shown to have a dramatic effect on increasing the levels of stress within families. Third, a household's lack of stable housing negatively impacts upon children's development, in particular their academic performance and overall health. Finally, affordable and decent-quality housing is critical in maintaining the vitality and sustainability of a neighborhood.

Given this, what can be done to strengthen the access that low-income Americans have to decent-quality affordable housing? Peter Kemp (2016) notes in his review of housing programs that there are two basic approaches to providing greater access. The first is through the building of lower-cost housing, while the second is through providing housing vouchers, which make it easier for lower-income families to acquire housing.

As indicated above, there is a clear need to increase and strengthen the country's stock of affordable and modestly priced housing. Both new construction as well as renovation of existing housing stock need to be undertaken. Tax incentives should be strengthened to encourage the private market to build and renovate existing housing stock (such as the Low Income Housing Tax Credit of 1986), and where private construction is not feasible, the federal and state governments need to become more directly involved in housing construction.

One source for stimulating and funding such efforts has been the establishment of the National Housing Trust Fund in 2008. It represents "The first new federal housing resource in a generation, and it is exclusively targeted to help build, preserve, rehabilitate, and operate housing affordable to people with the lowest incomes" (National Low Income Housing Coalition 2020, 1). It is based upon the successful examples of various state, county, and city housing trust funds that are operating throughout the United States. It allows states and communities to preserve and increase their supply of rental housing for low-income households and to increase homeownership for such households.

Consideration should be given to increasing the amount of revenue currently available for the National Housing Trust Fund. One approach would be to cap the home mortgage deduction at a lower level than is currently the case. Individuals are now able to deduct up to one million dollars of interest on their itemized income tax returns. The question to ask ourselves is why should the federal government subsidize the building or buying of million dollar homes? A more equitable approach would be to lower the home mortgage deduction to $500,000. This is still much higher than the median sales value of a new or existing home in the United States (Federal Reserve Bank of St. Louis 2020). If individuals want to buy or build a house for $800,000 or $1,000,000, they certainly can do so, but there is not a compelling reason for why our country should subsidize this activity. Rather, the increased revenue that would be raised through lowering the home mortgage deduction could go into a National Trust Fund that would then be used to assist lower-income renters and homeowners and used toward the construction of affordable housing.

A second venue for increasing the accessibility of affordable housing to lower-income households is through the expansion and more effective use of housing vouchers. Currently there are approximately 2.2 million households using Section 8 housing vouchers in the country (Center on Budget and Policy Priorities 2019b). The program is designed to allow families with low income to rent private housing on the open market from those landlords who will accept the vouchers and whose rental units qualify for the program. Individuals pay no more than 30 percent of their income toward their rent, with the government making up the difference. The program has generally been considered a success in opening up the housing market to lower-income families. It allows individuals some flexibility and movement in terms of their housing decisions. Unfortunately, it has become increasingly difficult for families to find landlords who are willing to accept the vouchers. Policies should be put in place to encourage and increase landlord participation, as well as modifying the program to expand and strengthen it.

A third avenue for reducing the economic burden of housing costs is to provide some form of a refundable housing tax credit that would be directed to low-income households (Kimberlin, Tach, and Wimer 2018). As noted earlier, current tax policy allows home owners to deduct the interest paid on their mortgages. This has helped millions of Americans by reducing the overall costs of owning a home. Yet in order to qualify for the deduction, households must itemize their income tax returns. The problem is that many low-income families do not itemize and therefore cannot take advantage of the deduction. Furthermore, the deduction is nonrefundable. That is, it can only be used to reduce the overall amount of taxes that are owed. Consequently, if your taxes are fairly low to begin with (as is the case for low-income earners), this deduction does not provide any economic relief.

What is needed is a refundable credit targeted to low-income home owners and renters. An example is Wisconsin's Homestead Credit, which was designed to ease the impact that rent and property taxes have upon low-income households (Wisconsin Department of Revenue 2020). The benefit can be taken either as an income tax credit or as a direct refund. The amount received depends upon the income level of a household (for 2019 tax filers, households had to be below $24,680 in order to qualify) and the amount they have paid in rent or property tax during the year. Larger credits and refunds go to those who have earned less but have paid more in housing costs. In this fashion, assistance is provided to both renters and home owners at the lower levels of the income distribution.

Finally, one cannot discuss the issue of housing and its accessibility without discussing the issue of race. Racial minorities (particularly African Americans) have historically been discriminated against in the housing market. Research has indicated that black and Hispanic renters are more likely to be excluded from housing made available to white renters, black and Hispanic home buyers learn about fewer available homes than white home buyers, and blacks and Hispanics are more likely to be turned down for a home loan than their white counterparts (Feagin 2010; Shapiro 2004, 2017). In each case these effects are present after taking into account any group differences in demographic or socioeconomic attributes. The result of such housing market discrimination is higher rent burdens, poorer quality housing, and increased residential segregation for African Americans and Hispanics.

In order to address racial and ethnic discrimination in the housing market, there is a need for strong enforcement of antidiscrimination legislation such as the Fair Housing Act of 1968 and the Fair Housing Amendments Act of 1988, as well as enforcement of fair lending legislation such as the Equal Credit Opportunity Act of 1974 and the Community Reinvestment Act of 1977 (Jargowsky, Din, and Fletcher 2019). It is also critical to provide those agencies charged with enforcing antidiscriminatory practices the resources to fully do so (such as the Department of Housing and Urban Development and the Justice Department). Without sufficient resources, antidiscriminatory laws are often rendered impotent.

Concluding Thoughts

In thinking about the three key public goods and services discussed in this chapter, they represent the foundation for enabling individuals to lead what I have referred to in other work as a "livable life." Such a life is one in which "an individual is able to thrive and develop in a healthy manner across their lifetime to reach their full potential" (Rank 2020c, 10). Having access to quality education, health care, and housing are the building blocks to enable such a life.

As mentioned at the start of this chapter, in some respects the poor in the United States are worse off than their counterparts in the other OECD countries. In nearly all of these countries, individuals and families are able to fully access these key resources, whereas in the United States having access is largely determined by one's income. Such policies are shortsighted in that investing in individual well-being results in a more productive and innovative workforce. It also creates a more healthy and cohesive society.

One of the reasons why the United States has failed to provide quality education, health care, and housing to all of its citizens is because these resources are often viewed as more of a privilege than a right. As a result, we leave it up to the individual to do their best in acquiring these goods and services. In contrast, many of the other OECD nations believe that every citizen should be entitled to the benefits of good education, health care, and housing. They are viewed as a cornerstone to a fulfilling and livable life, and as such, should be made available to all.

ONLINE ACTIVITIES

confrontingpoverty.org

In this chapter, we have been exploring the importance of three key social and public resources: education, health care, and housing. In order to further appreciate the significance of these resources for those living in or near poverty, our online activity involves watching a documentary entitled, "Waging a Living."

To access the documentary, go to the *Confronting Poverty* website and click on the "Discussion Guide." Then click on "Module 7" and on the sidebar, click the "Waging a Living" link. The documentary focuses on the lives of four individuals who are employed but struggling to keep their heads above water. It provides great insight into the lives of people who are struggling paycheck to paycheck. Another interesting aspect of the documentary is that for each individual, the filmmaker follows up with them after approximately six months to see how they are doing.

The film vividly illustrates the impact of not having access to the three resources discussed in this chapter. Although the specifics vary from individual to individual, there is an overall theme of the difficulty surviving in the absence of these key assets. As we have discussed throughout this chapter, the United States is an outlier in terms of not having universal health-care coverage. It is also an outlier in not providing access to affordable childcare or housing.

After you have watched the documentary, consider the types of policies that would have made life more sustainable for these four persons. Imagine the situations of these individuals if the United States provided universal health-care coverage, quality education to every citizen, affordable housing, and quality childcare (examined in the next chapter). Having access to these fundamental resources lays a strong foundation for allowing individuals and families to build a livable life. For each family in the film, they would undoubtedly vastly improve their overall quality of life.

CHAPTER

12 Supporting All Families

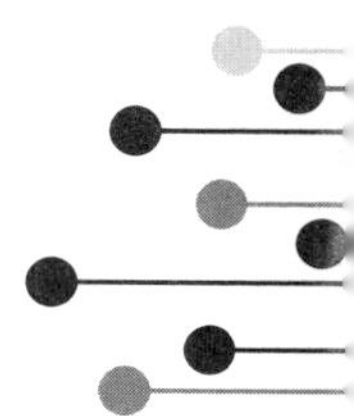

A third strategy for reducing American poverty is to address the much higher risk that single-parent families have of falling into poverty (Cancian and Meyer 2018). An underlying value behind this (as well as the earlier strategies) is that the economic well-being of children should be a top priority. No child should suffer from poverty, regardless of the type of family that a child has grown up in. Therefore, putting in place policies to increase the number of decent-paying jobs helps all household heads support their children—whether married or not. Likewise, increasing the access to fundamental resources such as health care and housing helps all children and their families. But beyond these sets of policies, we can also consider strategies that provide greater support to families with young children and specifically to single-parent families (National Academies of Sciences, Engineering, and Medicine 2019).

It is important to recognize that what constitutes "the family" has changed dramatically over the past 70 years (Cherlin 2020). There is much more variation today in the types of families in which children reside, and social policy must recognize and confront these realities. As we saw earlier in Chapter 3, single-parent families with children are at a much greater risk of poverty than married couple families. Yet it does not have to be this way. We can implement policies that will have the effect of reducing poverty for these families.

Child Support Policies

American families have experienced substantial change over the past several decades. One of the most profound of these changes has been the rising incidence of divorce, out-of-marriage births, and single-parent families. In 1970, 12 percent of all children were living in single-parent families, while in 2018 the percentage had increased to 27 percent (Smock and Schwartz 2020).

As a result, child support and its enforcement have become an increasing concern. As more and more children experience the separation and divorce of their parents, and as increasing numbers of children are born to single parents, the issue of noncustodial parent's financial responsibility takes on greater importance. The detrimental economic effects of divorce and single parenthood on women and their children have been extensively documented over the past three decades (Cooper and Pugh 2020; Raley and Sweeney 2020).

This body of work has demonstrated that newly created female-headed households with children are at a significant risk of poverty. For example, a divorced woman's standard of living tends to fall between 23 and 40 percent within a year following divorce (Tach and Eads 2014).

One reason for the sharp decline in the economic well-being of households headed by mothers is that they often fail to receive the court-ordered child support payments that are due to them. For example, in 2015, 43.5 percent of custodial parents (80 percent of whom are mothers) received the full amount of court-ordered child support payments, 25.8 percent received a partial payment, and 30.7 percent received no payment (U.S. Census Bureau 2020d). Of the $33.7 billion due to custodial parents in child support payments in 2015, $20.1 billion were actually received (U.S. Census Bureau 2020d).

Receiving the court-ordered amount of child support can make a significant difference in the economic well-being of single-parent families. For example, "among custodial parents below poverty who were receiving full payments, the mean annual child support received ($5,445) represented over half (58.0 percent) of their mean personal income" (U.S. Census Bureau 2020d, 13).

Since the mid-1970s, a series of changes in federal laws have attempted to make child support enforcement more effective. This was particularly the case with the 1996 welfare reform changes. States are now required to operate a child support program that meets federal mandates (e.g., expanded efforts in income withholding, paternity establishment, enforcement of orders, and use of central registries). Failing to do so disqualifies a state from grant monies under the Temporary Assistance for Needy Families program. Nevertheless, in spite of these changes, the percentage of custodial parents receiving child support has not increased (U.S. Census Bureau 2020d).

From a policy perspective, several approaches might be considered in order to make the system of child support more effective. Irwin Garfinkel (1992) has argued that the current system could be strengthened into a child support assurance program that would provide far greater protection for mothers and their children (Cancian and Meyer 2018). Such a system would contain three key elements. First, noncustodial parents would pay a set percentage of their income for child support. For example, if a noncustodial parent had one child, he or she might pay 15 percent of their income for child support. If there were two children, the noncustodial parent would pay 22 percent of their income for child support, and so on. The amount taken out would be capped at some upper limit (i.e., 33 percent) as would the total amount of income to be taxed (i.e., $100,000). Such an approach would greatly simplify the current situation that we have surrounding the process of court-ordered child support and would treat all noncustodial parents equally. The amount of child support transferred would be dependent upon the number of children that one has and the amount of earned income. All noncustodial parents are therefore treated the same.

Second, the support payments would be automatically withheld from the noncustodial parent's paycheck in the same manner as Social Security payments. Using the above formula, if a nonresident parent were earning 3,000 dollars a month from their job, 450 dollars (or 15 percent of their earnings) would be withheld and transferred each month to the custodial parent. This effectively takes the option of paying or not paying child support out of the hands of the nonresident parent and would dramatically increase the amount of court-ordered child support payments that would find its way to American children. Just as we do not leave the option to workers as to whether they should pay or not pay into the Social Security system, similarly we should not leave it up to the noncustodial parent as to whether or not they should pay their court-ordered child support payments. Transferring these payments directly from the nonresidents' paycheck deals with this problem simply and effectively.

A third component of a revamped child support system would assure that all children are guaranteed a minimum benefit level. Thus, if a noncustodial parent were not making enough income to meet this level, the government would then make up the difference. The exact amount of such a level can be debated, but for purposes of illustration let us assume that for one child this would be 5,000 dollars. In this case, if a noncustodial parent were earning 20,000 dollars a year, and 15 percent of their income was utilized for supporting that child, 3,000 dollars would be transferred during the year for child support. However, this would fall short of the minimum level of 5,000 dollars, and therefore the government would make up the additional 2,000 dollars in order to assure the child's minimum level of 5,000 dollars a year. In this fashion, children in single-parent households would not be allowed to fall below an economic floor in terms of financial support.

It should be noted that the above system would apply to all parents who father or mother a child, regardless of whether they were married or not. The underlying value here is that if you become a parent, you have a financial obligation to your children. Thus, if two unwed individuals have a child, and that child lives with their mother, the father of the child still has a financial obligation to support his son or daughter. A certain income percentage would be removed from the father's paycheck until his children reached the age of 18 years. In addition, the system would be applied equally to men and women. Although the vast majority of women have custody of children, if a father has custody, then it would be the mother who would be paying child support out of her paycheck.

The above system has the potential to significantly reduce poverty among mothers and their children. Various simulations have resulted in a range of poverty reductions resulting from such an approach (Cancian and Meyer 2018). In addition, it enforces and strengthens the parent's economic responsibility for child support, which can produce federal and state savings through reduced welfare payments. Finally, it may ensure more responsibility in terms of early sexual behavior through the knowledge that one will be held financially responsible toward supporting a child for 18 years.

Childcare

Good-quality and affordable childcare represents a second key ingredient for supporting families, and specifically single-parent families. As most new parents quickly realize, finding childcare that contains both of these attributes is a challenge (Collins 2019). It is particularly challenging for lower-income working parents. Some will turn to relatives such as grandparents to help watch younger children, others may use organized day care, while still others will rely upon a family day care operation run out of a neighbor's home. The Census Bureau indicates that for poor households who are making childcare payments, their expenses on average are 30 percent of their income (U.S. Census Bureau 2013). Families that were below the poverty line in 2011 who were paying for childcare had an average weekly expenditure of 93 dollars, while their average weekly pay was $310 (U.S. Census Bureau 2013).

At the same time, much of the childcare offered today in the United States is of mediocre quality. For example, the National Institute of Child Health and Human Development (2006) conducted a national study evaluating the overall quality of childcare in ten sites across the country, which included a wide range of childcare providers. Their conclusion was that "Fewer than 10 percent of arrangements were rated as providing very high quality child care" (2006, 11).

As with the previous topics of education, health care, and housing, reforming childcare represents a huge policy issue that simply cannot be adequately covered here. A number of researchers and policy analysts have put forth directions and initiatives to consider in terms of reforming childcare (Greenberg 2007; Child Care Aware 2019). As the 1990 National Research Council Report suggests, the overall goals of a revamped childcare system should include striving for quality within childcare services and arrangements, improving the accessibility to quality childcare services for families, and enhancing the affordability of childcare services for low- and moderate-income families (Hayes, Palmer, and Zaslow 1990).

Two initial steps can be taken to move toward these goals with respect to lower-income families. First, greater subsidies should be provided to support a family's use of quality childcare programs and arrangements. There are several types of subsidies currently available, but they are primarily delivered through the tax code as deductions and therefore fail to provide much relief to lower-income families. The Child Care and Development Block Grant program exists to help lower-income families with childcare needs, but only 15 percent of eligible children receive such assistance (Chien 2019).

David Blau (2001) suggests a more targeted use of childcare vouchers directed to lower-income families. Similar to our earlier discussion of housing vouchers, childcare vouchers would allow lower-income families to seek out a variety of childcare options and receive immediate assistance with regard to reducing their costs of childcare. In addition, vouchers could be structured in a manner such that they would increase in value depending upon the quality of the childcare used. For example, if a family were to utilize an unaccredited source of childcare, they might receive a subsidy of 40 percent of the average cost of care; if they used a provider that was accredited and of good quality they would receive a 60 percent subsidy, and if they utilized an accredited childcare provider of excellent quality, they would receive an 80 percent subsidy. As Blau notes, this has the advantage of encouraging and rewarding families to seek higher-quality childcare, and it provides an incentive for childcare providers to offer higher-quality care in order to attract consumers.

A second step for increasing lower-income families' access and affordability of quality childcare would be to expand the Head Start and Early Head Start programs. Head Start currently serves only approximately one-third of eligible children (848,000) between the ages of three and five years (Child Trends 2018), while approximately 211,000 infants and toddlers are served by the Early Head Start Program. Although they vary in design across localities, the programs are widely accepted as representing a high-quality experience for children. Head Start focuses on improving the learning skills, health, nutrition, and social competence of children.

Yet many more eligible children could be in the programs but are not. The reason for this is twofold. First, the programs lack the funding to include all such children. This can be directly resolved through increasing the federal funding for both the Head Start and Early Head Start Programs. The second reason is that they operate as part-day programs. Having a child in a program only part of the day often does not mesh well with a working parent's schedule. An important step to increasing Head Start's accessibility would be to integrate it with community childcare programs in order to provide extended day care for children whose parents are employed. Thus, children would receive the benefit of the Head Start Program, and lower-income working parents would be able to meet their childcare needs as well.

Preventing Teenage Pregnancies

Having a child at an early age and out of wedlock significantly increases the risk of poverty for both the mother and her child. Unmarried teen mothers are much more likely to experience poverty and receive public assistance than their counterparts who do not give birth. Having a child at an early age also leads to a much greater risk of dropping out of high school, and having less marketable skills, which in turn will have an impact upon the mother's ability to work her way out of poverty (Zweig and Falkenburger 2017). This can then affect the education and skills that her child acquires, as well as increasing the risk of the child becoming a teen mother and therefore repeating the cycle (Assini-Martin and Green 2015).

The good news is that teen births have come down substantially over the past 30 years. The birth rate per 1,000 women aged 15 to 19 years in 1960 was 89, and by 2018 it was 17. Since 1991, the birthrate for teenagers between the ages of 15 and 19 years has fallen by 72 percent (Child Trends 2019; Martin et al. 2019). Nevertheless, when compared to other industrialized countries, the United States remains at the high end (Sedgh et al. 2015). Consequently, there is still room for improvement in terms of reducing the number of unplanned teenage births.

By further reducing the rate of teenage pregnancy, the extent of poverty will also be reduced (Wu and Mark 2018). Research indicates that three critical components are necessary for such a reduction. First, providing medically accurate education regarding sexuality is essential. Programs that are age appropriate and contain balanced and realistic content regarding delaying sex until older ages, as well as promoting safer sex practices for those who become sexually active, have been shown to reduce the likelihood of teenage pregnancy (Planned Parenthood 2013).

Second, providing access to contraception and family planning services can significantly reduce the rate of teenage pregnancy (Wu and Mark 2018). For example, a comparative study by the Alan Guttmacher Institute indicated that the major reason teen pregnancy and childbearing rates were so much higher in the United States than in Canada and several other European countries was largely because of the differences in contraceptive use. Sexually active teens in the United States were less likely to use contraception, and when they did, they were more likely to utilize less effective methods than their European and Canadian counterparts (Darroch et al. 2001). Having access to both family planning services and effective contraceptive methods has been shown to be critical in preventing teenage pregnancy.

Third, the motivation for teens to avoid pregnancy must be present. This is particularly the case for teenagers who are residing in areas marked by high levels of concentrated poverty and bleak future prospects—in a world of negatives, having a child early might be viewed as a positive. Developing real opportunities for such adolescents is therefore critical in providing a strong motivation to delay childbearing. These opportunities would encompass several of the earlier discussed topics such as creating adequate-paying jobs, having access to quality education, as well as building both individual and community assets. As has been often noted, the best contraceptive is a real future.

Unfortunately, current U.S. policy has largely ignored these fundamental points, resulting in our high rates of teenage pregnancy. In many respects children are exposed to the worst combination of messages. On one hand they are bombarded with daily images from the media that sex is exciting, fun, and spontaneous. On the other hand, they are frequently denied the education and tools to engage in responsible sexual behavior. Rather, they are told to "just say no." The result, of course, is the highest rate of teen pregnancy in the developed world. Public policy needs to be based upon the above three principles in order to reduce our rates of teen pregnancy to those of our European and Canadian neighbors. Doing so will significantly reduce the number of Americans falling into poverty at an early age.

An example of such an approach is the Children's Aid Society—Carrera Adolescent Pregnancy Prevention Program, developed by Michael Carrera. The program combines education regarding sexuality, comprehensive health care that includes reproductive health services and contraception, and strong efforts to develop brighter futures for teens in the program. This includes providing academic assessment, help with homework, tutoring, preparation for standardized exams, and assistance with college entrance applications. The program also helps to improve work prospects through the use of a job club, assistance in finding employment, and career awareness. The program thus combines the above three principles.

A three-year evaluation of the 12 sites located in poor neighborhoods nationwide found that participants had significantly delayed the onset of sex, increased the use of condoms and other effective methods of contraception, and had one-third fewer pregnancies and births than those in the control group (Kirby 2001). As one teenager explained, she had just assumed that she would become a teenage mother as her older sister had done. But after being in the program for three years, her expectations were changed.

> *I wasn't thinking about college when I was young. But I changed when I was about 14. This program changed me. I have a life. I have things to do. I'm going to be a nurse. Will I have babies? No time soon. (Rank 2004, 226)*

The Children's Aid Society—Carrera Adolescent Pregnancy Prevention Program, illustrates that the principles discussed here can effectively reduce the high rates of teenage pregnancy and childbirth in this country, and thereby reduce the risk of poverty for millions of adolescents and young adults.

Concluding Thoughts

One of the significant changes that has occurred over the past 50 years is that more children will find themselves for some period of time living with only one parent. In most cases, this is with the mother. Such families are at an elevated risk of poverty for at least three reasons: (1) mothers generally earn less than fathers; (2) child support may not be forthcoming; and (3) childcare may be expensive and difficult to find.

In order to address these problems, several policy ideas were discussed, including reforming the child support system and making childcare more accessible and affordable. These policies have the potential to improve the economic well-being of mothers and their children.

Single-parent families do not have to be mired in poverty. Other countries provide a robust set of policies designed to protect all children from poverty, regardless of the type of household they may reside in. By doing so, they help ensure that the next generation are allowed to grow up healthy and capable of reaching their full potential.

ONLINE ACTIVITIES

confrontingpoverty.org

For the past 50 years, the Children's Defense Fund has advocated on behalf of America's children. In particular, the organization has focused much of its efforts on raising awareness around the issue of childhood poverty.

As discussed in this chapter, children are at a particularly high risk of poverty in the United States. This is the result of several factors. Many children are living in single-parent homes, and these families are at a much greater risk of poverty. One of the reasons these families are at a greater risk of poverty is due to our national and state policies failing to provide adequate support. As David Brady has argued, the United States has chosen to punish such families rather than to support them.

Let us go to the "Discussion Guide" of the *Confronting Poverty* website, and click on "Module 10." Now click on the Children's Defense Fund report. For our online activity, spend some time going through this report. It lays out a number of concrete ideas and policies that would reduce childhood poverty by 60 percent. Many of these policies are discussed throughout Chapters 11–15. However, there are additional ideas worth considering as well.

As we saw in Chapter 9, and as this report points out, the economic cost of childhood poverty to the nation is substantial. The question is therefore not whether we will pay for child poverty but rather how we will pay. Currently we are paying the very high price of dealing with the economic and social consequences of child poverty. This includes a less economically productive workforce, higher health-care costs, and so on.

A much more effective approach would be to reduce child poverty in the first place. As discussed in Chapter 9, for every dollar spent on reducing poverty among children, we would save at least seven dollars by reducing the fallout costs associated with poverty.

After you have read the report, consider the range of policies that we might consider to reduce childhood poverty. Most OECD countries have fairly robust systems in place to protect children from poverty. Discuss why it is that the United States does not.

CHAPTER 13 Employment and Universal Basic Income Policies

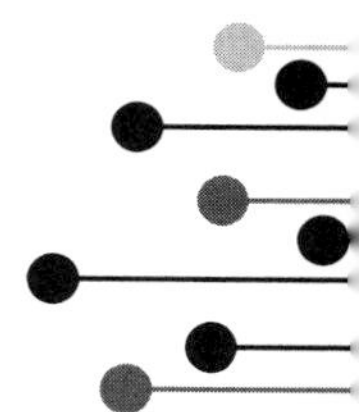

Essential to any overall strategy of reducing poverty are policies that will increase the number and availability of jobs that can support a family above the poverty line. As Bradley Schiller notes, "Jobs—in abundance and of good quality—are the most needed and most permanent solution to the poverty problem" (2008, 296).

In addition, as we look into the future, there may be a need to consider policies that address a reduced importance for certain kinds of work. The rise of automation and artificial intelligence could limit the number of workers in certain industries. A universal basic income is one important approach for dealing with such a shortage.

Creating Enough Good-Paying Jobs

The problem of not enough jobs has played itself out somewhat differently within an American versus a European context. Within the United States, the economy over the past 40 years has actually done quite well in terms of creating new jobs. The problem is that many of these jobs are low paying and/or lacking in basic benefits such as health care. The result has been that although unemployment rates have stayed relatively low in the United States (often averaging between 4 and 6 percent), working full-time does not ensure that a family will be lifted out of poverty or near poverty. Research has indicated that 40 percent of all jobs in the United States are considered low-paying, that is less than 16 dollars an hour (Ross and Bateman 2019).

In contrast, the European economies have been more sluggish in terms of creating new jobs over the past 40 years, resulting in unemployment rates much higher than in the United States. In addition, workers have remained out of work for longer periods of time. However, for those who are employed, employees are generally paid more and have greater benefits than their American counterparts, resulting in substantially lower rates of poverty (Alesina and Glaeser 2004).

What then can be done to address the problems of jobs that do not pay enough to support a family, and not enough jobs in the first place? Two broad initiatives would appear essential. The first is transforming the existing job base such that it will support a family. The second is the creation of enough jobs to employ all who are in need of work.

Raising the Minimum Wages of Current Jobs

Within the context of the United States, one might begin with the following benchmark—individuals who are employed full-time throughout the year (defined as working 40 hours per week over a 50-week period) should be able to generate earnings that will enable them to lift a family of three above the near-poverty threshold (150 percent of the poverty line). Such a family might include a married couple with one child, a one-parent household with two children, or a three-generation household of mother, grandmother, and child. The 2019 near-poverty threshold for a family of three in the United States was set at $30,503. Consequently, in order to lift such a family above the poverty line, an individual needs to be earning approximately $15.25 an hour. It is interesting that this calculation is nearly identical to the benchmark used for the Fight for $15 movement.

There are at least two specific ways of accomplishing this. One is to raise the minimum wage to a level that will support a family above the poverty line, and then index it to inflation so that it will continue to lift such a family over the poverty line in the future. This puts the onus of such an increase upon the employer. A second approach is to provide a tax credit (such as the Earned Income Tax Credit) that supplements workers' wages so that their total income for the year lifts them above the poverty line. This places the onus upon the taxpayer.

The minimum wage in the United States went into effect in October 1938 at an initial level of $.25 an hour. The basic concept was that no employee should fall below a certain wage floor. There was an underlying principle that workers should receive a fair wage for a fair day's work. However, unlike Social Security, the minimum wage has never been indexed to inflation; changes in the minimum wage must come through congressional legislation. Years often go by before Congress acts to adjust the minimum wage upward, causing it to lag behind the rising cost of living. The current minimum wage in the United States stands at $7.25 an hour, a rate that went into effect in July 2009. An individual working full-time during the year (50 weeks at 40 hours per week) would earn a total of $14,500, far short of the $30,503 needed to lift a family of three above the near poverty line.

As noted, to lift such a family above the near-poverty line, an individual needs to be earning at least $15 per hour. Consequently, what is needed is to raise the minimum wage to $15 per hour and then index this each year to the rate of inflation in order to maintain its purchasing power. The phase-in period to raise the minimum wage to $15 per hour might take place over several years in order to spread out the increase. Indeed, many states currently have a minimum wage much higher than the federal minimum wage.

The positive impact of tying the minimum wage to the poverty level for a family of three and then indexing it to the rate of inflation would be substantial. First, it would establish a reasonable floor below which no full-time worker would fall. Second, it would allow such a worker to support a family of three well above the official poverty line. Third, it would reinforce the value that Americans have consistently attached to work. Fourth, it would remove the political wrangling from the minimum wage debate. Fifth, it would address in a limited way the increasing inequities between CEOs who earn 300 or 400 times what their average paid workers earn.

One of the criticisms often mentioned when proposing to raise the minimum wage is that it leads to a rise in the unemployment rate. The argument is that as workers' labor becomes more expensive, employers hire fewer workers. The empirical research over the past 20 years has shown that this effect is small to nonexistent. However, it should also be mentioned that the bulk of this research has examined rather modest increases in the minimum wage.

It should also be noted that in today's dollars, the minimum wage in 1968 of $1.60 an hour would represent $11.86 in 2020. Consequently, raising the minimum wage to 15 dollars an hour is not out of line with its purchasing power in the past.

Earned Income Tax Credit

A second approach for supplementing and raising the earnings of low-income workers is through the tax structure, specifically through the use of tax credits. The primary example of such a credit in the United States is the Earned Income Tax Credit (EITC) (Hoynes and Patel 2018). The EITC was enacted in 1975 and underwent a significant expansion during the 1990s. In fact, it currently represents the largest cash antipoverty program in the United States and is frequently considered one of the more innovative American economic policy ideas (see Ventry 2002, for a historical and political background of the EITC).

The program is designed to provide a refundable tax credit to low-income workers, with the vast majority going to households with children. In 2018, a family with one child could qualify for the EITC if its earned income was below $40,320 (or $46,010 for married couples), while a family with three or more children could qualify if its household income was under $49,194 (or $54,884 for married couples). The maximum credit for a one-child family was $3,461; the benefit rose to $6,431 for a family with three or more children. The credit is normally received in a lump-sum payment as part of an overall tax refund for the previous year. Since it is a refundable credit, families receive the payment even if they do not owe any taxes.

The goals of the EITC are to deliver economic relief at the low end of the earnings distribution and to furnish a strong work incentive. An individual cannot qualify for the EITC without earned income, and the impact is particularly strong at the lower levels. For example, for a head of household with one child that was earning $7.50 an hour (and her total earnings were under $10,000), the EITC would effectively raise her wage by an additional $3.00 an hour, to $10.50 an hour.

The program thus provides a significant supplement to low earners as well as an incentive to work. In 2018, it was estimated that 28 million Americans benefitted from the EITC, and along with the Child Tax Credit, pulled approximately 10.6 million individuals above the poverty line who otherwise would have fallen into poverty (Center on Budget and Policy Priorities 2019c). For families that remain in poverty, the EITC has helped to reduce the distance between their household income and the poverty line. It has also enabled families to purchase particular resources that can improve their economic and social mobility (e.g., school tuition, a car, a new residence) or to meet daily expenses.

In order to make the EITC even more effective, its benefits should be expanded so that they provide greater assistance to low-income workers without children. The vast majority of the EITC benefits go to families with children. Yet there is no compelling reason why such benefits should not also be provided for individuals without children. Further research also needs to be done in order to examine the feasibility of receiving the EITC throughout the year, rather than as a lump sum during the tax season (although many families do prefer this way of receiving the EITC). Third, some households that qualify for the EITC fail to claim and take advantage of the tax credit. Better educating tax filers about the benefits of the EITC appears warranted. Fourth, state EITC programs should be encouraged as an additional antipoverty component on top of the federal EITC benefits. Finally, consideration should also be given to modestly increasing the size of the credits currently given to families.

The policy of an expanded EITC, in conjunction with the raising and indexing of the minimum to the level of a living wage, would substantially help working men and women in the United States who, in spite of their efforts, are unable to get themselves and their families out of poverty or near-poverty. In addition, such policies begin to address (although in a very limited way) the increasing inequalities and perceived unfairness of American income distribution and wage structure.

Job Creation

In terms of the problem of producing enough jobs, in many ways this is a much more difficult task than supplementing and raising the wages of existing jobs. Nevertheless, it is essential that a sufficient number of jobs be available to meet the demands of the existing labor pool.

Various labor demand policies have the potential to generate a more robust rate of job growth (Bartik 2016). Several approaches can be taken. First, economic policy should seek in a broad way to stimulate job growth. This would include fiscal policies such as increasing government expenditures, enhancing tax incentives for investment, or enacting consumer tax cuts. The strategy of investing in a "Green New Deal" could be one specific target of such investment. Monetary policy can also provide a stimulus by making access to credit easier and cheaper (Schiller 2008).

A second approach is to provide targeted wage subsidies to employers in order to stimulate job creation. Although the details of such programs can vary considerably, the basic concept is that an employer receives a monetary subsidy for creating a position and/or hiring an individual (often from a targeted population) that the employer might not have hired without such an incentive. This approach could be aimed at businesses and industries that are potential employers of individuals from lower-income or lower-skill backgrounds.

A third strategy for creating jobs is through public service employment (Paul et al. 2018). As David Ellwood and Elisabeth Welty (2000) note in their review of the effectiveness of public service employment programs, if done carefully and judiciously, they can help increase employment without displacing other workers, and they can produce genuinely valuable output. Such an approach appears particularly pertinent for those out of work for long periods of time.

Taken as a whole, an overall strategy for reducing poverty must begin with a set of policies that will increase the availability of jobs that can economically support families above the poverty threshold. To a large extent, poverty is the result of not having a job, or having a job that is not able to viably support a family. Policies must address these shortcomings within the high-economy free market societies.

Universal Basic Income

An alternative policy strategy that approaches income in a substantially different manner than the employment policies we have been discussing is what is known as a universal basic income or guaranteed income (Kenworthy 2019). The concept has been proposed at various times over the past few centuries. In fact, Thomas Paine, the author of *Common Sense* in 1776, was an early proponent of a guaranteed income.

The basic structure would be that every citizen in the United States is guaranteed a set amount of income from the government. This income would be received on a monthly or bimonthly basis. Every adult would be entitled to this income, regardless of whether they were employed or not. Advocates argue that such an approach is a straightforward and effective way of addressing poverty—since poverty is a lack of income, providing a guaranteed minimal income can substantially reduce poverty directly. In addition, the argument is made that this represents a possible solution to a future in which automation and artificial intelligence are likely to dominate the workplace, potentially reducing the number of jobs. On the other hand, opponents point out the possible work disincentives embedded in such a program as well as the overall cost.

The United States seriously considered the idea of a guaranteed income in the early 1970s with President Richard Nixon proposing to Congress a variant of this idea. Currently, several countries have been exploring the feasibility of such a policy, most notably Finland and Switzerland. In addition, the idea has been gaining some traction within the progressive wing of the Democratic Party. For example, Democratic candidate Andrew Yang made it the focal point of his 2020 bid for the presidency. Yang proposed giving all U.S. citizens over the age of 18 years a guaranteed payment of $1,000 per month, or $12,000 for the year. He argued that such assistance would dramatically cut the rate of poverty.

There have been a number of experiments and trials that have sought to examine the feasibility and effects of a universal basic income. What these studies have generally found is that increasing the amount of income to poverty-stricken families makes a significant difference in the well-being of children and parents. As Jeff Madrick writes, recent research,

> *has increasingly shown that low income itself is key, and arguably the major cause of the debilitating outcomes in cognition, emotional stability, and health for poor children. The countless studies reinforcing this claim are an important breakthrough.... Now we know that there is growing evidence that universal cash transfers, money itself, can solve or mitigate many problems. (2020, 134–35)*

Consequently, programs that direct additional income to such families see significant gains in the physical and mental well-being of children and adults.

The concept of a child cash allowance is a similar idea. Throughout most European countries, families with children under 18 years receive a monthly cash payment. This applies to all children, regardless of their circumstances. The idea behind this policy is that parents with young children are in need of additional economic help in raising their children and that such assistance allows parents to spend more time with their children.

Nevertheless, such policies face an uphill battle in the United States. Given our deep-seated values around rugged individualism, the idea of giving people money without something in return may not be palatable in at least the near future.

Concluding Thoughts

Key to any policy strategy for reducing poverty is the importance of ensuring enough livable wage jobs for all who need them. It would appear patently wrong that many Americans are working and yet still find themselves in the throes of poverty. This violates the basic principle that hard work should be the means for getting ahead in life.

Too many Americans find themselves working hard yet falling further behind. Wages have stagnated over the past 50 years, benefits have shrunk, and job security has become more tenuous. It is no wonder that more Americans are facing the prospect of economic insecurity.

A major policy focus on supporting workers and their families is clearly in order. In the past, unions had played an important role in protecting worker's rights and benefits. Yet union membership has fallen from a high of 35 percent of all workers to its current level of 6 percent (discussed in the next chapter).

In order to alleviate poverty, policies must focus on supporting lower-wage workers. As reviewed in this chapter, such strategies include raising the minimum wage, strengthening the Earned Income Tax Credit, and pursuing macroeconomic demand policies. In addition, a universal basic income and child allowances are policies that may become more important as the nature of work is transformed in the future.

ONLINE ACTIVITIES

confrontingpoverty.org

For this chapter's online activity, we will read an article published in *Salon* that was excerpted from my *Chasing the American Dream* book. Go to the "Research" page of the *Confronting Poverty* website, and under "Articles" select "From High Hopes to Low Wages: What Happened to the American Dream."

One of the core premises of the American Dream has been the availability of jobs that can support a family. During the 1950s and 1960s, the country saw rising standards of living, and the growth of good-paying jobs. Many of these jobs also had benefits attached to them, such as health insurance, retirement benefits, paid vacations, and sick leave.

However, with the advent of the 1970s, this began to change. As the United States faced increasing pressure from a more global economy, employers began looking for ways to cut their production costs. The result was lower wages, fewer benefits, and off-shoring jobs where labor costs were cheaper.

As you go through this article, the centrality of decent-paying jobs as a poverty-reduction strategy should be obvious. The million-dollar question is how do we move forward to a future where a household can be adequately supported through one's place of work? This question will become even more important in the years ahead as we face the challenge of increased automation and artificial intelligence. While there will surely be significant benefits to such developments, there will also be significant costs. Consider how we will be able to address these costs. How might the nature of work change in the future? Should benefits be tied to one's job, or should a different system be developed? These are some of the questions for you to consider after reading this article.

CHAPTER 14 Organizing for Social Change

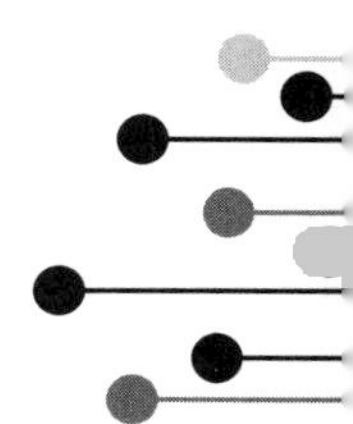

A final strategy for addressing and alleviating poverty is through the collective action of organizing. Those lacking in power can gain leverage and strength by coming together with people of similar interests and goals. Although political influence and power often derive from money, they can also be acquired through organizing large numbers of people around an issue.

Such organizing can take place on a variety of levels, but in this chapter we focus on three—at the job; in the community; and across the nation. As we think about ways to address poverty, organizing for better working conditions, stronger communities, and a greater federal effort in addressing poverty would appear excellent places to begin.

Labor Unions and Unionization

Labor unions represent one way in which workers have been able to gain better pay and benefits. The basic idea is that in order to partially correct for the power imbalance between employers and employees, a union representing the rights of workers is necessary. The purpose of such a union is to protect its members, through what is known as collective bargaining, and by negotiating for healthy working conditions and livable wages and benefits.

Labor unions began in the United States toward the end of the nineteenth century and reached their zenith during the 1950s. At that time, approximately one-third of all workers were represented by a union. Since then, union membership has steadily fallen, such that only 6 percent of workers today are unionized (Rosenfeld 2019).

One of the reasons for this decline has been that much of the unionized segment of the economy has traditionally been located in the manufacturing sector. Many of these jobs have dried up as we moved from a manufacturing-based economy to a more service-based economy. Nevertheless, unions are still active in the United States, particularly in public sector work such as government jobs, teaching, and city employees.

Research has shown that unions can have both a direct and an indirect effect on reducing poverty. The direct effect is through increasing the wages and benefits for workers in specific low-paying occupations. These increased wages have been able to pull households above the poverty threshold. In addition, research has shown that in localities with heavier organized labor, the wages for those in nonunion jobs are also raised. This effect is the result of nonunion employers needing to remain competitive in attracting qualified employees. In order to do so, they may offer higher wages and benefits than they might otherwise have offered in the absence of a union presence.

In addition, there are indirect effects that unions have on reducing poverty. Much of this is through the lobbying efforts of organized labor to influence antipoverty legislation such as minimum wage laws and greater coverage of health care. For example, in "many European nations, powerful labor movements helped establish and subsequently enlarge and protect generous welfare states" (Rosenfeld and Laird 2016, 816).

Indeed, countries with higher levels (70–80 percent) of unionization (such as Finland, Denmark, and Sweden) have lower rates of poverty, whereas countries with low rates of unionization (such as the United States) tend to have higher rates of poverty. This pattern also holds when looking at individual states within the United States.

Furthermore, higher levels of unionization have been shown to have a moderating effect on overall economic inequality. The rise of inequality in the United States over the past 50 years is partially attributed to the decline of unions during this same period.

Consequently, one important area of organizing is centered around the workplace. Workers in unionized jobs tend to have higher wages and benefits than their counterparts in similar types of nonunionized work. Organized labor has also been instrumental in helping to support the various living wage and minimum wage campaigns that have taken place in various municipalities and states across the country, thereby improving the conditions for all lower-income workers (Rosenfeld 2019).

Community Organizing

Just as individuals thrive with the acquisition and development of income and assets, so too do communities. As discussed in Chapter 8, poor neighborhoods are often characterized by their lack of strong community assets, such as quality schools, decent housing, adequate infrastructure, economic opportunities, available jobs, and so on. These, in turn, then affect the life chances of residents in such communities. A trip to any poor inner city or impoverished rural area makes this abundantly clear. Yet what can be done to improve this situation?

A first step is to recognize and build upon the abilities, strengths, and energy of residents within a neighborhood. One innovative idea is the use of a time-based currency. The idea is to allow neighbors to help each other and themselves through a service barter system. It works in the following way. For each hour that a resident gives in helping someone else, they are able to receive back an hour of help from another resident. One person may build their "time dollars" by providing childcare assistance, while they in turn may use their acquired time dollars to "purchase" a different service, perhaps a neighbor's home fix-it skills. In this fashion, residents are able to tap into the wealth of resources and talents found within a neighborhood, as well as helping each other and themselves. This type of activity represents a beginning avenue through which the assets of lower-income communities are being built and strengthened.

Ultimately the impetus to address neighborhood issues and problems must come from the neighbors themselves. Across the country, there has been a revitalization of grassroots community development and neighborhood organizations that have involved hundreds of thousands of residents. They can be found from the low-income neighborhoods of the South Bronx in New York City, to the bootheel region in southern Missouri, to Chinatown in San Francisco, California. As Paul Grogan and Tony Proscio note, residents in these communities,

> *have used these organizations to invest in their assets rather than nurse old wounds.... They have built and renovated thousands of houses and apartments, recruited businesses into their neighborhoods, organized child-care centers and charter schools, and formed block watches and civic clubs. As individual groups, their achievements are sometimes laughably modest. In aggregate, they are becoming monumental.* (2000, 4)

The rapid growth of nearly 5,000 Community Development Corporations around the country is vivid evidence that residents in lower-income communities have been coming together to produce tangible and pragmatic improvements in the asset base of their neighborhoods (Erekani 2014).

Yet such activity and development frequently need political capital and financial resources in order to accomplish specific community goals. Whether it be affordable housing, adequately supplied schools, or improved municipal services, these objectives do not happen in their absence. Therefore, a second step in revitalizing and strengthening the assets of lower-income neighborhoods is through the development of coalitions and leadership from within such communities that are able to exert political pressure and gain entry into the local and state decision-making process. Power can be obtained through organized money, but it can also be obtained through organized people. This is the principle that drives community development and grassroots organization efforts. When residents of communities are able to educate and organize themselves regarding specific issues of concern, they are better able to create positive change through the political process. Yet such a task is far from easy, especially in light of the daily turmoils of poverty that were discussed earlier.

Particular institutions are often needed to assist in this task. Historically one of the most important has been that of religious organizations. They have provided the moral foundation for such development (i.e., that of social justice), along with the organizational and resource capabilities necessary to foster and build community leadership skills. Other organizations exist as well. One in particular that has been instrumental in helping to develop such local leadership and coalition building has been that of the Industrial Areas Foundation (IAF). The IAF was founded in 1940 by perhaps the most influential community organizer during the past century, Saul Alinsky. Since that time, the IAF has expanded considerably. There are currently over 65 affiliated organizations in the United States network, along with affiliated organizations in Canada and Great Britain. As Ernesto Cortez, one of the most well-known and effective organizers notes, "The central role of the IAF organizations is to build the competence and confidence of ordinary citizens and taxpayers so that they can reorganize the relationship of power and politics in their communities, allowing them to reshape the physical and cultural face of their neighborhoods" (1996, 175). These groups may start with smaller issues and then work their way up. As Cortez describes,

> *They begin with small, winnable issues—fixing a streetlight, putting up a stop sign. They move into larger concerns—making a school a safe and civil place for children to learn. Then they move to still larger issues—setting an agenda for a municipal improvement budget; strategizing with corporate leaders and members of the city council on economic growth policies; developing new initiatives in job training, health care, and public education. When ordinary people become engaged and begin to play large, public roles, they develop confidence in their own competence. (1996, 186–87)*

Examples of such local organizations can be found throughout the country. The community-based group known as Communities Organized for Public Service/Metro Alliance (or COPS/Metro), has successfully mobilized low-income communities in and around San Antonio over the past 60 years. They have achieved major victories in influencing the power structure and acquiring municipal investments (such as storm sewers, adequate schools, and street repairs) that had long bypassed their communities.

Similarly, the Nehemiah Homes Project in Brooklyn and the Bronx was able to acquire the necessary resources from the city of New York in order to build thousands of new single-family homes for working families. In the lower delta region, the Mississippi Choctaws have revitalized their community through building upon their initial success of attracting federal and private investments. They have become one of the ten largest employers in Mississippi, with assets including an industrial park, a major shopping center, and more recently a casino (this in a county that had been the state's poorest). Through effective political and economic leadership, the tribe has been able to transform its community from abject poverty into an economically vibrant environment. These and countless other examples demonstrate that effective community organizing and leadership can provide leverage and ultimately a working relationship with larger political entities such as city hall or the statehouse.

A third step for revitalizing economically distressed neighborhoods is attracting businesses and economic opportunities into such communities. The primary approach in the past has been to entice such movement through the creation of tax incentives targeted to businesses who choose to locate in a specified impoverished area. This has been the logic behind both the Enterprise Zone and Empowerment Zone programs, as well as the Tax Increment Financing (or TIF) programs found at the state level. In theory, the idea makes considerable sense. If economic opportunities are lacking in a particular community, why not increase the financial incentives so that it is to a business's advantage to locate in such areas? However, the limited amount of research that has been conducted on enterprise zones indicates that they are not a particularly effective way of stimulating job and economic opportunities (Ferguson 2001). Providing a tax incentive is simply not enough to overcome the reluctance of businesses to move into impoverished areas, and when they are used they often do not benefit those whom the programs were designed to help.

More important would appear to be that of strengthening the assets of communities. In order for a business to move to a particular location, it must be seen as profitable and to its advantage. Consequently, building communities that are attractive to investment is a step along this path. As Ronald Ferguson notes, "The main focus of local economic development strategies should be removing unnecessary barriers to business location and growth and getting the long-term fundamentals right with regard to infrastructure, taxation, regulation, and education" (2001, 442).

Developing and building the assets of lower-income communities is vital in attracting economic opportunities. Gaining access to financial credit, such as through the Community Reinvestment Act, is also an important step in attracting such opportunities. If, in addition to this, the federal or state government is willing to provide further tax incentives for business to develop opportunities in lower-income communities, so much the better. But first the fundamentals must be in place. In doing so, communities that were once routinely bypassed by the banking establishment and the private sector are now being seen as important investment opportunities in their own right (Park and Quercia 2020).

Social Movements

A third way of thinking about organizing is on a much broader scale. The goal is to create a widespread social movement focused on reducing poverty and inequality. Such an effort obviously involves considerable effort, but such large-scale action is possible. One can point to many recent movements that have arisen to address various problems. For example, the environmental movement has gathered considerable momentum in the past few decades. The growing concern about climate change and environmental degradation has resulted in many groups organizing to help reverse these trends.

In a similar fashion, the growing number of Americans at risk of poverty and economic instability could be a focal point for a new social and economic movement. We saw glimpses of this with the Occupy movement, which captured the attention of many with its focus on the 1 and 99 percent. It is likely that in the future, more Americans will be facing economic uncertainty, thereby increasing the visibility of the issue.

Social movements have the ability to change the very culture of a society. As Edwin Amenta and Francesca Polletta write in their review of social movements,

> *The enduring impacts of social movements are often cultural. Movements change the way we live and work. They make some behaviors socially inappropriate and others newly appealing. They create new collective actors, alter lines of social cleavage, and transform what counts as expertise. (2019, 280)*

However, it should be recognized that there are at least two unique obstacles that hinder the ability of those in or near poverty to organize. The first is that there remains a considerable amount of stigma and shame connected with being poor. As we have discussed in earlier chapters, individuals in poverty generally do not want to be identified as such. For many people, it is a mark of economic failure. This undermines the ability of the poor to think collectively and to organize around the issues of poverty and inequality. As Frances Fox Piven and Lorraine Minnite write,

> *No matter their hardship, before people can mobilize for defiant collective action, they have to develop a proud and angry identity. They have to go from being hurt and ashamed to being angry and indignant. In the 1930s, many of the jobless tried to hide their travails; hangdog unemployed workers swung empty lunch boxes as they strode down the street so the neighbors would not know. But many of the unemployed also harbored other ideas, half-formed perhaps, about who was to blame for their plight. When those ideas were evoked they could be rallied to rise up with others in anger over their condition. (2016, 765)*

They go on to note,

> *Time and again in history even the poor have found the outrage to proclaim not only that their hardships are not of their own making, but that they themselves by their defiance can compel action to alleviate those hardships. (p. 765)*

Consequently, as we have demonstrated in earlier chapters, there is a need to show that poverty is by and large a failure at the structural level. With such an understanding, individuals may be more likely to transfer their personal pain into positive collective action. Such action can potentially exert pressure upon the status quo in order to create necessary and constructive change.

A second obstacle to organizing around the issue of poverty is that those who are poor or near poor generally do not have the time or resources to expend on such an effort. Individuals are often just trying to survive on a day-to-day basis, making it difficult to be concerned about issues beyond one's immediate needs. However, it is also true that the vast majority of the poor will be in poverty for only a relatively short period of time. Therefore, while they may not have the ability to focus on organizing opportunities in the present, they may have such an ability in the future.

As we have seen, when individuals effectively organize themselves in groups devoted to specific issues of concern, much can be accomplished. Such groups can be found in a wide array of settings, including local communities, churches, student groups, national organizations, and so on. As we discussed in the prior section, many examples exist of grassroots organizations that are working on issues with the potential to increase opportunities at the structural level, including groups focusing on living wage campaigns, child- and health-care legislation, racial inequities in policing, affordable housing, and asset-building initiatives.

At the same time, what is needed is a national focus on the issues of poverty and economic inequality. These are topics that underlie and pull together many of the concerns that various groups are attempting to redress. Building coalitions across racial and gender lines, socioeconomic classes, community boundaries, and various interest groups is essential for developing a strong political focus upon the problem of poverty. As we have seen throughout this book, poverty is not an issue of them but rather an issue of us. It is a problem that will affect most Americans in one way or another. Understanding this and acting politically upon such information is critical. As Paul Rogat Loeb observes,

> *The lesson here is not to stop challenging injustices that arise from people's particular identities and backgrounds. But to promote human dignity, we need to build coalitions that are as broad as possible. In addition to the important task of staking out rights for specific marginalized groups, we also need to organize around issues that affect everyone, such as the unprecedented gap between rich and poor, the corrupting influence of unaccountable wealth, the threats to our environment, and the general sense of powerlessness that pervades America today. (1999, 219)*

Concluding Thoughts

We have reviewed in this chapter various strategies around the idea of collectively organizing in order to redress the problems surrounding poverty. Within a democratic society, the potential exists for well-organized groups of individuals to mobilize and begin to exert pressure for social change. This can occur at various levels, such as in the workplace, within the community, or on a broader societal level.

These efforts move our nation toward one in which more individuals and families are able to live a livable life. Such a life is one in which all members of society are able to thrive and reach their full potential. As we have seen in earlier chapters, poverty seriously undermines a person's ability to do so. Collective organizing is one way in which to work toward the achievement of a more equitable and just society.

ONLINE ACTIVITIES

confrontingpoverty.org

In this chapter, we have reviewed the strategy of organizing as a way of addressing poverty. We have looked at unionization, community organizing, and the building of social movements as examples of creating coalitions.

But we can also think of organizing on a very micro level—that is, you. We will pick up this theme in more detail in Chapter 15, but for our online activity, go to the "Discussion Guide" page of the *Confronting Poverty* website, and click on "Module 12." Then click on the Oxfam link.

This is a very helpful toolkit detailing some of the practicable steps that anyone can take in working to create change. After you have gone through the toolkit, consider the ways in which you can take the information and knowledge you have gained from this book, and put them to use.

Sharing the link to the *Confronting Poverty* website that we have been using throughout all of our online activities might be a simple first step. The site is being used in a wide variety of settings to better inform and educate individuals and groups to the realities of poverty. What other steps could you take to begin having an effect on changing the conditions of poverty?

One action would be to get involved in directly assisting those in or near poverty. There are many groups working on a daily basis to provide such assistance. Yet we also need to focus our attention on changing the conditions that lead people into poverty in the first place. As we have discussed, these include the lack of living wage jobs, few social supports to protect families from poverty, racial disparities across a range of vital indicators, and many others. Drawing attention to these structural constraints is vitally important to any long-range strategy designed to alleviate poverty. Such attention can help build coalitions designed to pressure the political structure to act in addressing these shortcomings.

CHAPTER

15 Confronting Poverty

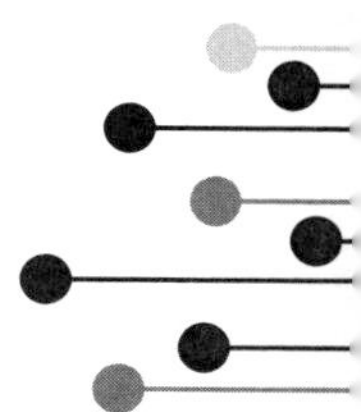

Our text has been organized around answering four questions: (1) What is the nature, extent, and makeup of poverty; (2) Why does poverty exist and persist; (3) What are the effects and consequences of poverty; and (4) How can we address and alleviate poverty? The answers to each of these questions were designed to provide you with a strong foundation for understanding poverty in the United States.

A Brief Review

We began by exploring the various ways in which poverty might be defined and measured. Regardless of the definition or measure, the underlying concept is that those in poverty lack the basic goods and resources necessary to lead a minimally adequate life. This is most often expressed in terms of a lack of income.

Using the official U.S. measure of poverty, we learned that a majority of Americans will at some point experience at least a year below the poverty line. However, the amount of time spent in poverty is often short, perhaps one or two years. Those more likely to experience poverty tend to have characteristics that put them at a greater disadvantage vis-à-vis the labor market. These include individuals with less education, a disability, single-parent families, nonwhites, women, and those residing in economically depressed areas.

We then turned to the question of why poverty exists. The most common explanations are those that emphasize individual deficiencies, such as laziness or bad decision-making. Although these perspectives have little empirical support, they nevertheless remain quite popular in the public imagination. We also reviewed several theories that were structural in nature. These explanations focus on failings at the economic or political level as the reasons behind poverty. We then explored the structural vulnerability explanation that puts various pieces of the puzzle together in order to explain poverty.

Our next section examined the effects and consequences of poverty upon individuals, communities, and the nation as a whole. We learned that the costs of poverty are extremely high. Impoverished individuals and communities are more likely to be plagued by a range of social problems, while the drag on the national well-being is significant.

Finally, we reviewed a range of strategies designed to reduce and alleviate poverty. These included strengthening the social safety net, providing key social resources, programs aimed at helping single-parent families, policies to increase the number of livable wage jobs, and various organizing strategies. Taken as a whole, these strategies have the potential to pull millions of Americans out of poverty.

With this knowledge, you are now in a stronger position to develop solid arguments for taking action to address the widespread poverty found in America. Yet how might we as individuals or as members of groups begin to construct positive change? This is our final topic to explore.

Becoming a Change Agent

How do we as a society, and how do I as an individual, create the kinds of social change that will allow us to effectively understand, confront, and alleviate poverty? These are questions that I do not pretend to have the definitive answers to. However, what I can provide are some thoughts and suggestions on ways in which we might begin the process of changing both the mindset surrounding poverty as well as our approach toward addressing poverty. We touched upon this briefly in the last chapter. Here I expand upon the topic.

I should start by noting that during the past 10 years there has been a growing awareness and concern regarding the issue of economic inequality broadly defined. Beginning with the Occupy movement in 2011 and 2012, considerable discussion has taken place around the concept of the 1 and 99 percent. This rising tide of inequality discourse has also washed into mainstream political debates across the country. Presidential candidates on the progressive side of the aisle routinely discuss the alarming trend of growing income and wealth inequality in the United States.

The Black Lives Matter movement has cast a further spotlight upon racial inequality in the United States, while the Fight for $15 has been garnering support for lifting the wages of fast-food workers. In addition, cities and states around the country have been raising their minimum wages in recognition of the need to assist those in low-paying jobs.

So the good news with respect to changing the country's understanding of poverty and inequality is that we have made a solid start in the last 10 years. There is a growing recognition that poverty and inequality are problems rooted at the structural or policy level, rather than primarily at the individual level. As such, there is a push to consider more fundamental change in our policy approaches to solving poverty. Nevertheless, there are many miles to go before such a realization becomes a consensus. How might we move further in such a direction?

Raising Awareness and Connections

One key factor to shifting the status quo is for more people to feel a personal connection to the issue of poverty. This has been true for many, if not most, social movements in the past. To take but one example, the rise and growing support of the environmental movement over the past 50 years have been based upon the realization that we all have a personal stake in the health and well-being of the planet. Furthermore, we have come to recognize that in one way or another, we all impact and are impacted by the environment. It has become painfully clear that each of us has a serious stake in halting both the acceleration of climate change and the degradation of our planet.

Support for other social movements has also hinged upon feelings of personal connection and urgency to an issue. That connection may be through one's sense of justice, or through one's sense of self-interest. In either case, individuals generally must feel some connection to a social problem in order to be motivated enough to become involved.

Such is the case with poverty. Too often the attitude regarding poverty has been, "I don't see how it affects me, so why be concerned?" Yet as I have hopefully demonstrated throughout this book, poverty is an issue that in one way or another affects us all. In addition, more Americans are feeling a sense of economic insecurity, and yet they may not be aware of the source of this insecurity. Consequently, there is a need to raise an awareness regarding the connections that each of us have to the issue. How might we accomplish this?

To begin, I should note that given our current political climate and age of "alternative facts" and "fake news," the idea of moving research evidence into the hands of a wider audience has taken on an added importance. There is a growing need to base our understanding of social issues upon well-supported and well-documented research evidence. Yet too often in higher education we wind up talking only to our fellow academics. This must change. Now, more than ever, there is a need to lift our research into the public arena.

This idea has a long history behind it. For example, the land grant universities were established in 1862 with the mission of translating academic research into practical applications at the state level. The 1914 federal initiative of building cooperative extension networks was designed to further extend the land grant universities' knowledge and research to the broader constituencies of practitioners and nonacademics.

The discipline of sociology in particular has begun to think seriously about this issue. In his 2004 American Sociological Association's presidential address, Michael Burawoy called for elevating the visibility of public sociology in the field. He explained the concept and impetus by noting, "We have spent a century building professional knowledge, translating common sense into science, so that now, we are more than ready to embark on a systematic back-translation, taking knowledge back to those from whom it came, making public issues out of private troubles, and thus regenerating sociology's moral fiber. Herein lies the promise and challenge of public sociology" (2005, 261).

Yet how might we extend this idea further with respect to poverty? Can we begin to actively awaken our fellow citizens to what sociologist C. Wright Mills described as understanding one's personal troubles within the context of the sociological imagination? That context is, providing the public with the knowledge that the issues and problems facing them often have a societal context and that rather than individual failure, many of these issues are the result of structural processes. Such knowledge can begin to shift the paradigm from one of status quo to active change. In addition, can we begin to facilitate an individual's understanding of their personal connection to the issue?

One example of an attempt to accomplish this has been the development of the poverty website that we have explored with the exercises and activities throughout these chapters. The website itself has received hundreds of thousands of visitors from over 200 countries around the globe. Its use has also entered into a number of different settings, including high school classrooms, university courses, community and civic agencies, and many more.

This represents but one example of bringing research evidence into the public arena in order to reshape general perceptions to align better with the actual realities rather than the myths of poverty. We might think of many other creative ways in which to bring evidence to bear. For example, social media provides a particularly powerful outlet for getting the word out regarding social issues and problems. The #MeToo movement is a prime example of how social media has been used effectively in order to spread awareness, experiences, and action toward sexual harassment and assault. Similarly, the Black Lives Matter movement has raised awareness of abusive policing around the United States and the world. This has been aided significantly through the use of social media.

Another striking example of the power of social media was the uprisings known as the Arab Spring. A series of protests and rebellions spread across North Africa and the Middle East demanding governmental reforms. The role of social media was crucial for disseminating the news of successful efforts and facilitating the ability of people to organize and stage rallies against these regimes.

Beyond being active on social media, there are many other ways for us to begin to take action in confronting poverty. For example, we can continue to learn about the dynamics of poverty and share this newfound knowledge with others. We can get involved in our community with those organizations that are assisting low-income families. We can mobilize a group of our friends and acquaintances to begin to consider the ways in which to stand up to poverty and injustice. We can make our voices heard to legislators and policy makers in our community, state capital, and Washington, D.C. We can vote.

In short, there are many ways in which each of us can work toward being proactive in creating a positive change. Such change begins with conversations in our daily lives. The well-known phrase "Think globally, act locally" epitomizes the idea that when thinking about widespread change, it is helpful to put it into the context of our local environment.

Change Does Occur, Sometimes Quickly

Yet oftentimes it can feel as if social change is glacial—that nothing really happens over the course of decades and that the problems of yesterday are the problems of today and the problems of tomorrow. And in fact, it is true that significant change often does take a considerable amount of time.

However, it is also true that social and policy change can occur over relatively short periods of time as well. For example, the mid-1930s saw a dramatic change in the role of the federal government providing long-term economic protections to its citizens. Among the array of programs begun during this time period were the Social Security and Unemployment Insurance Programs. As a result of the catastrophic economic conditions of the Great Depression, President Franklin Roosevelt was able to sign into law many of his New Deal initiatives.

Likewise, during the 1960s, President Johnson was able to legislate many of his Great Society and War on Poverty programs in a very short period of time. These included major civil rights legislation along with the Medicare and Medicaid programs (Shlaes 2020).

One could point to other examples as well. The point being that laying the groundwork for social change often involves years of determination and hard work but that it is also possible to see rapid change over fairly short periods of time.

I feel that it is quite possible we are entering such a time with respect to poverty and inequality. Of course, it is difficult to predict the future, but I see hopeful signs that fundamental change could be on the horizon. As I noted earlier, there is a growing awareness surrounding the issues of inequality and poverty. There is also an increasing sense of injustice with respect to the schism between the haves and have-nots, with the have-nots becoming more plentiful and more vulnerable. These realizations have been brought to the fore through the organizing efforts of many grassroots groups around the country.

In my *American Dream* book, a gathering of rural, upstate New Yorkers were brainstorming about how positive change can come about on a national level. After much discussion, one of the focus group members had the floor:

> *So what do you do that lets you go beyond the local level? And I can't give precise answers to that, but I can give a generic answer. And that is, organization. I think the history of the country and the world show that in any society at any time there is a struggle between those who want to dominate politically, socially, economically, and control everything.*

And those who want to live their lives in a broader, comfortable way, but they don't feel the need to own vast amounts. They just want enough. And some call that class struggle. And the only thing that has ever won, the larger numbers of people win against the small group that controls the money and the power has been organization.

And Mary made a comment a little while ago, that she'll be dust before we see major social change. And I think that's a mistake. Again, I think if you look at history, what I see is that social change has come very rapidly when it's come. And usually to everyone's surprise. People are always trying to organize, and every once in a while, something clicks and it all happens. And I can't explain what it's going to take to make it click, all I can say is that you keep trying to organize. But you look at—Jim Crow was around for a hundred years, and it collapsed in about five. The Soviet Union was around for 70 or 80 years and it fell apart in months. And I think there's a very real possibility that things like that can happen. And I don't know when they'll happen, or what's going to trigger them, and what's going to make it work. But when it happens it'll surprise you, and it'll be fast. (Rank, Hirschl, and Foster 2014, 174)

Over 130 years ago, the damaging effects of American poverty were documented in Jacob Riis's landmark 1890 book, *How the Other Half Lives*. Riis detailed in both words and photographs the impoverished conditions of tenement families in an area known as "the Bend" in New York City. He wrote about the difficulty of eliminating the wretched conditions of those living in that neighborhood. There were times when it appeared very little was being accomplished. Yet as Riis observed, regarding such feelings of discouragement,

When nothing seems to help, I go and look at a stonecutter hammering away at his rock perhaps a hundred times without as much as a crack showing in it. Yet at the hundred and first blow it will split in two, and I know it was not that blow that did it—but all that had gone before.

This relates back to what our focus group member was discussing in terms of rapid change occurring after years of the status quo. Oftentimes we may feel as if little is being accomplished, when in fact we have been laying the foundation for a profound shift to occur.

Concluding Thoughts

Having completed the chapters in this book, you should now have a firm understanding into the issues of poverty and economic hardship. I would encourage you, my readers, to use this information as a valuable tool in creating the kind of changes we have been discussing in this book. Diagnosing the scope and cause of a problem is a first step toward addressing that problem. A second step is using that diagnosis to shift the prevailing status quo mentality to one of social action. A third step is building the momentum to leverage a change in how we address the problem.

Ultimately, such change begins with each of us. As Margaret Mead once poignantly remarked, "Never doubt that a small group of committed citizens can change the world. Indeed, it is the only thing that ever has." As we look into the future, let us create a community and a country that are transformed by the knowledge that poverty can and must be eradicated, once and for all.

References

Abramsky, Sasha. 2013. *The American Way of Poverty: How the Other Half Still Lives*. New York: Nations Books.

Alesina, Alberto, and Edward L. Glaeser. 2004. *Fighting Poverty in the US and Europe: A World of Difference*. New York: Oxford University Press.

Alexander, Michelle. 2020. *The New Jim Crow: Mass Incarceration in the Age of Colorblindness*. New York: The New Press.

Amenta, Edwin, and Francesca Polletta. 2019. "The Cultural Impacts of Social Movements." *Annual Review of Sociology* 45: 279–99.

Anacker, Katrin B. 2015. *The New American Suburb: Poverty, Race and the Economic Crisis*. Burlington, VT: Ashgate Publishing.

Anderson, Joan B. 2003. "The U.S.–Mexico Border: A Half Century of Change." *The Social Science Journal* 40: 535–54.

Anderson, Gerard F., Peter Hussey, and Varduhi Petrosyan. 2019. "It's Still the Prices, Stupid: Why the US Spends So Much on Health Care, and a Tribute to Uwe Reinhardt." *Health Affairs* 38: 87–95.

Andersson, Fredrik, John C. Haltiwanger, Mark J. Kutzbach, Henryo Pollackoski, and Daniel H. Weinberg. 2018. "Job Displacement and the Duration of Joblessness: The Role of Spatial Mismatch." *Review of Economics and Statistics* 100: 203–18.

Angel, Ronald J. 2016. "Social Class, Poverty and the Unequal Burden of Illness and Death." In *The Oxford Handbook of the Social Science of Poverty*, edited by David Brady and Linda M. Burton, 660–83. New York: Oxford University Press.

Assini-Martin, Luciana C., and Kerry M. Green. 2015. "Long-Term Consequences of Adolescent Parenthood Among African-American Urban Youth: A Propensity Score Matching Approach." *Journal of Adolescent Health* 56: 529–35.

Atkinson, Anthony B. 2015. *Inequality: What Can Be Done?* Cambridge, MA: Harvard University Press.

Balestra, Carlotta, and Richard Tonkin. 2018. "Inequalities in Household Wealth Across OECD Countries: Evidence From the OECD Wealth Distribution Database." OECD Statistics Working Papers 2018/01. OECD, Paris.

Bane, Mary J., and David T. Ellwood. 1986. "Slipping Into and Out of Poverty: The Dynamics of Spells." *Journal of Human Resources* 34: 1–23.

Barrett, Christopher B., and Erin C. Lentz. 2016. "Hunger and Food Insecurity." In *The Oxford Handbook of the Social Science of Poverty*, edited by David Brady and Linda M. Burton, 602–22. New York: Oxford University Press.

Bartik, Timothy J. 2016. "Labor-Demand-Side Economic Development Incentives and Urban Opportunity." In *Shared Prosperity in America's Communities*, edited by Susan M. Wachter and Lei Ding, 129–50. Philadelphia: University of Pennsylvania Press.

Becker, Gary S. 1981. *A Treatise on the Family*. Cambridge, MA: Harvard University Press.

Becker, Gary S. 1993. *Human Capital: A Theoretical and Empirical Analysis With Special Reference to Education*. Chicago: University of Chicago Press.

Beeghley, Leonard. 2000. *The Structure of Social Stratification in the United States*. Boston: Allyn and Bacon.

Bentron, Richard A., and Lisa A. Keister. 2017. "The Lasting Effect of Intergenerational Wealth Transfers: Human Capital, Family Formation, and Wealth." *Social Science Research* 68: 1–14.

Bhattacharya, Jayanta, Thomas DeLeire, Steven Haider, and Janet Currie. 2002. "Heat or Eat? Cold Weather Shocks and Nutrition in Poor American Families." Paper presented at the USDA Food Assistance Research Development Grants Workshop, Northwestern University, Evanston, IL, April 19.

Bills, David B., Valentina Di Stasio, and Klarita Gerxhani. 2017. "The Demand Side of Hiring: Employers in the Labor Market." *Annual Review of Sociology* 43: 291–310.

Blank, Rebecca M. 1997. *It Takes a Nation: A New Agenda for Fighting Poverty*. Princeton, NJ: Princeton University Press.

Blau, David M. 2001. *The Child Care Problem: An Economic Analysis*. New York: Russell Sage Foundation.

Bloome, Deirdre. 2014. "Racial Inequality Trends and the Intergenerational Persistence of Income and Family Structure." *American Sociological Review* 79: 1196–225.

Bok, Derek. 1996. *The State of the Nation: Government and the Quest for a Better Society*. Cambridge, MA: Harvard University Press.

Bowles, Samuel, Steven N. Durlauf, and Karla Hoff. 2006. *Poverty Traps*. New York: Russell Sage Foundation.

Bowles, Samuel, Gerbert Gintis, and Melissa Osborne Groves. 2005. *Unequal Chances: Family Background and Economic Success*. New York: Russell Sage Foundation.

Brady, David. 2009. *Rich Democracies, Poor People: How Politics Explain Poverty*. New York: Oxford University Press.

Brady, David. 2019. "Theories of the Causes of Poverty." *Annual Review of Sociology* 45: 155–75.

Brady, David, Agnes Blome, and Hanna Kleider. 2016. "How Politics and Institutions Shape Poverty and Inquality." In *The Oxford Handbook of the Social Science of Poverty*, edited by David Brady and Linda M. Burton, 117–40. New York: Oxford University Press.

Brady, David, Ryan M. Finnigan, and Sabine Hubgen. 2017. "Rethinking the Risks of Poverty: A Framework for Analyzing Prevalences and Penalties." *American Journal of Sociology* 123: 740–86.

Braga, Anthony A., Rod K. Brunson, and Kevin M. Drakulich. 2019. "Race, Place, and Effective Policing." *Annual Review of Sociology* 45: 535–55.

Brand, Jennie E. 2015. "The Far-Reaching Impact of Job Loss and Unemployment." *Annual Review of Sociology* 41: 359–75.

Bullard, Robert D. 2000. *Dumping in Dixie: Race, Class, and Environmental Quality*. New York: Routledge.

Burawoy, Michael. 2005. "2004 American Sociological Presidential Address: For Public Sociology." *The British Journal of Sociology* 56: 259–94.

Cai, Xixia, and Timothy Smeeding. 2019. "Deep and Extreme Poverty in Rich and Poor Nations: Lessons From Atkinson for the Fight Against Child Poverty." LIS Working Paper Series, No. 780. Luxembourg Income Study, Luxembourg.

Calnitsky, David. 2018. "Structural and Individualist Theories of Poverty." *Sociological Compass* 12: e12640.

Cancian, Maria, and Daniel R. Meyer. 2018. "Reforming Policy for Single-Parent Families to Reduce Child Poverty." *The Russell Sage Foundation Journal of the Social Sciences* 4: 91–112.

Caplovitz, David. 1968. *The Poor Pay More: Consumer Practices of Low-Income Families*. New York: Free Press.

Cellini, Stephanie Riegg, Signe-Mary McKernan, and Caroline Ratcliffe. 2008. "The Dynamics of Poverty in the United States: A Review of Data, Methods, and Findings." *Journal of Policy Analysis and Management* 27: 577–605.

Center on Budget and Policy Priorities. November 18, 2019a. "Policy Basics: Federal Tax Expenditures." https://www.cbpp.org/research/federal-tax/policy-basics-federal-tax-expenditures

Center on Budget and Policy Priorities. January 3, 2019b. "Where Families With Children Use Housing Vouchers: A Comparative Look at the 50 Largest Metropolitan Areas." https://www.cbpp.org/research/housing/where-families-with-children-use-housing-vouchers

Center on Budget and Policy Priorities. October 31, 2019c. "Child Tax Credit and Earned Income Tax Credit Lift 10.6 Million People out of Poverty in 2018." Off the Charts: Policy Insight Beyond the Number. https://www.cbpp.org/research/federal-tax/policy-basics-the-earned-income-tax-credit

Century Foundation Task Force on the Common School. 2002. *Divided We Fail: Coming Together Through Public School Choice*. New York: Century Foundation Press.

Chaudry, Ajay, and Chirstopher Wimer. 2016. "Poverty Is Not Just an Indicator: The Relationship Between Income, Poverty, and Child Well-Being." *Academic Pediatrics* 16: S23–29.

Cherlin, Andrew J. 2020. "Degrees of Change: An Assessment of the Deinstitutionalization of Marriage Thesis." *Journal of Marriage and Family* 82: 62–80.

Chetty, Raj, David Grusky, Maximilian Hell, Nathaniel Hendren, Robert Manduca, and Jimmy Narang. 2017. "The Fading American Dream: Trends in Absolute Mobility Since 1940." *Science* 356: 398–406.

Chetty, Raj, Nathaniel Hendren, Maggie R. Jones, and Sonya R. Porter. 2020. "Race and Economic Opportunity in the United States: An Intergenerational Perspective." *Quarterly Journal of Economics* 135: 711–83.

Chetty, Raj, Michael Stepner, and Sarah Abraham. 2016. "The Association Between Income and Life Expectancy in the United States, 2001–2014." *JAMA* 315: 1750–66.

Chien, Nina. October 2019. "Factsheet: Estimates of Child Care Eligibility and Receipt for Fiscal Year 2016." Office of the Assistant Secretary for Planning and Evaluation, U.S. Department of Health and Human Services.

Child Care Aware. 2019. "The US and the High Price of Child Care: An Examination of a Broken System." 2019 Report. https://www.childcareaware.org/our-issues/research/the-us-and-the-high-price-of-child-care-2019/

Child Trends. December 27, 2018. "Head Start." https://www.childtrends.org/indicators/head-start

Child Trends. May 24, 2019. "Teen Births." https://www.childtrends.org/indicators/teen-births

Children's Defense Fund. 2015. "Ending Child Poverty Now." Children's Defense Fund Report. https://www.childrensdefense.org/wp-content/uploads/2018/06/Ending-Child-Poverty-Now.pdf

Chung, Chanjin, and Samuel L. Myers. 2005. "Do the Poor Pay More for Food? An Analysis of Grocery Store Availability and Food Price Disparities." *Journal of Consumer Affairs* 33: 276–96.

Coleman-Jensen, Alisha, Matthew P. Rabbitt, Christian A. Gregory, and Anita Singh. 2019. "Household Food Security in the United States in 2018." ERR-270. U.S. Department of Agriculture, Economic Research Service, Washington, DC.

Collins, Caitlyn. 2019. *Making Motherhood Work: How Women Manage Careers and Caregiving*. Princeton, NJ: Princeton University Press.

Conley, Dalton. 1999. *Being Black, Living in the Red: Race, Wealth, and Social Policy in America*. Berkeley, CA: University of California Press.

Connolly, Marie, Miles Corak, and Catherine Haeck. 2019. "Intergenerational Mobility Between and Within Canada and the United States." *Journal of Labor Economics* 52: 595–641.

Cooper, Marianne, and Allison J. Pugh. 2020. "Families Across the Income Spectrum: A Decade in Review." *Journal of Marriage and Family* 82: 272–99.

Corak, Miles. 2010. "Chasing the Same Dream, Climbing Different Ladders: Economic Mobility in the United States and Canada." Economic Mobility Project. The Pew Charitable Trusts, Philadelphia, PA.

Cortes, Ernesto, Jr. 1996. "Reweaving the Fabric: The Iron Rule and the IAF Strategy for Power and Politics." In *Reducing Poverty in America: Views and Approaches*, edited by Michael R. Darby, 175–98. Thousand Oaks, CA: SAGE Publications.

Cottle, Thomas J. 2001. *Hardest Times: The Trauma of Long Term Unemployment*. Westport, CT: Praeger.

Council on Community Pediatrics. 2016. "Poverty and Child Health in the United States." *Pediatrics* 137: 1–14.

Crowder, Kyle, and Scott J. South. 2003. "Neighborhood Distress and School Dropout: The Variable Significance of Community Context." *Social Science Research* 32: 659–98.

Cynamon, Barry Z., and Steven M. Fazzari. 2015. "Rising Inequality and Stagnation in the US Economy." *European Journal of Economics and Economic Policies: Intervention* 12: 170–82.

Dahl, Gordan B., Andreas Raundal Kostol, and Magne Mogstad. 2014. "Family Welfare Culture." *Quarterly Journal of Economics* 129: 1711–52.

Darling-Hammond, Linda, and Laura Post. 2000. "Inequality in Teaching and Schooling: Supporting High-Quality Teaching and Leadership in Low-Income Schools." In *A Nation at Risk: Preserving Public Education as an Engine for Social Mobility*, edited by Richard D. Kalenberg, 127–67. New York: The Century Foundation Press.

Darroch, Jacqueline E., Jennifer J. Frost, Susheela Singh, and The Study Team. November 2001. "Teenage Social and Reproductive Behavior in Developed Countries: Can More Progress Be Made?" Occasional Report No. 3. Alan Guttmacher Institute, New York.

David, Jonathan, and Bhashkar Mazumder. 2020. "The Decline in Intergenerational Mobility After 1980." Working Paper No. WP-2017-5. Federal Reserve Bank of Chicago, Chicago. https://www.chicagofed.org/publications/working-papers/2017/wp2017-05

Davidai, Shai. 2018. "Why Do Americans Believe in Economic Mobility? Economic Inequality, External Attributions of Wealth and Poverty, and the Belief in Economic Mobility." *Journal of Experimental Psychology* 79: 138–48.

Davis, James J., Vincent J. Roscigno, and George Wilson. 2015. "American Indian Poverty in the Contemporary United States." *Sociological Forum* 31: 5–28.

Desmond, Matthew. 2016. *Evicted: Poverty and Profit in the American City*. New York: Random House.

Desmond, Matthew. 2018. "Heavy Is the House: Rent Burden Among the American Urban Poor." *International Journal of Urban and Regional Research* 42: 160–70.

Desmond, Matthew, and Bruce Western. 2018. "Poverty in America: New Directions and Debates." *Annual Review of Sociology* 44: 305–18.

DiPrete, Thomas A. 2020. "The Impact of Inequality on Intergenerational Mobility." *Annual Review of Sociology* 46: 1–29.

Domina, Thurston, Andrew Penner, and Emily Penner. 2017. "Categorical Inequality: Schools as Sorting Machines." *Annual Review of Sociology* 43: 311–30.

Duina, Francesco. 2018. *Broke and Patriotic: Why Poor Americans Love Their Country*. Stanford, CA: Stanford University Press.

Duncan, Cynthia M. 2014. *Worlds Apart: Poverty and Politics in Rural America*. New Haven, CT: Yale University Press.

Duncan, Greg J., and Jeanne Brooks-Gunn. 1997. *Consequences of Growing Up Poor*. New York: Russell Sage Foundation.

Duncan, Greg J., and Richard J. Murnane. 2011. *Whither Opportunity? Rising Inequality, Schools, and Children's Life Chances*. New York: Russell Sage Foundation.

Duncan, Greg J., and Richard J. Murnane. 2016. "Rising Inequality in Family Incomes and Children's Educational Outcomes." *The Russell Sage Foundation Journal of the Social Sciences* 2: 142–58.

Durlauf, Steven N. 2001. "The Membership Theory of Poverty: The Role of Group Affiliations in Determining Socioeconomic Status." In *Understanding Poverty*, edited by Sheldon H. Danziger and Robert H. Haveman, 392–416. New York: Russell Sage Foundation.

Durlauf, Steven N. 2006. "Groups, Social Influences, and Inequality." In *Poverty Traps*, edited by Samuel Bowles, Steven N. Durlauf, and K. Hoff, 141–75. New York: Russell Sage Foundation.

Dwyer, Rachel E. 2018. "Credit, Debt, and Inequality." *Annual Review of Sociology* 44: 237–61.

Edin, Kathryn. 2005. "More Than Money: The Role of Assets in the Survival Strategies and Material Well-Being of the Poor." In *Assets for the Poor: The Benefits of Spreading Asset Ownership*, edited by Thomas M. Shapiro and Edward N. Wolff, 206–31. New York: Russell Sage Foundation.

Edin, Kathryn J., and Laura Lein. 1997. *Making Ends Meet: How Single Mothers Survive Welfare and Low-Wage Work*. New York: Russell Sage Foundation.

Edin, Kathryn J., and H. Luke Shaefer. 2015. *$2.00 a Day: Living on Almost Nothing in America*. Boston: Houghton Mifflin Harcourt.

Ellwood, David T., and Elisabeth D. Welty. 2000. "Public Service Employment and Mandatory Work: A Policy Whose Time Has Come and Gone and Come Again?" In *Finding Jobs: Work and Welfare Reform*, edited by David E. Card and Rebecca M. Blank, 299–372. New York: Russell Sage Foundation.

Eppard, Lawrence M., Mark Robert Rank, and Heather E. Bullock. 2020. *Rugged Individualism and the Misunderstanding of American Inequality*. Bethlehem, PA: Lehigh University Press.

Erekani, Rachid. September 17, 2014. "What Is a Community Development Corporation?" National Alliance of Community Economic Development Associations. https://www.naceda.org/index.php?option=com_dailyplanetblog&view=entry&category=bright-ideas&id=25%3Awhat-is-a-community-development-corporation-&Itemid=171

Ermisch, John, Markus Jantti, and Timothy Smeeding. 2012. *From Parents to Children: The Intergenerational Transmission of Advantage*. New York: Russell Sage Foundation.

Evans, Gary W., and Pilyoung Kim. 2012. "Childhood Poverty, Chronic Stress, Self-Regulation, and Coping." *Child Development Perspectives* 7: 43–48.

Fabbre, Vanessa D., Eleni Gaveras, Anna Goldfarb Shabsin, Janelle Gibson, and Mark R. Rank. 2020. "Confronting Stigma, Discrimination, and Social Exclusion." In *Toward a Livable Life: A 21st Century Agenda for Social Work*, edited by Mark Robert Rank, 70–93. New York: Oxford University Press.

Fankenhuis, Willem E., and Daniel Nettle. 2019. "The Strengths of People in Poverty." *Current Directions in Psychological Science* 29: 16–21.

Feagin, Joe R. 2010. *Racist America: Roots, Current Realities, and Future Reparations*. New York: Routledge.

Federal Reserve Bank. May 2020. "Report on the Economic Well-Being of U.S. Households in 2019, Featuring Supplemental Data From April 2020."

https://www.federalreserve.gov/publications/files/2019-report-economic-well-being-us-households-202005.pdf

Federal Reserve Bank of St. Louis. 2020. "Median Sales Price of Houses Sold for the United States." Economic Research Data, New Residential Sales. https://fred.stlouisfed.org/series/MSPUS

Feeding America. 2014. "Hunger in America 2014: National Report Prepared for Feeding America." http://help.feedingamerica.org/HungerInAmerica/hunger-in-america-2014-full-report.pdf

Ferguson, Ronald F. 2001. "Community Revitalization, Jobs and the Well-Being of the Inner-City Poor." In *Understanding Poverty*, edited by Sheldon H. Danziger and Robert H. Haveman, 417–43. New York: Russell Sage Foundation.

Fisher, Gordon M. 1992. "The Development and History of the Poverty Thresholds." *Social Security Bulletin* 55: 3–14.

Fox, Liana, Florencia Torche, and Jane Waldfogel. 2016. "Intergenerational Mobility." In *The Oxford Handbook of the Social Science of Poverty*, edited by David Brady and Linda M. Burton, 528–54. New York: Oxford University Press.

Frankenberg, Erica, Jongyeon Ee, Jennifer B. Ayscue, and Gary Orfield. May 10, 2019. "Harming Our Common Future: America's Segregated Schools 65 Years After *Brown*." The Civil Rights Project. https://www.civilrightsproject.ucla.edu/research/k-12-education/integration-and-diversity/harming-our-common-future-americas-segregated-schools-65-years-after-brown/Brown-65-050919v4-final.pdf

Furstenberg, Frank F. 2020. "Kinship Reconsidered: Research on a Neglected Topic." *Journal of Marriage and Family* 82: 364–82.

Gale, William G., and John Karl Scholz. 1994. "Intergenerational Transfers and the Accumulation of Wealth." *Journal of Economic Perspectives* 8: 145–60.

Gallup Poll. 2013. "Americans Say Family of Four Needs Nearly $60K to 'Get By'." https://news.gallup.com/poll/162587/americans-say-family-four-needs-nearly-60k.aspx

Gans, Herbert. 1972. "Positive Functions of Poverty." *American Journal of Sociology* 78: 275–89.

Gans, Herbert. 1991. *People, Plans, and Policies: Essays on Poverty, Racism, and Other National Urban Problems*. New York: Columbia University Press.

Gans, Herbert. 2012. "The Benefits of Poverty." *Challenge* 55: 114–25.

Garfinkel, Irwin. 1992. *Assuring Child Support*. New York: Russell Sage Foundation.

Gibson-Davis, Christina M. 2016. "Single and Cohabiting Parents and Poverty." In *The Oxford Handbook of the Social Science of Poverty*, edited by David Brady and Linda M. Burton, 417–37. New York: Oxford University Press.

Gilbert, Neil. 2017. *Never Enough: Capitalism and the Progressive Spirit*. New York: Oxford University Press.

Gilder, George. 1981. *Wealth and Poverty*. New York: Basic Books.

Gilens, Martin. 1999. *Why Americans Hate Welfare: Race, Media, and the Politics of Antipoverty Policy*. Chicago: University of Chicago Press.

Glasmeier, Amy. 2020. "MIT Living Wage Calculator." livingwage.mit.edu.

Glennerster, Howard. 2002. "United States Poverty Studies and Poverty Measurement: The Past Twenty-Five Years." *Social Service Review* 76: 83–107.

Gokhale, Jagdeesh, and Lawerence J. Kotlikoff. 2002. "Simulating the Transmission of Wealth Inequality." *American Economic Review* 92: 265–69.

Goldstein, Amy. 2017. *Janesville: An American Story*. New York: Simon and Schuster.

Gould, Elise. May 19, 2015. "Poor People Work: A Majority of Poor People Who Can Work Do." Economic Snapshot. Economic Policy Institute, Washington, DC.

Greenberg, Mark. 2007. "Next Steps for Federal Child Care Policy." *The Future of Children* 17: 73–96.

Gregory, Christian A., and Alisha Coleman-Jensen. July 2017. "Food Insecurity, Chronic Disease, and Health Among Working-Age Adults." ERR-235. U.S. Department of Agriculture, Economic Research Service, Washington, DC.

Grogan, Paul S., and Tony Proscio. 2000. *Comeback Cities: A Blueprint for Urban Neighborhood Revival*. Boulder, CO: Westview Press.

Gundersen, Craig, and James P. Ziliak. 2018. "Food Insecurity Research in the United States: Where We Have Been and Where We Need to Go." *Applied Economic Perspectives and Policy* 40: 119–35.

Gurley, Lauren. 2016. "Who's Afraid of Rural Poverty? The Story Behind America's Invisible Poor." *American Journal of Economics and Sociology* 75: 589–604.

Hair, Nicole L., Jamie L. Hanson, and Barbara L. Wolfe. 2015. "Association of Child Poverty, Brain Development, and Academic Achievement." *JAMA Pediatrics* 169: 822–29.

Hanson, F. Allan. 1997a. "Why Don't We Care about the Poor Anyway?" *Humanist* 57: 11–14.

Hanson, F. Allan. 1997b. "How Poverty Lost Its Meaning." *Cato Journal* 17: 189–209.

Harrell, Erika, Lynn Langton, Marcus Berzofsky, Lance Couzens, and Hope Smiley-McDonald. 2014. "Household Poverty and Nonfatal Violent Victimization, 2008–2012." *Bureau of Justice Statistics*, NCJ 248384.

Hartwell, R. M. 1986. "The Long Debate on Poverty." Paper presented at the Political Economy Seminar Series, Washington University, St. Louis, MO.

Harvey, David L. 1993. *Potter Addition: Poverty, Family, and Kinship in a Heartland Community*. New York: Aldine de Gruyter.

Hattery, Angela, and Earl Smith. 2007. "Social Stratification in the New/Old South: The Influences of Racial Segregation on Social Class in the Deep South." *Journal of Poverty* 11: 55–81.

Haveman, Robert. 1988. *Starting Even: An Equal Opportunity Program to Combat the Nation's New Poverty*. New York: Simon and Schuster.

Hayes, Cheryl D., John L. Palmer, and Martha J. Zaslow. 1990. *Who Care for America's Children: Child Care Policy for the 1990s*. Washington, DC: National Academy Press.

Herrnstein, Richard J., and Charles Murray. 1994. *The Bell Curve: Intelligence and Class Structure in American Life*. New York: Free Press.

Hertel, Florian Rolf, and Fabian T. Pfeffer. 2020. "The Land of Opportunity? Trends in Social Mobility and Education in the United States." In *Education and Intergenerational Social Mobility in Europe and the United States*, edited by Richard Breen and Walter Muller, 29–68. Stanford, CA: Stanford University Press.

Hochschild, Jennifer, and Nathan Scovronick. 2003. *The American Dream and the Public Schools*. New York: Oxford University Press.

Hodson, Randy, and Robert J. Kaufman. 1982. "Economic Dualism: A Critical Review." *American Sociological Review* 47: 727–39.

Holdt, Jacob. 1985. *American Pictures: A Personal Journey Through the American Underclass*. Copenhagen, Denmark: American Pictures Foundation.

Holzer, Harry J. 2013. "Workforce Development Programs." In *Legacies of the War on Poverty*, edited by Martha J. Bailey and Sheldon Danziger, 121–50. New York: Russell Sage Foundation.

Housing and Urban Development Summer. 2016. "Neighborhoods and Violent Crime." Evidence Matters. Office of Policy Development and Research, Washington DC.

Hout, Michael. 2018. "Americans Occupational Status Reflects Both of their Parents." *Proceedings of the National Academy of Sciences of the United States of America* 115: 9527–32.

Hoynes, Hillary W., and Ankur J. Patel. 2018. "Effective Policy for Reducing Poverty and Inequality? The Earned Income Tax Credit and the Distribution of Income." *Journal of Human Resources* 53: 859–90.

Hudson, Darrell L., Sarah Gehlert, and Shanta Pandey. 2020. "Tackling the Social Determinants of Ill Health." In *Toward a Livable Life: A 21st Century Agenda for Social Work*, edited by Mark Robert Rank, 16–44. New York: Oxford University Press.

Hughes, Michelle, and Whitney Tucker. 2018. "Poverty as an Adverse Childhood Experience." *North Carolina Medical Journal* 79: 124–26.

Hunt, Matthew O., and Heather E. Bullock. 2016. "Ideologies and Beliefs About Poverty." In *The Oxford Handbook of the Social Science of Poverty*, edited by David Brady and Linda M. Burton, 93–116. New York: Oxford University Press.

Iceland, John. 2005. "Measuring Poverty: Theoretical and Empirical Considerations." *Measurement: Interdisciplinary Research and Perspectives* 3: 199–235.

Iceland, John. 2013. *Poverty in America: A Handbook*. Berkeley: University of California Press.

Jantti, Markus, Bernt Bratsberg, Knut Roed, Oddbjorn Raaum, Robin Naylor, Eva Osterbacka, Anders Bjorklund, and Tor Eriksson. 2006. "American Exceptionalism in a New Light: A Comparison of Intergenerational Earnings Mobility in the Nordic Countries, the United Kingdom and the United States." Discussion Paper 1938. Institute for the Study of Labor, Bonn.

Jargowsky, Paul A. 2003. "Stunning Progress, Hidden Problems: The Dramatic Decline of Concentrated Poverty in the 1990s." The Living Cities Census Series. The Brookings Institution, Washington, DC.

Jargowsky, Paul A. 2015. "Concentration of Poverty in the New Millennium: Changes in Prevalence, Composition, and Location of High Poverty Neighborhoods." A Report by The Century Foundation, New York and Rutgers Center for Urban Research and Education, New Brunswick, NJ.

Jargowsky, Paul A. 2019. "Racial and Economic Segregation in the US: Overlapping and Reinforcing Dimensions." In *Handbook of Urban Segregation*, edited by Sako Musterd, 151–68. London: Edward Elgar Publishing.

Jargowsky, Paul A., Lei Din, and Natasha Fletcher. 2019. "The Fair Housing Act at 50: Successes, Failures, and Future Directions." *Housing Policy Debate* 29: 694–703.

Johnson, Lyndon B. 1965. "The President's Inaugural Address, January 20, 1965." In *Public Papers of the Presidents of the United States: Lyndon B. Johnson, 1965*, vol. 1, entry 27, 71–74. Washington, DC: U.S. Government Printing Office.

Johnson, Sara B., Jenna L. Riis, and Kimberly G. Noble. 2016. "State of the Art Review: Poverty and the Developing Brain." *Pediatrics* 137: 1–16.

Joint Center for Housing Studies of Harvard University. 2017. "America's Rental Housing 2017." Report by the Joint Center for Housing Studies of Harvard University, Cambridge, MA.

Jonson-Reid, Melissa, Brett Drake, Patricia L. Kohl, and Wendy F. Auslander. 2020. "Preventing Child Maltreatment." In *Toward a Livable Life: A 21st Century Agenda for Social Work*, edited by Mark Robert Rank, 152–92. New York: Oxford University Press.

Kahlenberg, Richard D. 2002. "Economic School Integration: An Update." Century Foundation Issue Brief Series. Century Foundation, New York.

Kalleberg, Arne L. 2011. *Good Jobs, Bad Jobs: The Rise of Polarized and Precarious Employment Systems in the United States, 1970s to 2000s*. New York: Russell Sage Foundation.

Karney, Benjamin R., and Thomas N. Bradbury. 2020. "Research on Marital Satisfaction and Stability in the 2010s: Challenging Conventional Wisdom." *Journal of Marriage and Family* 82: 100–16.

Karoly, Lynn. 2001. "Investing in the Future: Reducing Poverty Through Human Capital Investments." In *Understanding Poverty*, edited by Sheldon H. Danziger and Robert H. Haveman, 314–56. New York: Russell Sage Foundation.

Kemp, Peter A. 2016. "Housing Programs." In *The Oxford Handbook of the Social Science of Poverty*, edited by David Brady and Linda M. Burton, 820–42. New York: Oxford University Press.

Kenworthy, Lane. 2014. *Social Democratic America*. New York: Oxford University Press.

Kenworthy, Lane. 2019. *Social Democratic Capitalism*. New York: Oxford University Press.

Killewald, Alexandia, Fabian T. Pfeffer, and Jared N. Schachner. 2017. "Wealth Inequality and Accumulation." *Annual Review of Sociology* 43: 379–404.

Kim, Hyunil, and Brett Drake. 2018. "Child Maltreatment Risk as a Function of Poverty and Race/Ethnicity in the USA." *International Journal of Epidemiology* 47: 780–87.

Kimberlin, Sara, Laura Tach, and Christopher Wimer. 2018. "A Renter's Tax Credit to Curtail the Affordable Housing Crisis." *The Russell Sage Foundation Journal of the Social Sciences* 4: 131–60.

Kirby, Douglas. 2001. *Emerging Answers: Research Findings on Programs to Reduce Teen Pregnancy*. Washington, DC: National Campaign to Prevent Teen Pregnancy.

Kneebone, Elizabeth, and Alan Berube. 2013. *Confronting Suburban Poverty in America*. Washington, DC: Brookings Institution Press.

Kravitz-Wirtz, Nicole, Samantha Teixeira, Anjum Hajat, Bongki Woo, Kyle Crowder, and David Takeuchi. 2018. "Early-Life Air Pollution Exposure, Neighborhood Poverty, and Childhood Asthma in the United States, 1990–2014." *International Journal of Environmental Research and Public Health* 15: 2–14.

Krueger, Alan B. 2002. "Economic Scene; The Apple Falls Close to the Tree, Even in the Land of Opportunity." *New York Times*, November 14, Section C, p. 2.

Lacy, Karyn. 2016. "The New Sociology of Suburbs: A Research Agenda for Analysis of Emerging Trends." *Annual Review of Sociology* 42: 369–84.

Landers, Ashley L., Domenica H. Carrese, and Robin Spath. 2019. "A Decade in Review of Trends in Social Work Literature: The Link Between Poverty and Child Maltreatment in the United States." *Child Welfare* 97: 65–96.

Lee, Cheol-Sung, and In-Hoe Koo. 2016. "The Welfare States and Poverty." In *The Oxford Handbook of the Social Science of Poverty*, edited by David Brady and Linda M. Burton, 709–32. New York: Oxford University Press.

Leidenfrost, Nancy B. 1993. "An Examination of the Impact of Poverty on Health." Report prepared for the Extension Service, U.S. Department of Agriculture, Washington, DC.

Levin, Josh. 2019. *The Queen: The Forgotten Life Behind an American Myth*. New York: Little, Brown and Company.

Lewis, Oscar. 1959. *Five Families: Mexican Case Studies in the Culture of Poverty*. New York: Basic Books.

Lewis, Oscar. 1966a. *La Vida: A Puerto Rican Family in the Culture of Poverty*. New York: Random House.

Lewis, Oscar. 1966b. "The Culture of Poverty." *Scientific American* 215: 19–25.

Lobao, Linda, Minyu Zhou, Mark Partridge, and Michael Betz. 2016. "Poverty, Place, and Coal Employment Across Appalachia and the United States in a New Economic Era." *Rural Sociology* 81: 343–86.

Loeb, Paul Rogat. 1999. *Soul of a Citizen: Living With Conviction in a Cynical Time*. New York: St. Martin's Griffin.

Luker, Kristin. 1996. *Dubious Conceptions: The Politics of Teenage Pregnancy*. Cambridge, MA: Harvard University Press.

Madrick, Jeff. 2020. *Invisible Americans: The Tragic Cost of Child Poverty*. New York: Alfred A. Knoff.

Martin, Joyce A., Brady E. Hamilton, Michelle J. K. Osterman, and Anne K. Driscoll. November 27, 2019. "Births: Final Data." *National Vital Statistics Reports* 68: 1–47.

Martin, Philip, Michael Fix, and J. Edward Taylor. 2006. *The New Rural Poverty: Agriculture and Immigration in California*. Washington, DC: The Urban Institute Press.

Marx, Ive, Brian Nolan, and Javier Olivera. 2015. "The Welfare State and Antipoverty Policy in Rich Countries." In *Handbook of Income Distribution*, edited by Anthony B. Atkinson and Francois Bourguignon, 2063–109. Amsterdam: Elsevier.

Marx, Karl, and Friedrich Engels. 1968. *Selected Works*. New York: International Publishers.

Massey, Douglas S. 1996. "The Age of Extremes: Concentrated Affluence and Poverty in the Twenty-First Century." *Demography* 33: 395–412.

Massey, Douglas A. 2007. *Categorically Unequal: The American Stratification System*. New York: Russell Sage Foundation.

Massey, Douglas A. 2016. "Segregation and the Perpetuation of Disadvantage." In *The Oxford Handbook of the Social Science of Poverty*, edited by David Brady and Linda M. Burton, 369–93. New York: Oxford University Press.

Massey, Douglas S., and Nancy A. Denton. 1993. *American Apartheid: Segregation and the Making of the Underclass*. Cambridge, MA: Harvard University Press.

Mauer, K. Whitney. 2016. "Indian Country Poverty: Place-Based Poverty on American Indian Territories, 2006–10." *Rural Sociology* 82: 473–98.

Maynard, Rebecca A. 1997. *Kids Having Kids: Economic Costs and Social Consequences of Teen Pregnancy*. Washington, DC: The Urban Institute Press.

Mazumder, Bhaskar. 2018. "Intergenerational Mobility in the United States: What We Have Learned from the PSID." *The ANNALS of the American Academy of Political and Social Science* 680: 213–34.

McCord, Collin, and Harold P. Freeman. January 18, 1990. "Excess Mortality in Harlem." *New England Journal of Medicine* 322: 1606–7.

McEwen, Bruce S. 2017. "Neurobiological and Systemic Effects of Chronic Stress." *Chronic Stress* 1: 1–11.

McKee-Ryan, Frances M., and Robyn Maitoza. 2018. "Job Loss, Unemployment, and Families." In *The Oxford Handbook of Job Loss and Job Search*, 87–97. New York: Oxford University Press.

McLaughlin, Michael, and Mark R. Rank. 2018. "Estimating the Economic Cost of Childhood Poverty in the United States." *Social Work Research* 42 (2): 73–83.

McLeod, Jane D., and Michael J. Shanahan. 1993. "Poverty, Parenting, and Children's Mental Health." *American Sociological Review* 58: 351–66.

McMurrer, Daniel P., and Isabel V. Sawhill. 1998. *Getting Ahead: Economic and Social Mobility in America*. Washington, DC: Urban Institute Press.

Merton, Robert K. 1949. *Social Theory and Social Structure*. New York: Free Press.

Merton, Robert K. 1968. "The Matthew Effect in Science: The Reward and Communication System of Science." *Science* 199: 55–63.

Merton, Robert K. 1988. "The Matthew Effect in Science, II: Cumulative Advantage and the Symbolism of Intellectual Property." *Isis* 79: 606–23.

Mettler, Suzanne. 2002. "Bringing the State Back Into Civic Engagement." *American Political Science Review* 96: 351–65.

Mettler, Suzanne. 2005. *Soldiers to Citizens: The G.I. Bill and the Making of the Greatest Generation*. New York: Oxford University Press.

Millennial Housing Commission. 2002. *Meeting Our Nation's Housing Challenges*. Washington, DC: Bipartisan Millennial Housing Commission.

Mills, C. Wright. 1959. *The Sociological Imagination*. New York: Oxford University Press.

Minsky, Hyman P. 1986. *Stabilizing an Unstable Economy*. New Haven, CT: Yale University Press.

Mishel, Lawrence, and Julia Wolfe. August 14, 2019. "CEO Compensation Has Grown 940% Since 1978." Economic Policy Report. Economic Policy Institute, Washington, DC.

Moffitt, Robert A. 2015. "The Deserving Poor, the Family, and the U.S. Welfare System." *Demography* 52: 729–49.

Morduch, Jonathan, and Rachel Schneider. 2017. *The Financial Diaries: How American Families Cope in a World of Uncertainty*. Princeton, NJ: Princeton University Press.

Morelli, Niccolo, and Robert J. Sampson. 2020. "Lessons and Current Challenges for Urban Sociologists: A Conversation with Robert J. Sampson." *Sociologica* 14: 249–61.

Morrissey, Taryn, and Katie M. Vinopal. 2017. "Neighborhood Poverty and Children's Academic Skills and Behavior in Early Elementary School." *Journal of Marriage and Family* 80: 182–97.

Muller, Christopher, Robert J. Sampson, and Alix S. Winter. 2018. "Environmental Inequality: The Social Causes and Consequences of Lead Exposure." *Annual Review of Sociology* 44: 263–82.

Murray, Charles. 1984. *Losing Ground: American Social Policy 1950–1980*. New York: Basic Books.

National Academies of Sciences, Engineering, and Medicine. 2019. *A Roadmap to Reducing Child Poverty*. Washington, DC: National Academies Press.

National Center for Education Statistics. 2020. "Back to School Statistics." https://nces.ed.gov/fastfacts/

National Center for Employee Ownership. September 2019. "Employee Ownership by the Numbers." https://www.nceo.org/articles/employee-ownership-by-the-numbers

National Institute of Child Health and Human Development. 2006. "The NICHD Study of Early Child Care and Youth Development." NIH Publication No. 05-4318.

National Low Income Housing Coalition. 2019. "Out of Reach 2019." https://reports.nlihc.org/sites/default/files/oor/OOR_2019.pdf

National Low Income Housing Coalition. 2020. "National Housing Trust Fund Fact Sheet." https://files.hudexchange.info/resources/documents/National-Housing-Fund-Trust-Factsheet.pdf

Newman, Katherine. 1999. *No Shame in My Game: The Working Poor in the Inner City*. New York: Knopf.

Noble, Charles. 1997. *Welfare as We Knew It: A Political History of the American Welfare State*. New York: Oxford University Press.

O'Connell, Heather, Katherine J. Curtis, and Jack DeWaard. 2018. "Population Change and the Persistence of the Legacy of Slavery." Paper presented at the Rural Poverty Research Conference, March 21–22, Washington, DC.

O'Connor, Alice. 2001. *Poverty Knowledge: Social Science, Social Policy, and the Poor in Twentieth-Century U.S. History*. Princeton, NJ: Princeton University Press.

O'Connor, Alice. 2016. "Poverty Knowledge and the History of Poverty Research." In *The Oxford Handbook of the Social Science of Poverty*, edited by David Brady and Linda M. Burton, 169–92. New York: Oxford University Press.

Okun, Arthur M. 1975. *Equality and Efficiency: The Big Tradeoff*. Washington, DC: The Brookings Institution.

Orfield, Gary, and Chungmei Lee. 2005. "Why Segregation Matters: Poverty and Educational Inequality." The Civil Rights Project. Harvard University, Cambridge, MA.

Orshansky, Mollie. 1965. "Counting the Poor: Another Look at the Poverty Profile." *Social Security Bulletin* 28: 3–29.

Owens, Ann. 2018. "Income Segregation Between School Districts and Inequality in Students Achievements." *Sociology of Education* 91: 1–27.

Pappas, Gregory, Susan Queen, Wilbur Hadden, and Gail Fisher. 1993. "The Increasing Disparity in Mortality Between Socioeconomic Groups in the United States, 1960 and 1986." *New England Journal of Medicine* 329: 103–15.

Park, Kevin A., and Roberto G. Quercia. 2020. "Who Lends Beyond the Red Line? The Community Reinvestment Act and the Legacy of Redlining." *Housing Policy Debate* 30: 4–26.

Parolin, Zachary, and David Brady. 2019. "Extreme Child Poverty and the Role of Social Policy in the United States." *Journal of Poverty and Social Justice* 27: 3–22.

Paul, Mark, William Dairty Jr., Darrick Hamilton, and Khaing Zaw. 2018. "A Path to Ending Poverty by Way of Ending Unemployment: A Federal Job Guarantee." *The Russell Sage Foundation Journal of the Social Sciences* 4: 44–63.

Pettit, Becky, and Bruce Western. 2004. "Mass Imprisonment and the Life Course: Race and Class Inequality in U.S. Incarceration." *American Sociological Review* 69: 151–69.

Pfeffer, Fabian T., Paula Fomby, and Noura Insolera. 2020. "The Longitudinal Revolution: Sociological Research at the 50-Year Milestone of the Panel Study of Income Dynamics." *Annual Review of Sociology* 46: 1–26.

Pfeffer, Fabian T., and Alexandria Killewald. 2018. "Generations of Advantage: Multigenerational Correlations in Family Wealth." *Social Forces* 96: 1411–42.

Piketty, Thomas, and Emmanuel Saez. 2014. "Inequality in the Long Run." *Science* 344: 838–43.

Piven, Frances Fox, and Richard A. Cloward. 1971. *Regulating the Poor: The Functions of Public Welfare*. New York: Pantheon.

Piven, Frances Fox, and Lorraine C. Minnite. 2016. "Poor People's Politics." In *The Oxford Handbook of the Social Science of Poverty*, edited by David Brady and Linda M. Burton, 751–73. New York: Oxford University Press.

Planned Parenthood. July 2013. "Reducing Teenage Pregnancy." https://www.plannedparenthood.org/files/6813/9611/7632/Reducing_Teen_Pregnancy.pdf

Popkin, Susan J., Molly M. Scott, and Martha Galvez. 2016. "Impossible Choices: Teens and Food Insecurity in America." Research Report. Urban Institute, Washington, DC.

Prasad, Monica. 2018. *Starving the Beast: Ronald Reagan and the Tax Cut Revolution*. New York: Russell Sage Foundation.

Price, James H., Jagdish Khubchandani, and Fern J. Webb. 2018. "Poverty and Health Disparities: What Can Public Health Professionals Do?" *Health Promotion Practice* 19: 170–74.

Pula, Besnik. 2017. "Dual Labor Market/Dual Economy." In *The Wiley-Blackwell Encyclopedia of Social Theory*, edited by Bryan S. Turner, Chang Kyung-Sup, Cynthia F. Epstein, Peter Kivisto, J. Michael Ryan, and William Outhwaite. New York: John Wiley.

Putnam, Robert D. 2015. *Our Kids: The American Dream in Crisis*. New York: Simon and Schuster.

Raley, R. Kelly, and Megan M. Sweeney. 2020. "Divorce, Repartnering, and Stepfamilies: A Decade in Review." *Journal of Marriage and Family* 82: 81–99.

Rank, Mark R. 1994. *Living on the Edge: The Realities of Welfare in America*. New York: Columbia University Press.

Rank, Mark R. 2000. "Socialization of Socio-Economic Status." In *Handbook of Family Development: Dynamics and Therapeutic Interventions*, edited by William C. Nichols, Mary Anne Pace-Nichols, Dorothy S. Becvar, and Augustus Y. Napier, 129–42. New York: John Wiley.

Rank, Mark R. 2004. *One Nation, Underprivileged: Why American Poverty Affects Us All*. New York: Oxford University Press.

Rank, Mark R. 2009. "Measuring the Economic Racial Divide Across the Course of American Lives." *Race and Social Problems* 1: 57–66.

Rank, Mark R. 2020a. "Alleviating Poverty." In *Toward a Livable Life: A 21st Century Agenda for Social Work*, edited by Mark Robert Rank, 45–69. New York: Oxford University Press.

Rank, Mark R. 2020b. "Reducing Cumulative Inequality." In *Toward a Livable Life: A 21st Century Agenda for Social Work*, edited by Mark Robert Rank, 94–113. New York: Oxford University Press.

Rank, Mark R. 2020c. "Introduction." In *Toward a Livable Life: A 21st Century Agenda for Social Work*, edited by Mark Robert Rank, 1–15. New York: Oxford University Press.

Rank, Mark R., Lawrence M. Eppard, and Heather E. Bullock. 2021. *Poorly Understood: What America Gets Wrong about Poverty*. New York: Oxford University Press.

Rank, Mark R., and Thomas A. Hirschl. 1999a. "The Economic Risk of Childhood in America: Estimating the Probability of Poverty Across the Formative Years." *Journal of Marriage and the Family* 61: 1058–67.

Rank, Mark R., and Thomas A. Hirschl. 1999b. "Estimating the Proportion of Americans Ever Experiencing Poverty During Their Elderly Years." *Journal of Gerontology: Social Sciences* 54B: S184–93.

Rank, Mark R., and Thomas A. Hirschl. 2009. "Estimating the Risk of Food Stamp Use and Impoverishment During Childhood." *Archives of Pediatrics and Adolescent Medicine* 163: 994–99.

Rank, Mark R., and Thomas A. Hirschl. 2015. "The Likelihood of Experiencing Relative Poverty Across the Life Course." *PLOS One* 10: e01333513.

Rank, Mark R., Thomas A. Hirschl, and Kirk A. Foster. 2014. *Chasing the American Dream: Understanding What Shapes Our Fortunes*. New York: Oxford University Press.

Ravallion, M. 2016. *The Economics of Poverty*. New York: Oxford University Press.

Rawls, John. 1971. *A Theory of Justice*. Cambridge, MA: Harvard University Press.

Reardon, Sean F., and Kendra Bischoff. 2011. "Income Inequality and Income Segregation." *American Journal of Sociology* 116: 1092–153.

Reiman, Jeffrey. 1979. *The Rich Get Richer and the Poor Get Prison: Ideology, Class and Criminal Justice*. New York: John Wiley & Sons.

Riis, Jacob A. (1890) 1957. *How the Other Half Lives: Studies Among the Tenements of New York*. New York: Hill and Wang.

Rodgers, Joan R. 1995. "An Empirical Study of Intergenerational Transmission of Poverty in the United States." *Social Science Quarterly* 76: 178–94.

Rosenfeld, Jake. 2019. "US Labor Studies in the Twenty-First Century: Understanding Laborism Without Labor." *Annual Review of Sociology* 45: 449–65.

Rosenfeld, Jake, and Jennifer Laird. 2016. "Unions and Poverty." In *The Oxford Handbook of the Social Science of Poverty*, edited by David Brady and Linda M. Burton, 800–19. New York: Oxford University Press.

Ross, Martha, and Nicole Bateman. November 2019. "Meeting the Low-Wage Workforce." Metropolitan Policy Program at Brookings.

Royce, Edward. 2019. *Poverty and Power: The Problem of Structural Inequality*. New York: Rowman and Littlefield.

Rubin, Lillian B. 1994. *Families on the Faultline: America's Working Class Speaks About the Family, the Economy, Race, and Ethnicity*. New York: HarperCollins.

Ruiu, Maria L. 2014. "Differences Between Cohousing and Gated Communities: A Literature Review." *Sociological Inquiry* 84: 316–35.

Sampson, Robert J. 2012. *Great American City: Chicago and the Enduring Neighborhood Effect*. Chicago: University of Chicago Press.

Sampson, Robert J., S. W. Raudenbush, and Felton Earls. 1997. "Neighborhoods and Violent Crime: A Multilevel Study of Collective Efficacy." *Science* 227: 918–24.

Sandoval, Daniel A., Mark R. Rank, and Thomas A. Hirschl. 2009. "The Increasing Risk of Poverty Across the American Life Course." *Demography* 46: 717–37.

Sassler, Sharon, and Daniel T. Lichter. 2020. "Cohabitation and Marriage: Complexity and Diversity in Union-Formation Patterns." *Journal of Marriage and Family* 82: 35–61.

Sawhill, Isabel V. 2001. "The Behavioral Aspects of Poverty." *The Public Interest* 153: 79–93.

Schiller, Bradley R. 2008. *The Economics of Poverty and Discrimination*, 10th ed. Upper Saddle River, NJ: Prentice Hall.

Sedgh, Gilda, Lawrence B. Finer, Akinrinola Bankole, Michelle A. Eilers, and Susheela Singh. 2015. "Adolescent Pregnancy, Birth, and Abortion Rates Across Countries: Levels and Recent Trends." *Journal of Adolescent Health* 56: 223–30.

Sen, Amartya. 1992. *Inequality Reexamined*. New York: Russell Sage Foundation.

Shaefer, H. Luke, Sophie Collyer, Greg Duncan, Kathryn Edin, Irwin Garfinkel, David Harris, Timothy M. Smeeding, Jane Waldfogel, Christopher Wimer, and Hirokazu Yoshikawa. 2018. "A Universal Child Allowance: A Plan to Reduce Poverty and Income Instability Among Children in the United States." *The Russell Sage Foundation Journal of the Social Sciences* 4: 22–42.

Shaefer, H. Luke, Kathryn Edin, Vince Fusaro, and Pingui Wu. 2020. "The Decline of Cash Assistance and the Well-Being of Poor Households with Children." *Social Forces* 98: 1000–25.

Shapiro, Thomas M. 2004. *The Hidden Cost of Being African American: How Wealth Perpetuates Inequality*. New York: Oxford University Press.

Shapiro, Thomas M. 2017. *Toxic Inequality: How America's Wealth Gap Destroys Mobility, Deepens the Racial Divide, and Threatens Our Future*. New York: Basic Books.

Shapiro, Thomas M., and Heather Beth Johnson. 2000. "Assets, Race, and Educational Choices." Center for Social Development Working Paper, No. 00-7. Washington University, St. Louis, MO.

Shapiro, Thomas M., Tatjana Meschede, and Sam Ossoro. February 2013. "The Roots of the Widening Racial Wealth Gap: Explaining the Black–White Economic Divide." Research and Policy Brief. Institute on Assets and Social Policy, Brandeis University, Waltham, MA.

Shapiro, Thomas M., and Edward N. Wolff. 2001. *Assets for the Poor: The Benefits of Spreading Asset Ownership*. New York: Russell Sage Foundation.

Sharifi, Mona, Thomas D. Sequist, Sheryl L. Rifas-Shiman, Steven J. Melly, Dustin T. Duncan, Christine M. Horan, Renata L. Smith, Richard Marshall, and Elsie M. Taveras. 2016. "The Role of Neighborhood Characteristics and the Built Environment in Understanding Racial/Ethnic Disparities in Childhood Obesity." *Preventative Medicine* 91: 103–9.

Sheffield, Rachel, and Robert Rector. 2011. "Air Conditioning, Cable TV, and an Xbox: What Is Poverty in the United States Today?" Backgrounder Executive Summary, No. 2575. The Heritage Foundation, Washington, DC.

Sherman, Arloc. 1994. *Wasting America's Future: The Children's Defense Fund Report on the Costs of Child Poverty*. Boston: Beacon Press.

Shlaes, Amity. 2020. *Great Society: A New History*. New York: Harper.

Silber, Norman I. 2017. "Discovering That the Poor Pay More: Race, Riots, Poverty, and the Rise of Consumer Law." *Fordham Urban Law Journal* 44: 1319–28.

Small, Mario Luis, David J. Harding, and Michele Lamont. 2010. "Reconsidering Culture and Poverty." *The ANNALS of the American Academy of Political and Social Science* 629: 6–27.

Smeeding, Timothy. 2016. "Poverty Measurement." In *The Oxford Handbook of the Social Science of Poverty*, edited by David Brady and Linda M. Burton, 21–46. New York: Oxford University Press.

Smith, Adam. 1776. *An Inquiry Into the Nature and Causes of Wealth of Nations*. London: W. Strahan and T. Cadell.

Smith, Judith R., Jeanne Brooks-Gunn, and Pamela K. Klebanov. 1997. "Consequences of Living in Poverty for Young Children's Cognitive and Verbal Ability and Early School Achievement." In *Consequences of Growing Up Poor*, edited by Greg J. Duncan and Jeanne Brooks-Gunn, 132–89. New York: Russell Sage Foundation.

Smock, Pamela J., and Christine R. Schwartz. 2020. "The Demography of Families: A Review of Patterns and Change." *Journal of Marriage and Family* 82: 9–34.

Sohn, Heeju. 2017. "Racial and Ethnic Disparities in Health Insurance Coverage: Dynamics of Gaining and Losing Coverage Over the Life-Course." *Population Research and Policy Review* 36: 181–201.

Sommer, Teresa, Terri J. Sabol, Elise Chor, William Schneider, P. Lindsay Chase-Lansdale, Jeanne Brooks-Gunn, Mario L. Small, Christopher King, and Hirokazu Yoshikawa. 2018. "A Two-Generation Human Capital Approach to Antipoverty Policy." *The Russell Sage Foundation Journal of the Social Sciences* 4: 118–43.

Song, Xi, Catherine G. Massey, Karen A. Rolf, Joseph P. Ferrie, Jonathan L. Rothbaum, and Yu Xie. 2020. "Long-Term Decline in Intergenerational Mobility in the United States Since the 1850s." *Proceedings of the National Academy of Sciences of the United States of America* 117: 251–58.

Squires, Gregory. 2004. *Why the Poor Pay More: How to Stop Predatory Lending*. Westport, CT: Praeger.

Stack, Carol B. 1974. *All Our Kin: Strategies for Survival in a Black Community*. New York: Harper and Row.

Stevens, Ann Huff. 2012. "Transitions Into and Out of Poverty in United States." Vol. 1 (No. 1). Policy Brief. Center for Poverty Research, University of California–Davis, Davis, CA.

Stiglitz, George. 2012. *The Price of Inequality: How Today's Divided Society Endangers Our Future*. New York: W. W. Norton.

Tach, Laura, and Alicia Eads. 2014. "The Cost of Breaking Up." *Focus* 30: 15–20.

Tach, Laura, and Kathryn Edin. 2017. "The Social Safety Net After Welfare Reform: Recent Developments and Consequences for Household Dynamics." *Annual Review of Sociology* 43: 541–61.

Thurow, Lester C. 1996. *The Future of Capitalism: How Today's Economic Forces Shape Tomorrow's World*. New York: William Morrow.

de Tocqueville, Alexis. 1983. "Memoir on Pauperism." *The Public Interest* 70: 102–20.

Tridico, Pasquale. 2018. "The Determinants of Income Inequality in OECD Countries." *Cambridge Journal of Economics* 42: 1009–42.

Tuttle, Charlotte, and Timothy K. Beatty. 2017. "The Effect of Energy Price Shocks on Household Food Security in Low-Income Households." Economic Research Report 260484. United States Department of Agriculture, Economic Research Service, Washington, DC.

United Nations Development Programme. 2019. *Human Development Report 2019*. New York: United Nations.

U.S. Bureau of the Census. 2014. "Dynamics of Economic Well-Being: Poverty 2009–2011." Current Population Reports, Series P70-137. U.S. Government Printing Office, Washington, DC.

U.S. Bureau of the Census. 2015. "Dynamics of Economic Well-Being: Participation in Government Programs, 2009–2012: Who Gets Assistance?" Current Population Reports, Series P70-141. U.S. Government Printing Office, Washington, DC.

U.S. Bureau of the Census. 2016. "POV-28. Income Deficit or Surplus of Families and Unrelated Individuals by Poverty Status." https://www.census.gov/data/tables/time-series/demo/income-poverty/cps-pov/pov-28.2016.html

U.S. Bureau of the Census. April 9, 2019a. "Fertility of Women in the United States: 2018." *Fertility Tables*.

U.S. Bureau of the Census. 2019b. "Net Worth of Households: 2015." Current Population Reports, Series P70BR-164. U.S. Government Printing Office, Washington, DC.

U.S. Bureau of the Census. 2020a. "Income and Poverty in the United States: 2019." Current Population Reports, Series P60-270. U.S. Government Printing Office, Washington, DC.

U.S. Bureau of the Census. 2020b. "The Supplemental Poverty Measure: 2019." Current Population Reports, Series P60-272. U.S. Government Printing Office, Washington, DC.

U.S. Bureau of the Census. 2020c. "Health Insurance Coverage in the United States: 2019." Current Population Reports, Series P60-271. U.S. Government Printing Office, Washington, DC.

U.S. Bureau of the Census. 2020d. "Custodial Mothers and Fathers and Their Child Support: 2015." Current Population Reports, Series P60-262. U.S. Government Printing Office, Washington, DC.

U.S. Department of Education, Equity and Excellence Commission. 2013. *For Each and Every Child: A Strategy for Education Equity and Excellence*. Washington, DC: Education Publications Center.

U.S. Department of Health and Human Services. 2018. "Welfare Indicators and Risk Factors, Seventeenth Report to Congress." U.S. Government Printing Office, Washington, DC.

Ventry, Dennis J. 2002. "The Collision of Tax and Welfare Politics: The Political History of the Earned Income Tax Credits." In *Making Work Pay: The Earned Income Tax Credit and Its Impact on American Families*, edited by Bruce D. Meyer and Douglas Holtz-Eakin, 15–66. New York: Russell Sage Foundation.

Wachtel, Howard M. 1971. "Looking at Poverty From a Radical Perspective." *Review of Radical Political Economics* 3: 1–19.

Walker, Renee E., Christopher R. Keane, and Jessica G. Burke. 2010. "Disparities and Access to Healthy Food in the United States: A Review of Food Deserts Research." *Health and Place* 16: 876–84.

Wildsmith, Elizabeth, Jennifer Manlove, and Elizabeth Cook. August 8, 2018. "Dramatic Increase in the Proportion of Births Outside of Marriage in the United States from 1990 to 2016." *Child Trends*. https://www.childtrends.org/publications/dramatic-increase-in-percentage-of-births-outside-marriage-among-whites-hispanics-and-women-with-higher-education-levels

Wilkinson, Richard, and Kate Pickett. 2010. *The Spirit Level: Why Greater Equality Makes Societies Stronger*. New York: Bloomsbury Press.

Williams, Trina. 2000. "The Homestead Act: A Major Asset-Building Policy in American History." Working Paper 00-9. Center for Social Development, Washington University, St. Louis, MO.

Willie, Charles, and Michael Alves. 1996. *Controlled Choice: A New Approach to School Desegregated Education and School Improvement*. Providence, RI: Education Alliance Press.

Wilson, William Julius. 1987. *The Truly Disadvantaged: The Inner City, the Underclass, and Public Policy*. Chicago: University of Chicago Press.

Wilson, William Julius. 1996. *When Work Disappears: The World of the New Urban Poor*. New York: Knopf.

Wilson, William Julius. 2009. *More Than Just Race: Being Black and Poor in the Inner City*. New York: W. W. Norton.

Wilson, William Julius. 2016. "Urban Poverty, Race, and Space." In *The Oxford Handbook of the Social Science of Poverty*, edited by David Brady and Linda M. Burton, 394–413. New York: Oxford University Press.

Wisconsin Department of Revenue. 2020. "Claiming Homestead Credit." https://www.revenue.wi.gov/Pages/FAQS/ise-home.aspx

Wiswall, Matthew, and Basit Zafar. 2018. "Preference for the Workplace, Investment in Human Capital, and Gender." *Quarterly Journal of Economics* 133: 457–507.

Wolff, Edward N. November 2017. "Household Wealth Trends in the United States, 1962 to 2016: Has Middle Class Wealth Recovered?" National Bureau of Economic Research Working Paper Series, Working Paper 24085. NBER, Cambridge, MA.

World Bank. 2018. *Piecing Together the Poverty Puzzle*. Washington, DC: World Bank.

Wright, Erik O. 1994. *Interrogating Inequality: Essays on Class Analysis, Socialism, and Marxism*. London: Verso.

Wu, Lawrence L., and Nicholas P. E. Mark. 2018. "Could We Level the Playing Field? Long-Acting Reversible Contraceptives, Nonmarital Fertility, and Poverty in the United States." *The Russell Sage Foundation Journal of the Social Sciences* 4: 144–66.

Zedlewski, Sheila R., Linda Giannarelli, Joyce Morton, and Laura Wheaton. April 2002. "Extreme Poverty Rising, Existing Government Programs Could Do More." New Federalism, Series B, No. B-45. Urban Institute, Washington, DC.

Ziliak, James P. 2018. "Economic Change and the Social Safety Net: Are Rural Americans Still Behind." Discussion Paper Series, DP 2018-06. University of Kentucky Center for Poverty Research, Lexington, KY.

Ziliak, James P., and Craig Gundersen. May 14, 2019. "The State of Senior Hunger in America 2017: An Annual Report." Prepared for Feeding America, Chicago, IL.

Zweig, Janine M., and Elsa Falkenburger. September 6, 2017. "Preventing Teen Pregnancy Can Help Prevent Poverty." *Urban Wire: Poverty, Vulnerability, and the Safety Net*. Urban Institute, Washington, DC.

Index